The Borgarthing Law and the Eidsivathing Law

The Borgarthing Law and the Eidsivathing Law is dedicated to two closely linked medieval laws which were intended to cover adjacent legal provinces in eastern Norway, around and beyond the modern capital, Oslo.

The core of this book consists of new translations of the two laws, based on the recent editions and translations into modern Norwegian by Eyvind Fjeld Halvorsen and Magnus Rindal. Individual rules cover subjects such as Church rites, prohibitions, property, and payments, and shed light on medieval ideas relating to matters as diverse as disability, sexual relations, witchcraft, and forbidden foods. The volume contains a general introduction by Torgeir Landro and Bertil Nilsson, in addition to a translator's introduction by Lisa Collinson, summarizing in English some of the information on manuscripts and relevant linguistic studies outlined by Halvorsen and Rindal. The translated texts in English are also supplemented by footnotes, supplying key readings from the original, in some cases with significant variants from relevant manuscripts.

With a commentary on the individual chapters after each translation, drawing on recent scholarship on medieval law, Church history, and other relevant historical fields, this book is an ideal resource for students and scholars of medieval Norwegian legal history.

Lisa Collinson is Research Lead for Museums and Special Collections, University of Aberdeen. Her previous work has examined the legal and literary history of medieval Scandinavia and the British Isles.

Torgeir Landro is Associate Professor at NLA University College, Norway. His previous publications deal with the reception of canon law in medieval Norway.

Bertil Nilsson is Professor Emeritus of History of Christianity at the University of Gothenburg, Sweden. His previous publications deal with medieval canon law as well as the way in which the encounter between religions developed during the process of Christianization in the Scandinavian kingdoms.

Medieval Nordic Laws
Series editors: Stefan Brink and Ditlev Tamm

Medieval Nordic Laws, edited by **Stefan Brink and Ditlev Tamm,** is part of the ***Routledge Medieval Translations*** series. These translations are the first translations into English of the earliest laws of Scandinavia, and are some of the earliest written sources for Scandinavia. These translated laws emanate from an international project of the same name and have never before been introduced to an international audience.

Guta Lag and Guta Saga
The Law and History of the Gotlanders
Christine Peel

The Danish Medieval Laws
The Laws of Scania, Zealand and Jutland
Ditlev Tamm and Helle Vogt

The Liber legis Scaniae
The Latin Text with Introduction, Translation and Commentaries
Ditlev Tamm

The Borgarthing Law and the Eidsivathing Law
The Laws of Eastern Norway
Lisa Collinson, Torgeir Landro, and Bertil Nilsson

The Borgarthing Law and the Eidsivathing Law

The Laws of Eastern Norway

Translated and edited by
Lisa Collinson, Torgeir Landro, and Bertil Nilsson

Routledge
Taylor & Francis Group
LONDON AND NEW YORK

First published 2021
by Routledge
2 Park Square, Milton Park, Abingdon, Oxon OX14 4RN

and by Routledge
52 Vanderbilt Avenue, New York, NY 10017

Routledge is an imprint of the Taylor & Francis Group, an informa business

British Library Cataloguing-in-Publication Data
A catalogue record for this book is available from the British Library

Library of Congress Cataloging-in-Publication Data
Names: Collinson, Lisa, translator, editor. | Landro, Torgeir, translator, editor. | Nilsson, Bertil, 1951– translator, editor.
Title: The Borgarthing law and the Eidsivathing law : the laws of Eastern Norway / translated and edited by Lisa Collinson,Torgeir Landro, and Bertil Nilsson.
Description: Milton Park, Abingdon, Oxon ; New York, NY : Routledge, 2021. | Includes bibliographical references and index.
Identifiers: LCCN 2020031516 | ISBN 9780367646424 (hardback) | ISBN 9781003125617 (ebook)
Subjects: LCSH: Law, Medieval—Norway—Sources. | Law—Norway—History—Sources.
Classification: LCC KKN125 .B67 2021 | DDC 349.48109/021—dc23
LC record available at https://lccn.loc.gov/2020031516

ISBN: 978-0-367-64642-4 (hbk)
ISBN: 978-0-367-64644-8 (pbk)
ISBN: 978-1-003-12561-7 (ebk)

Typeset in Times New Roman
by Apex CoVantage, LLC

Contents

A general introduction to the *Medieval Nordic Laws* translations

The oldest laws of the Nordic countries were written in the vernacular. The earliest manuscripts stem from the thirteenth century and are younger than the texts of the laws, some of which date back to the twelfth century. They are, of course, important for the fields of Nordic law and legal history, but are equally significant for other fields, being amongst the oldest written sources for medieval Nordic social history (including household, administrative, ecclesiastical, and agrarian matters), as well as for philology, as some of the oldest written documents we have in the vernacular.

For a long time, these laws were intensely studied by legal historians as the foundation of national law. During the last decade, there has been a revival of interest in these early laws in the Nordic countries, manifested in, for example, an influential conference series on early law at the Carlsberg Academy in Denmark, and the initiative of an interdisciplinary network project, called *Medieval Nordic Laws* (*MNL*), funded by The Leverhulme Trust and based at the University of Aberdeen, along with some other local initiatives. In order to open up the floodgates to international interest and research on these laws and to facilitate comparison, the decision was made in the *MNL* project to translate the laws into English. Besides the obvious scoop of international interest in the laws based on new translations, another gain with this initiative was the rethinking of the position of the laws in connection with the redaction of new introductions to the laws. The Nordic medieval laws were earlier subjected to thorough analysis from both legal and historical points of view and have been translated into modern Nordic languages. This happened mainly in the 1930s and 40s, but the laws have long played a central role in Nordic legal history. In the second part of the nineteenth century, the Nordic laws were seen in German scholarship as important expressions of the so-called *Germanenrechte*, and intense learning was used in developing and describing a specific Nordic variant of such law. This approach was never fully accepted in the Nordic countries, and a more critical study of the laws based on the idea that they reflected both older and newer layers of law started in the 1920s and continued to the 1980s in Scandinavia. Today's legal historians in the Nordic countries tend to see the laws in a European context and generally as new law written down as such. Most Nordic scholarship, however, has only been published in Nordic languages. Research into the medieval legal world has continued in later years; these translations and introductions in English thus make the newest research accessible to an international public. Iceland holds a somewhat different position and has already seen two of the old law codes, *Grágás* and *Jónsbók*, given modern translations and introductions recently. The edition of the old Icelandic law has been an inspiration for the present project.

The work has been pursued on a national basis by local teams with occasional meetings to discuss the project. The original plan for these new translations was for the work to be done either by individuals already acquainted with the relevant laws or by teams of scholars with appropriate expertise. To assist these translators, reference groups were assembled, with some of the most prominent scholars in the fields of law, legal history, canon law, history, and philology. A crucial question when dealing with translations of this kind is, of course, in each case to find a 'normative' text on which to base the translation, chosen from the potentially many (sometimes diverging) manuscripts which contain the law. It has been up to each team or translator to make this decision. It would have been desirable but technically very complicated to include the original text. To make the volumes accessible to a broader readership, we have therefore decided not to include the Old Nordic texts, which can, in most cases, be found online.

Stefan Brink
Professor of Scandinavian Studies
University of Aberdeen

Ditlev Tamm
Professor of Law
University of Copenhagen

Foreword

This volume contains translations of the two oldest versions of the Church Law Sections of the eastern Norwegian *Borgarthing Law* and *Eidsivathing Law*, which are the only parts of these laws that survive to the present day. The translations have been supplemented both with footnotes highlighting key readings and manuscript variants, and with in-depth end-note commentaries on their contents. Lisa Collinson (Aberdeen) worked mainly on the translations and footnotes, and Torgeir Landro (Bergen) and Bertil Nilsson (Lund) on commentaries, but all parts of the finished text were created through fruitful and stimulating discussions between all three. Anne Irene Riisøy (Oslo) also made many useful contributions during the early stages of this project.

Lisa Collinson, Torgeir Landro, and Bertil Nilsson
Aberdeen, Bergen, and Lund, June 2020

Part I General introduction

Torgeir Landro and Bertil Nilsson

Thing organization and the Church

At the turn of the first millennium, Norway was divided into four legal provinces, each called a *lǫg* or *lag* ('legal district', 'law-area'). Each *lǫg* had its own law, jurisdiction, and assembly (*þing*, anglicized as 'thing'). The *Borgarthing Law* and the *Eidsivathing Law* were two of the four provincial laws of Norway and were valid in the southeastern parts of Norway. They are amongst the earliest extant written records from the kingdom as a whole. The *kristinnréttr* ('Church Law Section') was but one of several *balkar* ('books' or 'sections') of law material contained within the laws. The *kristinnréttr* was also called the *kristinsdómsbalkr*, and contained Christian legal material, written down in the wake of the early eleventh-century conversion of Norway (Rindal 2004).

The contents of the Church Law Sections include regulations relating to baptism rituals; building and maintenance of churches and churchyards; tithes; burial customs; the liturgical year, with its days of feasting or fasting; marriage regulations; holiday regulations; dietary regulations; and prohibitions against heathen customs. In general, the provisions are quite typical for a newly converted kingdom with a rudimentary Church organization; the initiation rites of the new religion are explained, and it is made clear that churches and churchyards must be maintained, and that heathen customs must cease.

The geographical boundaries of Church districts (dioceses) were established soon after the conversion. The newly established Church was first organized under the archbishopric of Hamburg-Bremen, and from 1103 or 1104 under the archbishopric of Lund (Denmark). Finally, the Norwegian kingdom became an archdiocese of its own with the establishment of the archbishopric of Niðaróss in 1152 or 1153. Interestingly enough, in Norway, ecclesiastical law was not shaped by diocese boundaries. Instead, Church organization was adapted to fit the existing thing organization, with its hierarchy of lower and higher thing assemblies. Consequently, the bishop of Oslo presided over both the Eidsivathing *lǫg* and the Borgarthing *lǫg* until 1152 or 1153, when the diocese of Hamar was created from part of the diocese of Oslo.

The organization of thing assemblies

The eastern part of Norway was split into two different areas: the Borgarthing *lǫg* covering the coastal area around the Oslofjord, and the Eidsivathing *lǫg* for the inner part of eastern Norway. However, by the twelfth century, thing assemblies had operated more locally for centuries. These were held in meeting places of social and religious importance and were used for discussing and resolving conflicts – later as legislative and judicial bodies – with the farmers in charge (Øyrehagen Sunde 2010: 81–96). These so-called *bygðarstefnur* ('community meetings') were quite numerous and scattered, and every local man had a right and a duty to attend (Helle 2001: 27). By contrast, the later *lǫg* thing assemblies were representative bodies for larger geographical areas (Helle 2001: 32), with the thing-sites either strategically located in the fjords along the coastal shipping route or near internal waterways, such as the location of the Eidsivathing close to Mjøsa, the largest lake in Norway. And while the local thing assemblies were established to meet the needs of farmers, it would seem reasonable to regard the Church and kings as driving forces behind the development of the *lǫg* thing assemblies (*lǫgþing*, in both singular and plural forms). The creation of a hierarchical structure with the *lǫg* thing assemblies at the top happened along with the Christianization and the unification of the kingdom, which is why Church and kingdom play a rather prominent role in the laws (Helle 2001: 209–218). Hákon inn góði (r. ca. 933–961), one of the first kings to introduce Christianity into Norway, was allegedly the organizer of the Gulathing in western Norway (Helle 2001: 30–37). However, each of the four *lǫg* thing assemblies has a rather unique history. Although Hákon helped organize the Gulathing, it seems likely that the Frostathing in northern Norway came into being quite early, perhaps in the ninth century, without any initiative from either Church or kingdom (Hagland & Sandnes 1994: XII–XVII). The Borgarthing, on the other hand, was probably first established as a *lǫg* thing assembly around the middle of the twelfth century.

The Eidsivathing was originally a thing assembly for a smaller geographical area (Hedmark and Mjøsbygdene) with the thing site located outside Hamar. Saga tradition credits both Hálfdan svarti (ca. 810–860) and Hákon inn góði as organizers. In the beginning of the eleventh century, the legal district was extended and the meeting place moved to Eid (modern Eidsvoll) – a reorganization for which Óláfr Haraldsson (St Óláfr) was allegedly responsible (Norseng et al. 2003: 506). From this time onwards there was a single *lǫg* thing covering eastern – as opposed to southeastern – Norway (the Eidsivathing *lǫg*).

When did the Borgarthing reach the status of a *lǫg* thing assembly in the southeast? The so-called 'Process of Sigurðr Hranason', which outlines a legal dispute involving the king Sigurðr Jórsalafari around 1115, states that Norway consisted of only three legal districts at that time (Brandt 1880: 166–167). This suggests that the Borgarthing had not yet become a *lǫg* thing assembly by the early 1100s, and most scholars agree that the change of status took place in the decades around 1150 (Brandt 1880: 166–167; Eliassen & Norseng 2005: 34). Prior to the establishment of the archbishopric of Niðaróss in 1152/53, the bishop of Oslo had presided over all of eastern Norway, but Hamar then became a bishopric in its own right. This incident might have coincided with, or paved the way for, the acquisition of *lǫg* thing assembly status for the Borgarthing. Whether or not this was the case, in 1164, the *jarl* Erlingr skakki summoned a 'four-*fylki*-thing' at Borg (Eliassen & Norseng 2005: 33), probably modern Sarpsborg, which makes clear that the Borgarthing had become the centre of a wider geographical area by this time. *Historia Norwegiæ*, a Latin history of Norway probably written sometime between 1150 and 1200, also mentions *Sinus orientalis* ('The Bay in the East') as one of the main legal districts in Norway (Eliassen & Norseng 2005: 33). The process thus seems to reveal a deliberate attempt to harmonize the boundaries of the bishoprics with the legal districts of eastern Norway. Eliassen and Norseng argue that both ecclesiastical and secular motives might lie behind the reorganization: both Church and monarchy wanted tighter control and more efficient organization (Eliassen & Norseng 2005: 34).

Although the Borgarthing became a *lǫg* thing assembly as late as the 1150s, it had probably been a thing assembly of some importance in the preceding period. According to sagas, both Knútr inn ríki and Haraldr harðráði ('the Ruthless') were hailed as kings at the Borgarthing assembly in 1028 and 1047 respectively – incidents which might indicate that the Borgarthing had a prominent position in the eastern coastal area (Eliassen & Norseng 2005: 32). Besides, a law-learned man called Bessi, who probably lived in the area around Borgarthing in the late eleventh century, is referred to in one of the paragraphs in two copies of the *Borgarthing Law* (AM 31 8o and Holm 28 4o). This provision strengthens the suspicion that legal activities of enduring character took place at the Borgarthing as early as the eleventh century (Eliassen & Norseng 2005: 32).

A mix of secular and ecclesiastical law

The term 'canon law' usually refers to independent ecclesiastical legislation (Ericsson 1967: 1–2). In this respect, the various Norwegian Church Law Sections cannot be labelled as canon law in the strictest sense of the term. The Norwegian Church Law Sections belong, in their written form, to secular law; each is the first section in a lost legal compilation comprising various sections dealing with topics such as inheritance and commercial law, and presumably promulgated and sanctioned by a secular thing assembly. There is no evidence for the existence of ecclesiastical courts in the first couple of centuries after the conversion, and the *Eidsivathing Law* explicitly witnesses that the farmers (*bœndr*) were in charge of judging violations at the thing. Fines were to be divided into three, and one third had to go to the 'farmers who were involved in the judgement' (E 25). Thus, adaptation of ecclesiastical law to Norwegian conditions meant that it became mixed with secular law (Hellström 1971: 143).

Based on supposed contributions by the laity to Norwegian Church law (both as judges of transgressions and as active participants in the formulation of the Church Law Sections) some scholars have advanced a theory that the Norwegian Church laws were the products of compromises between the clergy and the laity.

According to this theory, the laity had a great deal of say in legal matters, and scholars have contended finding evidence of strong and resistant Norwegian farmers in the regulations in the Church Law Sections concerning diet, procedure, and infant exposure (Seip 1942: 17; Jochens 1998: 90–92; Sanmark 2004: 225–227; Landro 2010: 23–24). This notion has been strongly contested, since many of the regulations supposedly forced through by the laity actually have parallels within medieval canon law (Landro 2010: 210–219). This does not mean, however, that there are no lay elements in the Norwegian Church laws. Concepts and terms borrowed from secular law do provide evidence of lay participation. But this probably took the form of peaceful and cooperative collaboration between clerics and people with special knowledge of local secular law (Foote 2003: 12). In fact, passages in the provincial laws provide glimpses of the collaboration in practice. The *Frostathing Law* states that Cardinal Nicholas Breakspear (later Pope Adrian IV (1154–1159) and Archbishop Jón of Niðaróss (archbishop 1152–1157) advised that amendments should be formulated 'together with the wisest men', bearing in mind the good of all the inhabitants of the province. Also, the same law testifies that Archbishop Eysteinn of Niðaróss (archbishop 1161–1188) gave advice and prescriptions 'with the approval of the wisest men', which seems to describe exactly the same procedure. The Church thus seems to have followed a deliberate strategy to involve people who were especially knowledgeable about local law in the processes of shaping and authorizing legislation (Landro 2010: 129–130).

Another facet to be considered is the term *kristinnréttr* itself. Why is the Old Norse term *réttr* preferred to denote the Church Law material, and not *lag/lǫg* ('law'), which is more common in medieval Scandinavian laws (Vogt 2005: 38–39)? In line with the distinction between the Latin legal terms, *lex* and *ius*, one would expect 'law' to be used in this case. *Lex* was used to denote a single law or a book of law, while the term *ius* more often referred to what is just, or, as Murphy puts it: 'to the body of law as a whole, or indeed, to the rule of law in general' (Murphy 2006: 111; Landro 2013: 125). The distinction between *lex* and *ius* is still present in most modern European languages, except in English: the Germans distinguish between *Gesetz* (*lex*) and *Recht* (*ius*), likewise the French between *loi* and *droit*, the Italians between *legge* and *diritto*, and the Scandinavians between *lov/lag* and *rett* (Murphy 2006: 108; Landro 2013: 125). Helle Vogt has suggested that *kristinnréttr* could refer to 'the Christian legal order', without giving any further explanation of what this might imply (Vogt 2005: 39). Perhaps a statement from *Archbishop Jón's Church Law* from the thirteenth century sums up the meaning of this legal concept: 'God's law in every Christian country' (NgL II: 372, § 46). If so, was the term *kristinnréttr* deliberately chosen to underline the fact that the Church Laws, unlike secular laws, belonged to a different legal order, with roots outside the Norwegian provinces (Landro 2013: 126)?

Another way to approach the concept of *kristinnréttr* is to take into account the variations and synonyms found in the manuscripts (Landro 2005: 20, 2013: 126). The final and concluding paragraph in the *Borgarthing Law* states: 'Now, the Christian Law (*kristinnréttr*), as we recall it, has been recounted' (Borg. 18). In one of the manuscripts, however, the term *kristinnréttr* has been replaced by *kristindomr* (*kristinndómr* ModE. 'Christendom'): 'Now, our Christendom, as we recall it, has been recounted' (AM 31 8o; Halvorsen & Rindal 2008: 198; NgL I: 363). Apparently, the term *kristinndómr* conveys the same meaning as *kristinnréttr*. It also appears in the introduction to one of the manuscripts of the *Eidsivathing Law*, 'Here is told of our old Christendom' (NB 317 4o; Halvorsen & Rindal 2008: 64), thus confirming that the alternation between these two terms should not be seen as an isolated case in the AM 31 8o copy of the *Borgarthing Law*. What does this mean? One should be careful and not draw overly dramatic conclusions based on this switch of terms alone, but the term *kristinndómr* evokes other associations and can be interpreted as a more all-encompassing concept, including doctrine in addition to the legal sphere of Christianity (NgL V: 364, s.v. *kristinn dómr*). There are admittedly few, if any, other traces of doctrine or dogma in the old Church laws. Nevertheless, this fact should not lead to a subordination of the laws as sources for medieval Christianity. The Norwegian historian Andreas Holmsen claimed that the laws were only concerned with outward conduct, and provided no clues to the question of whether the Norwegians were really Christians in the Middle Ages (Holmsen 1961: 188; Landro 2013: 127). He thus revealed an understanding, maybe inspired by Protestantism, of Christianity as mainly consisting of inner beliefs (Bagge 1998: 97, 108–110; Landro 2013: 128). Perhaps the occurrence of terms like *kristinnréttr* and *kristinndómr* (concepts which are rather vague and open in character) should be a warning not to interpret the content of the Church laws as a sphere of its own, distinct from dogma and doctrine, but as an integral and essential part of medieval Christianity as a whole.

Origins and development over time

The extant manuscripts of the *Borgarthing Law* and the *Eidsivathing Law* can be dated to the time period between 1300 and 1350, based on palaeographical evidence. In spite of this, the core of the content of the Norwegian Church laws has for generations been linked to the missionary and legal activities of Óláfr Haraldsson, king of Norway from 1015 until 1028. Óláfr was among the first Norwegian kings to make a serious attempt to promote Christianity and was killed in the battle of Stiklastaðir in 1030, thereby acquiring the status of martyr and saint. The notion that he lay behind the core of the Borgarthing Church Law Section is mainly based on two arguments. Firstly, four different chapters in the *Gulathing Law*, valid in the Gulathing legal district on the west coast of Norway, refer to St Óláfr and Grimkell, an English bishop, as lawgivers. Secondly, it has been claimed that comparison of Norwegian and Anglo-Saxon ecclesiastical laws reveals great similarities between these (Taranger 1890; Helle 2001: 180–182; Tveito 2007; Landro 2010: 20–21). Given Óláfr's connexions with England, this is then claimed to confirm the validity of the references in the *Gulathing Law* to St Óláfr as lawgiver.

St Óláfr is claimed to have promulgated laws first at a thing assembly in Moster in the current province of Vestland in 1024, and then through the provincial laws, after their contents were negotiated at all four provincial thing assemblies. These negotiated laws have traditionally been regarded as the basis for the four Church Law Sections (Seip 1942: 14–15). Furthermore, although the Borgarthing Church Law Section does not contain any specific references to St Óláfr, its relative brevity has been seen as an indication that it provides the best picture of the laws originally given by him (Taranger 1890: 208; Helle 2001: 179).

However, the role of St Óláfr as lawgiver should probably be played down. Some of the paragraphs attached to his name have been proven to be later additions (Landro 2010: 190). Besides, the tradition of crediting law paragraphs to mythical law-making kings from the distant past was well-established in medieval Europe. Later generations of legislators claimed the authority of kings, such as Valdemar II and Frode in Denmark (Vogt 2009: 78–79), King Erik in Sweden, and King Hywel Dda in Wales, in order to legitimize regulations (Pryce 2000: 34; Landro 2010: 189–191). References to St Óláfr as lawgiver should probably be seen in light of this phenomenon (Helle 2001: 18–19). In addition, the argument for Anglo-Saxon influence is weak, and recent scholarship has stressed the great methodological challenges involved in studying ecclesiastical law comparatively, undermining the possibility of tracing the Norwegian ecclesiastical norms back to any specific geographical area (Landro 2010: 227–229).

It is probably a better idea to regard the fourteenth-century manuscripts as end products of long and gradual processes of legislation, and it is generally assumed that these manuscripts therefore consist of several different strata (Hellström 1971: 7; Rindal 2004: 110). This is difficult to prove in many cases, but the *Borgarthing Law* provides a rare case in point. In chapter five, which deals with dietary regulations, it is actually possible to discern three different chronological layers. The underlying principle which initially lay behind these regulations was inspired by a canonical tradition originating in the East Frankish kingdom in the middle of the ninth century. However, later on in the chapter, it can be seen that this was replaced by a more recently introduced, Augustinian interpretation of the dietary regulations. In addition, the procedural content of the chapter seems to have been rearranged a number of times after 1200. This, together with the character of the legal procedure described by the law as a whole, reveals that, at some stage, quite extensive revision must have taken place (Landro 2010: 187–188).

It is first and foremost the *consistency* within its procedural arrangements which makes the *Borgarthing Law* stand out, compared with the other Norwegian Church Law Sections. The distinction between intentional and unintentional crime, the latter leading not to fines but to penance, reveals a methodical approach to legislation unknown in the other Norwegian Church Law Sections. Similar cases are treated equally and show that someone with legal training has gone through the entire law, chapter by chapter, and harmonized its procedural arrangements consistently. In the chapter dealing with dietary regulations (chapter five), for instance, the editor inserts a remark ('then he shall have five-days' grace, following the trial by hot iron, as would a witch') which guides the reader to a parallel case later on (chapter sixteen), in which witches are given the same treatment. Such a comment has obviously been inserted later on by someone familiar with the content of the entire law (Landro 2010: 154–155).

The juridical skills obviously possessed by the editor imply that the revision must have taken place sometime after 1150, when professional study of law gained momentum. Chapter seventeen seems to reflect knowledge of the inquisitorial procedure instituted by Pope Innocent III (1198–1216) at the Fourth Lateran Council in 1215; paragraphs 17.7–17.12 arguably display traces of both of the two procedural stages which characterize the inquisitorial procedure: *inquisitio famae* and *inquisitio veritatis* (Trusen 1988; Brundage 1996; Thijssen 1996; Landro 2010: 172–181). Also, the very same chapter prohibits double jeopardy (bringing the same lawsuit against the same defendant twice). The classical principle behind this, *non bis in idem*, was standard within the *ius commune* (Helmholz 1996: 286–290; Pennington 1997: 1108; Landro 2010: 178–179) and gives further reason to assume that someone learned in canon law was involved in the formulation of this paragraph. On the other hand, the revision of the *Borgarthing Law* was probably not carried out any later than 1250, since it still prescribed use of trial by ordeal in certain limited cases; clerical participation in ordeals was prohibited at the Fourth Lateran Council in 1215, but this was not enforced in Norway until 1247 during a visitation by the papal legate, Cardinal William of Sabina (Nilsson, Bertil 2001: 530). Taken together, all the evidence suggests that the revision of the *Borgarthing Law* was probably carried out at some point after 1215, but probably no later than 1250 (Landro 2010: 181). This timeframe makes Bishop Nikulás Árnason a possible candidate as the man behind the revision. Nikulás was bishop of Oslo between 1190 and 1225, and as Anne Duggan has pointed out, Pope Celestine III (1191–1198) explicitly stated that bishop Nikulás was 'learned in canon law' (Landro 2010: 182–184; Duggan 2011: 24).

Three centuries lay between the conversion and the writing of the extant manuscripts. There is not much hard evidence that can help pinpoint the dating of any given detail in the *Borgarthing Law* within this long timespan. As noted earlier, the existence of different strata in this text obviously implies that the legislation developed gradually; the revisions concerning procedure took place quite late within this period. Nevertheless, a series of indications suggest that the bulk of the content of the *Borgarthing Law* does date to the time prior to 1150. First, there is no mention of the archbishop or the archbishopric (established in 1152 or 1153) in the *Borgarthing Law*, unlike in the other Norwegian laws. Neither did this law incorporate an amendment of the baptismal rite (allowing women to perform baptism in emergency situations) made by the first archbishop, Jón – again, unlike the other provincial laws (Landro 2010: 212). Second, whereas the marriage regulations in the *Eidsivathing Law* reflect the consensus doctrine promoted by Pope Alexander III (1159–1181), there is no sign of this novelty in the *Borgarthing Law*. Third, when it comes to the question of who should be in charge of appointing local priests, the *Borgarthing Law* seems not to have been brought up to date with the other Church Law Sections; in these, the bishop is in charge, a responsibility he probably took over after a revision of the legislation by King Magnús Erlingsson (1161–1184) in the 1160s. The *Borgarthing Law*, by contrast, seems to reflect an earlier period, during which the farmers were in control not only of a priest's appointment, but also of his freedom of movement once appointed; a priest was not allowed to leave the parish without asking the farmers for permission in advance. The local priests in the *Borgarthing Law* still seem to be living under tightly controlled conditions, reminiscent of those described in a famous passage in the *Gulathing Law*, which states that 'we have abolished punishing them [the priests] by beating' (Gul. 15); this can be seen as evidence both for the conditions of the time prior to the writing of the *Gulathing Law* passage and for changes which took place after that point (Wisløff 1966; Landro 2010: 211–213). Fourth, only some of the manuscripts contain references to the Feast of St Thomas, venerating Archbishop Thomas Becket of Canterbury (d. 1170), who was canonized in 1173 (Halvorsen & Rindal 2008: xii–xiii). Although all four of these indicia are arguments *e silentio*, when taken together, they do give the impression that the Church Law Section of the *Borgarthing Law* has been modernized less than those of other provincial laws in terms of material content.

The early date of the material content of the *Borgarthing Law* leads, however, to another important question, namely why the manuscripts were still copied as late as the fourteenth century. Icelandic sources tell that king Magnús the Lawmender (r. 1263–1280) issued new editions of the Church Law for western Norway in 1267 and another law for eastern Norway in 1268. This information has been connected to a couple of law manuscripts which have been identified as the new Christian Laws of the *Gulathing* and the *Borgarthing*. These laws were a part of an attempt to harmonize the old provincial church laws and promulgate a national code. Nevertheless, the old Christian laws did not cease to circulate since copies are found from the fourteenth century. Why did new and old laws coexist for centuries? The historian Jens Arup Seip claimed to find the answer to this puzzle in the conflict between Church and Kingdom in the second half of the thirteenth century (Seip 1942: 158–160, 229–231; Bagge 2010: 294–306). The new archbishop, Jón rauði (1268–1282), elected in 1268, refused the king's involvement in ecclesiastical legislation and promulgated a Christian law of his own in 1273. An agreement was reached in the Concordat of Tunsberg (Tønsberg) in 1277, but when king Magnús died in 1280, the anti-clerical regency government that followed him revoked the concessions given to the Church in the Treaty of Tunsberg and re-issued the old Christian law (*forn kristin rettr*). Seip's interpretation, which admittedly has been questioned (Riisøy & Dale Spørck 1999), is that *forn kristin rettr* referred to the old Church Law Sections of the regional laws. If so, the circulation of presumably outdated law manuscripts in the early fourteenth century can be explained.

Without doubt, the fourteenth-century date of the manuscripts of the *Borgarthing Law* – combined with the existence of different chronological layers in the manuscripts and signs of a revision in the thirteenth century – suggest that the prominent position traditionally given to Óláfr Haraldsson as the creator of the Norwegian Church laws should be toned down. This does not, however, rule out the possibility that a thing assembly was held at Moster sometime in the early 1020s, and that basic principles were agreed upon then. An inscription on a runic monument called the Kuli Stone in the current province of Møre og Romsdal states that Christianity had been in Norway for twelve winters when it was erected – probably in the early 1030s (Hagland 1998; Spurkland 2005: 108–112, 133; Mikkelsen 2019: 86–87). This statement seems to refer to some special event which marked the beginning of a new era: quite possibly a thing assembly at which a decision was taken to accept Christianity and guiding principles were established. In this respect, it is still possible to regard the thing assembly at Moster and Óláfr Haraldsson's initiative as starting points for Norwegian ecclesiastical legislation. But the small number of clerics and the absence of a Church organization at that time, along with the fact that any legislation would have had to be transmitted orally until the laws were committed to writing around the turn of the eleventh century, suggest that a very limited quantity of legislation could have been carried forwards into the surviving *Borgarthing Law*. If a thing assembly did take place at Moster in the early 1020s, this should be conceived as the foundation stone for a rudimentary Church organization, which paved the way for more elaborate legislation later (Landro 2010: 191).

Part II Translator's introduction

Lisa Collinson

This introduction is intended as a basic guide to previous scholarship, which I hope will provide the general reader with some useful insights into the scribal and linguistic contexts in which the surviving manuscripts of the Church Law Sections were created in early fourteenth-century east and southeast Norway. Accordingly, I have tried to use readily understandable layman's terms wherever possible. Readers interested in delving into the specialist literature are advised to consult the bibliography provided. Individual manuscripts are mentioned in passing in the opening survey, and then described in more detail in a separate section later on. Where possible, I have offered pointers to images of the script in the texts under discussion, and I would encourage readers curious to understand the dating of those scripts to compare the recommended images with the tables of Norwegian letter types provided by Lars Svensson in *Nordisk paleografi* (Svensson 1974: 243–249). More detailed verbal descriptions of Norwegian script, along with longer samples, are to be found throughout Didrik Arup Seip's *Palæografi B: Norge og Island* (Seip 1954). (For an up-to-date general introduction to Old Norwegian palaeography, see Haugen 2002.)

Previous editions and translations

The present translations of the Church Law Sections of the *Older Borgarthing Law* and the *Eidsivathing Law* are based on a recent combined edition of these by Eyvind Fjeld Halvorsen and Magnus Rindal, published as *De eldste østlandske kristenrettene* (Halvorsen & Rindal 2008). Previously, the standard editions had been part of the first volume of the nineteenth-century series *Norges gamle Love indtil 1387* (usually abbreviated to NgL or NGL), edited by Peter Andreas Munch and Rudolph Keyser, which contained editions of the oldest Norwegian legal texts, printed in a dense Gothic font (NgL I). In that volume, the edition of the Borgarthing Church Law Section was based on the manuscript AM 78 4o, and that of the Eidsivathing Church Law Section on AM 68 4o, setting the pattern for the present work. Descriptions of the manuscripts consulted were published in a supplement to the series produced by Gustav Storm in 1885 (NgL IV).

The following year, the Norske Historiske Kildeskriftfond published a photographic facsimile of that part of one of the manuscripts (Codex Tunsbergensis

NKS 1642 4o) containing the Church Law Section of the *Older Borgarthing Law*, produced by Storm and others including Oluf Rygh (BÆK); this is now viewable online from the Bavarian State Library (Bayerische Staatsbibliothek, München), through the Europeana Foundation (www.europeana.eu/portal/). In 1914, Torleiv Olavsson published translations of the *Older Borgarthing* and the *Eidsivathing Law* into modern Norwegian, based on the NgL I edition (Olavsson 1914a, 1914b). Rudolf Meißner published translations of both Church Law Sections, also based on NgL I, into German in 1942 (Meißner 1942).

The recent work *De eldste østlandske kristenrettene* contains diplomatic editions of all surviving manuscripts of medieval provincial law from east and southeast Norway: Østlandet. (In this Introduction, 'east' and 'southeast' Norway will be kept distinct, with 'east Norway' referring to Oppland, Hedmark, and Buskerud, and 'southeast Norway' to the areas around the Oslofjord.) The most important of these editions, based on the same manuscripts prioritized in NgL I, are accompanied by translations into modern Norwegian. These also provide the basis for editorial division of the laws into chapters and paragraphs. Corresponding chapters and paragraphs in secondary manuscripts are labelled with the same numbers, even if they appear in different orders, aiding cross-referencing. Substantial clauses found in three of the secondary manuscripts of the *Older Borgarthing Law* but not in the main manuscripts are presented as numbered additions, translated in a separate section, near the end of the volume.

The present translations

Our translations follow the methods and numbering system adopted by Halvorsen & Rindal closely. We have agreed with their selections of primary manuscripts and translated from these into English, showing in footnotes interesting phrases and significant variations in secondary manuscripts. Fuller remarks on specific terms and matters of content are given in commentaries and a glossary. In most cases, we have also agreed with the interpretations of the Old Norwegian texts put forward by Halvorsen & Rindal, and by T. Olavsson and R. Meißner in their much earlier translations into modern Norwegian and German (Olavsson 1914a, 1914b; Meißner 1942). However, our detailed discussions of individual phrases have occasionally led to slightly different interpretations, which we offer as suggestions in this volume. The style of the translations has evolved since work on them began in 2009, becoming less literal but hopefully clearer and more useful along the way. In order to achieve this, my initial draft translation has been silently emended throughout in a number of ways. First, I have added articles, both definite and indefinite. Second, I have added commonly elided words, including verbs (especially forms of *vera* and *skulu*), pronouns, and conjunctions. Third, I have sometimes switched pronouns, to use whichever would be most natural in English (for example, swapping 'this' for 'that'). Fourth, I have converted some plurals into singular forms and vice versa, where number has appeared insignificant in the original texts and where such a change would improve the English. I have also ignored relatively insignificant variations and errors related to spelling, mood, grammatical consistency, and choice of synonyms, including the sometimes synonymous *ok* and *eða* (normally 'and' and 'or' respectively) and *vera* and *verða* ('to be' and 'to become'). More significantly, after much deliberation, I decided to translate *maðr* as 'man' (rather than 'person') except where this would have been entirely inappropriate. Similarly, in some cases, I have chosen to use the pronoun 'it' for a child. Finally, in certain rules, a particularly wide gap between the Old Norwegian and modern English has made rather free, although careful, translation necessary. However, patches of awkwardness remain, reflecting the opacity and unevenness of the original texts.

Writing in east and southeast Norway in the early fourteenth century

The Eidsivathing legal area is believed to have covered much of eastern and inner Norway, whilst the Borgarthing area covered the southeast. (Maps can be found in Jón Viðar Sigurðsson 2009: 77; Ødegaard 2013: 42.) The oldest surviving copies of the Church Law Sections of the *Eidsivathing Law* and the *Older Borgarthing Law* are thought to have been produced in the east and southeast during the early fourteenth century, and it may be helpful to consider their geographical and cultural backgrounds before introducing the texts themselves.

Throughout the High Middle Ages, the human geography of east and southeast Norway had been changing. Arable farming was especially important to this region, and forests were cleared to a greater extent than in the west (Helle 1995: 35, 42). In the Oslo area, for example, around half the known named estates can be dated to the forest-clearing period following the establishment of the town (Nedkvitne & Norseng 1991: 77). Particularly during the twelfth and thirteenth centuries, Østlandet grew in population and in new kinds of economic and political importance, partly due to changing patterns of foreign influence (Jón Viðar Sigurðsson 2009: 160).

Oslo, like Hamar further north, had long been an episcopal see, and therefore an economic centre; the bishopric of Hamar had been divided from that of Oslo in 1152–3, and Hamar had been regarded as a town since that century (Jón Viðar Sigurðsson 2009: 98; Helle 1995: 38). Oslo was probably originally the dominant Church centre and most likely remained so in the later thirteenth and earlier fourteenth centuries (Nedkvitne & Norseng 1991: 63). In addition, both Oslo and particularly Tønsberg were trading centres, from the thirteenth century dealing especially with the Hansa of Rostock (Jón Viðar Sigurðsson 2009: 164; Nedkvitne & Norseng 1991: 188–202). Indeed, from the middle of the thirteenth century, Oslo and Tønsberg had been two of the three biggest towns in Norway: by 1300, Oslo probably had a population of 3000, and Tønsberg 1500 (Jón Viðar Sigurðsson 2009: 160, 162; Nedkvitne & Norseng 1991: 104). (For an artist's impression of Oslo around 1350, see Nedkvitne & Norseng 1991: 310–311.) In both Olso and Tønsberg, versions of a dedicated *Town Law* issued by Magnús Lawmender in 1276 applied, probably from within a few years of its creation (Nedkvitne & Norseng 1991: 76). Further small towns included the old settlement of Skien in Telemark, on the western side of the Oslofjord, as well as Borg, Uddevalla, the port of Marstrand and the royal harbour, Konghelle to the east (Jón Viðar Sigurðsson 2009: 159; Helle 1995: 32, 39). However, the administrative importance of Oslo as a royal centre remained relatively modest during most of the twelfth and thirteenth centuries. Its significance began to grow during the 1280s and 1290s, when Hákon Magnússon, son of Magnús Lawmender, made Oslo the main residence of his dukedom, and increased still further after the duke became king (Hákon V) in 1299 (Nedkvitne & Norseng 1991: 133–152).

The rural population of the east and southeast also expanded during the thirteenth century, overtaking that of the west by around 1270 (Jón Viðar Sigurðsson 2009: 199). Perhaps in response to the seeds of such changes, Oslo had begun to develop as a royal administrative centre around 1200 (Nedkvitne & Norseng 1991: 139). Duke Hákon Magnússon declared Oslo his main residence in 1286.

In this developing region, writing was carried out in several places. In Oslo, some form of clerical education is likely to have been available from around 1100 (Nedkvitne & Norseng 1991: 291). By the early fourteenth century, documents were written at two churches, in particular: Hallvardskirken (St Hallvarðr's Cathedral, dedicated to the local saint) and the royal chapel Mariakirken (St Mary's Church). The oldest part of Hallvardskirken had probably been in use since the early twelfth century, and it was physically expanded quite extensively during the thirteenth century, with a new Gothic choir built in the 1260s (Nedkvitne & Norseng 1991: 66, 99, 312). A cathedral school provided opportunities for reading and possibly writing, at least in Latin (Nedkvitne & Norseng 1991: 291–292). Indeed, this is likely to have been the principal site of clerical education in the region, and it has been suggested that many of the scribes working at Hallvardskirken may have been from rural areas and had a tendency to include dialectal features characteristic of their areas of origin in their written language – at least when it came to letter writing. An important example of such a feature is modification (reduction) of unstressed /a/ to /ə/, /æ/ or /e/ after a long syllable (usually in a word ending). This was a characteristic of eastern and southeastern language from the end of the thirteenth century onwards; by the 1320s it was widespread enough that orthographic marking of the feature (using *æ* or *e*) had become the most distinctive feature of writing from Hallvardskirken (Grøtvedt 1939: 152, Hagland 1984: 119, 159–161, 226; Hagland 2002: 1016–1017).

The second important church in Oslo was the royal chapel Mariakirken. This lay closer to the royal estate and had been built in stone in the decades around 1100 on the site of an earlier wooden church (Nedkvitne & Norseng 1991: 40, 51, 136). A college of canons to provide royal administrative help was introduced by Hákon Magnússon (duke, then king) during the 1290s, and new building work on Mariakirken began around the same time and continued in the early 1300s, expanding it to 'cathedral dimensions' (Nedkvitne & Norseng 1991: 100, 145–146; Bagge 2001: 380). In 1314, Hákon made the provost of St Mary's in Oslo permanent chancellor. From at least this point, the church seems to have been a centre of legal learning and must have owned relevant books. In 1317, for example, the church lent four legal codices to a man travelling abroad to study (Rindal

2002: 805). A school was attached to the church from at least 1319; its purpose may have been to create literate men capable of carrying out various administrative duties (Nedkvitne & Norseng 1991: 291). Later, it certainly owned a fine copy of the *Town Law* of Oslo, produced around 1325. (A colour facsimile can be seen in Nedkvitne & Norseng 1991: 233.)

Mariakirken may itself have been the place of origin of many of the copies of laws produced in the early fourteenth century (Hagland 1984: 191). When it came to letter-writing from Mariakirken in the fourteenth century, one notable characteristic was retention of letter *a* in unstressed positions following long consonants, as in classical Old Norse (Hagland 1984: 159). This gave the language of letters from Mariakirken a distinctive look which has sometimes been seen as 'conservative' in its southeast Norwegian context but might simply suggest that the scribes working there were not local or chose not to show reduced */a/* in the same way as the scribes working at Hallvardskirken (Hagland 1984: 192–194).

Of course, some informal education, reading, and writing must have taken place at other religious institutions in southeast Norway, such as the Benedictine nunnery at Nonneseter in Oslo (Nedkvitne & Norseng 1991: 292). Outside Oslo was the Cistercian monastery, Hovedøya, and on an island near the small town of Skien was the Benedictine nunnery, Gimsøy. At Konghelle, there was the Augustinian Kastelle monastery, and there were Premonstratension foundations in Tønsberg and Bohuslän: St. Olav's and Dragsmark abbeys (Grøtvedt 1939: 10). Dominicans arrived in Olso a little before 1240, and then founded the twelve-man Olavskloster (Nedkvitne & Norseng 1991: 118). From the latter part of the thirteenth century onwards, there were also Fransiscans in Oslo, Konghelle, Tønsberg, and Marstrand (Jón Viðar Sigurðsson 2009: 75). However, there is no evidence that these provided significant formal education, and Norway was unusual amongst High Medieval Scandinavian and North European regions in that none of its towns, including Oslo, had a local secular school (Nedkvitne & Norseng 1991: 292).

Functional writing aside, by the early fourteenth century, Oslo seems to have been growing in importance as a centre of literary translation and copying (Lönnroth et al. 2003: 492). For the period 1299–1319, this may have been linked to a court culture focused on Hákon V, son of Magnús Lawmender, but also grandson of Hákon Hákonarson, around whom a similar court culture had emerged. The marriage of Hákon V to his continental queen Euphemia in 1299 is likely to have encouraged such a development, although conditions were probably favourable for it before this (Nedkvitne & Norseng 1991: 310).

Two now fragmentary copies of the handbook of royal behaviour, *Konungs skuggsjá*, were produced somewhere in the southeast in the late thirteenth century, perhaps around 1260–70 (Knudsen 1967: 43–70). A copy of *Barlams ok Josaphats saga* (in Stockholm, Kungliga biblioteket, 6 fol. (Holm. perg. 6 fol. or Sth. perg. fol. 6), dated to roughly 1250–75) may be eastern or southeastern (Rindal 1981: 18; Hagland 1984: 70). (For a script sample, see Haugen 2002: 828.) A little later, a scribe who, around 1320, contributed to the Codex Tunsbergensis – one of the Borgarthing manuscripts, NKS 1642 4o, discussed later – also wrote in a manuscript containing *Flores saga* (Seip 1954: 108). Given the existence of these small gems, it seems important to remember that although relatively few traces of non-functional literature survive from fourteenth-century east and southeast Norway, laws and official documents produced there were not created in a literary vacuum. By this stage, we know of several books (one psalter and three others unknown) in the ownership of private individuals in Oslo – as it happens, both women (Nedkvitne & Norseng 1991: 304).

The situation further north, in the bishop's seat of Hamar, is less easy to trace. However, the bishop (and possibly others) must have owned books, and there was certainly a cathedral school.

Writing law in east and southeast Norway in the early fourteenth century

The oldest surviving manuscripts of the Norwegian provincial laws have been dated to the thirteenth century: ten to the first half, and two to the second (Rindal 1987: 134). Those written around 1200–1250 record parts of the *Frostathing Law* (six) and *Gulathing Law* (three), and there is also a fragment of secular law from southeastern Norway (NRA 1 A, edited and translated in Halvorsen & Rindal 2008: 226–231). The two manuscripts from the latter part of the thirteenth century contain parts of the *Frostathing Law*. In all cases, there seems to be some correlation between the area to which a text pertained, and the dialectal character of its language (Rindal 1987: 135). In addition, a *National Law* was created in 1274, and several copies of this were made during the late thirteenth century, intended for different legal provinces including the Borgarthing and the Eidsivathing. Overall, these show relatively little dialectal variation, but both the Eidsivathing and the Borgarthing copies do feature linguistic traits which link them to east and southeast Norway (Hagland 1984: 44–81).

The oldest manuscripts containing the *Older Borgarthing Law* belong to the early fourteenth century. These were investigated by Per Nyquist Grøtvedt in his doctoral thesis of 1938 (published 1939). Grøtvedt studied seven law manuscripts which had earlier been dated by Gustav Storm to the relevant period (NgL IV). Most of these contained the *National Law* of 1274 and miscellaneous legal material including local town laws and additional laws, but three contained the Church Law Section of the *Older Borgarthing Law*: AM 78 4o, NKS 1642 4o and AM 31 8o. (AM 78 4o and NKS 1642 4o contain Version One of the law, whilst AM 31 8o contains Version Two, with some interesting additions.) Grøtvedt called these manuscripts A II, B, and C. He also looked at shorter official documents (diplomas), connected with kings and royal circles, clerics, law speakers, and a baron, all operating in the Borgarthing area in the first half of the fourteenth century. Finally, Grøtvedt considered features of more recent southeast Norwegian and west Swedish dialects. Taken together, this evidence allowed Grøtvedt to build up a detailed snapshot of scribal practice in the production of legal manuscripts in this region, during this specific period, with a particular focus on dialectal features.

In all cases, the script is basically Gothic; by this stage, thirteenth century changes to Norwegian law-book script were mainly complete. (For short samples see Haugen 2002: 828.) The normal methods of punctuation and abbreviation were used, although not consistently (Grøtvedt 1939: 28). The language is Old Norwegian, caught just before the opening of the phase known as Middle Norwegian, and – particularly in the Church Law Sections – incorporates many Nordic forms of loan words connected with the Church, such as 'priest', 'bishop', 'fast', 'mass', 'altar', and 'chrism' (*prestr, biskup, fasta, messa, krisma*). The spelling of the manuscripts tends to be quite mixed, with rather few indications that dialectal influence operated in any consistent way. One of the features Grøtvedt found most characteristic of written language from the Borgarthing area was vowel reduction, especially seen in /a/ written as *æ* or *e* (Grøtvedt 1939: 79, 152). Grøtvedt also produced evidence that the phenomenon called vowel harmony was an active influence on the language of the Borgarthing area law manuscripts. This was a much-debated feature of Old Norwegian and some dialects of Old Swedish, including that of Västergötland in the east, and involved matching (or partially matching) the qualities of vowels (especially /i/ and /u/) in unstressed syllables to preceding non-adjacent vowels (for example, *manne*). Grøtvedt gave a large number of examples from the Church Law Section of AM 78 4o and NKS 1642 4o (66–71) and the Borgarthing Version Two manuscript AM 31 8o. However, it has recently been pointed out that vowel harmony is probably a less reliable clear indicator of dialect than was generally thought, so the continuing value of Grøtvedt's evidence for this remains to be seen (Ottosson 2002: 792; Schulte 2002: 891–892).

Another feature known as 'younger *u*-umlaut' (vowel change under the influence of a later /u/) was represented quite inconsistently in the legal manuscripts Grøtvedt studied. At present, unmarked younger *u*-umlaut of /a/ is seen as a feature of the dialect of Oppland in the east (Hagland 2002: 1016). Although marked younger *u*-umlaut was sometimes present in Grøtvedt's *Borgarthing Law* manuscripts Grøtvedt also found many unmarked cases in his southeast Norwegian sources, including the *Borgarthing Law* manuscripts AM 78 4o, NKS 1642 4o and AM 31 8o (Grøtvedt 1939: 53–55). (AM 78 4o, for instance, used both *lagh um* and *logum* as dative plural forms of 'law'.)

In addition, Grøtvedt investigated two more apparently distinctive and easily spotted characteristics of southeast Norwegian (For recent views on these, see Hagland 2002). One was absence of *i*-umlaut in present tense strong verbs (showing up in forms like *takr, komr, gangr*), found in AM 78 4o and AM 31 8o (Grøtvedt 1939: 47). Another was preservation of *v* in the consonant cluster *vr* where it occurred initially; he concluded that the scribe of AM 78 4o probably came from an area where this feature had been retained, but that he at times omitted it (*ruæiði*), due to some external influence (Grøtvedt 1939: 110). In addition, Grøtvedt looked for a feature linked to southeast Norwegian dialect: use of *mn* rather than *fn* in words like *namn*. He found that although east Norwegian *mn* was seldom used in AM 78 4o or AM 31 8o, NKS 1642 4o showed 'rich variation' between *mn, fn*, and similar forms (Grøtvedt 1939: 115). As expected, he also found that all the *Borgarthing Law* manuscripts tended to represent the privative prefix ('un-') as *u* rather than *o*: a trait shared by east and southeast Norwegian texts of this period; however NKS 1642 4o did contain many examples of *o*: the choice normally made in Old Icelandic, Trøndelag, and Northwest Norwegian manuscripts (Grøtvedt 1939: 117).

Finally, it is worth noting here that Grøtvedt proposed that the manuscripts he studied could show differences in language within the Borgarthing area. For instance, he argued that svarabhakti vowels tended to appear as *a* in the south of the Borgarthing area, but *e* or *æ* farther north – in other words, towards the east Norwegian area (Grøtvedt 1939: 96–97). (Again, it should be mentioned as an aside that this an imperfect indicator of regional origin. See Schulte 2002: 891.) On the western side of the Oslofjord, around Tønsberg and beyond, Grøtvedt saw especially strong tendencies towards vowel rounding (*rǫttyndi*), loss of *l* (*fygdar halld*), and loss of *r* (*borgha þings*), all reflected in NKS 1642 4o. He also suggested that there were differences between written language produced in the Borgarthing area, which was dominated by an official 'chancery norm' originating in Mariakirken, and written language from the area which reflected local spoken language more closely (Grøtvedt 1939: 9). However, Jan Ragnar Hagland's more recent research on the early fourteenth century has suggested that the evidence for the existence of a strict chancery norm linked to Mariakirken is slim (Hagland 1984: 228–229). Instead, documents from across the area seem to display some natural smoothing out of dialectal features, perhaps connected with activities such as the copying of law-books by scribes exposed to a variety of dialects from both Norway and Iceland (Hagland 2002: 1017).

Although dialect boundaries did not correspond exactly with the boundaries of legal areas, in general terms, the Eidsivathing area was the home of a dialect now known as East Norwegian, which differed slightly from the Southeast Norwegian spoken in the Borgarthing area. East Norwegian is believed to have had some features in common with Southeast Norwegian as well as with the dialect of Trøndelag, which lies to the north and west: the Frostathing legal area. Features of Old East Norwegian shared with some apparently southeastern texts seem to have included unmarked *u*-umlaut of short /a/ before preserved /u/ (yielding *hafum* as opposed to *hofum*); which has been linked to Oppland as well as other parts of Norway; *mn* rather than *fn* in words like *namn* (amongst the southeastern texts, mainly in Codex Tunsbergensis, NKS 1642 4o); *u* as privative prefix (in common with most Old Norwegian dialects); svarabhakti vowel *e*/*æ* as in most varieties of written Old Norwegian (with some exceptions from western parts of the southeast); and weakening of unstressed /a/ after long syllables (*hiærtæ*). Unlike Southeast Norwegian, East Norwegian did not have unmarked *i*-umlaut in present tense strong verbs, and so gave standard *tekr*, for example, rather than *taker*. Similarly, unlike Southeast Norwegian, East Norwegian failed to preserve the *w*/*v* in the consonant cluster *vr*, where this appeared initially (Hagland 2002: 1016–1017). Old East Norwegian also had vowel harmony, although, as noted earlier, this may have been a general Norwegian trait. As yet, no monograph covering the Eidsivathing area and matching Grøtvedt's work on the Borgarthing manuscripts has been published. However, for more detailed information, interested readers may consult the items listed in the bibliography.

The Church Law Section of the Borgarthing Law: versions and manuscripts

The *Older Borgarthing Christian Law* survives in two versions. The present translation gives Version One, along with some additions found in Version Two manuscripts (AM 31 8o, Holm 28 4o and Holm 29 4o). Version One has been preserved in three manuscripts, one of which (AM 78 4o) underlies our translation. The other Version One manuscripts (NKS 1642 4o and AM 68 4o) are described next, and variants from these are given in footnotes. (For details of the Version Two manuscripts not discussed here, see Halvorsen & Rindal 2008: xxx–xxxi.)

AM 78 4o

Our translation of the text of the *Borgarthing Law* (Version One) has been founded on the same manuscript taken as the basis for the 1846 NgL edition, and for the translation by Halvorsen & Rindal: AM 78 4o in Den Arnamagnæanske Samling, University of Copenhagen, which can be viewed online through the website of the Handrit.is project (https://handrit.is/en/). This is the manuscript designated AII in Grøtvedt's study. Keyser and Munch dated it to the first quarter of the fourteenth century, Storm to the beginning of the fourteenth century, and Halvorsen & Rindal considered a date of around 1300 reasonable (NgL I: 338; NgL IV: 569; Halvorsen & Rindal 2008, xxviii–xxix). The main script of this manuscript (called 'A' by Keyser and Munch and '*a*' by Storm) has been identified with that in three further legal manuscripts, all dated to around 1300: AM 302 fol., AM 305 fol., and AM 56 4o; Storm noted similarities in their orthography and language (NgL IV: 569). Storm's descriptions of the scripts in the first and last of these emphasize their fineness and clarity and the attractive colouring of their initials (NgL IV: 473–76, 477–482, 539–541). Samples of the script in these can be seen in NgL IV: Plate XI: 1 and Seip 1954: 107 fig. 36 (AM 302 fol.) and Rindal 2002: 828, fig. 95.6 (AM 305) and Grøtvedt 1939: Plates I, III, and IV (all).

In one of these linked manuscripts (AM 302 fol.) the scribe named himself as *Thorgerus haquini*: Þorgeirr Hákonsson. This means that the scribe of AM 78 4o was one of fewer than a handful of Norwegian codex (as opposed to diploma) scribes of the period up to 1350 known by name (Haugen 2002: 831; Rindal 2002: 804). Since AM 302 fol. and AM 305 fol. contain additions which concern the Borgarthing town of Skien, it has been suggested that Þorgeirr had links to the town and produced manuscripts intended to be used and kept there (Hagland 1984: 49; Grøtvedt 1939: 14). Attempts to identify more about Þorgeirr Hákonsson have proved inconclusive (Hagland 1984: 48–49).

AM 78 4o itself is a parchment codex of 276 x 205mm (Kålund, 1889–94: I, 389, nr 730). It has lost many folios, and now contains sixty-nine (Halvorsen & Rindal 2008: xxviii). Its writing falls into two columns and it has been rubricated, with some of the initials highly ornamented and coloured red, blue, and green; in other words, it contains a level of decoration similar to that found in the three other manuscripts of which Þorgeirr Hákonarson seems to have been amongst the scribes. Indeed, Storm thought that AM 78 4o and AM 56 4o must originally have constituted a single codex, as suggested by their similar formats and complementary contents, and had not been divided until the middle of the sixteenth century (NgL IV: 571). Images of AM 78 4o were supplied by both Storm and Grøtvedt (NgL IV: Plate XI: 2; Grøtvedt 1939: Plate II).

The *Borgarthing Law* is to be found in the first eight folios of AM 78 4o, which also contains further Christian laws (*Archbishop Jón's Christian Law*, *Sverrir's Christian Law*), the *Town Law* of Bergen, and some additional laws attributed to the kings Hákon Hákonarson and Eiríkr Magnússon (NgL IV: 569–70; Kålund, 1889–94: 389–390, nr 730). Þorgeirr Hákonarson's other manuscripts contain copies of the *National Law*, and some additional laws (Halvorsen & Rindal 2008: xxviii; Hagland 1984: 47; Grøtvedt 1939: 15; Kålund 1889–94: I, 256 nr 457; 258 nr 460; 375 nr 699).

Didrik Arup Seip believed that the language of Þorgeirr Hákonarson's manuscripts was southeastern, and connected this with Skien, partly due to the non-linguistic evidence mentioned earlier (Hagland 1984: 49). Grøtvedt showed that the language in both AM 78 4o and the other manuscripts attributed to Þorgeirr does seem characteristic of southeast Norway: southern Østlandet. Salient features he found in AM 78 4o included examples of weakening of vowels (particularly /a/) in word endings, *a* as svarabhakti vowel, and possible retention of *v* in initial *vr* (Grøtvedt, 1939: 79, 96, 110–111). Less clear in meaning was the dominance of western *fn* over eastern *mn*, but this trait is shared with another potential southeastern manuscript: AM 31 8o (Grøtvedt 1939: 115). A 1981 dissertation by Elin Aa confirmed that the language of the Defence Sections of the *National Law* in the other three manuscripts linked to Þorgeirr seemed southeastern and suggested that these might have been produced in Oslo (Halvorsen & Rindal 2008: xxix).

Codex Tunsbergensis (NKS 1642 4o)

Codex Tunsbergensis is an alternative name for Nye Kongelige Samlinger, Det Kongelige Biblioteket København 1642 4o. (Storm described it in NgL IV: 425–34; Grøtvedt labelled it B, as had NgL I.) As previously mentioned, a digital copy of a nineteenth-century facsimile is available from the Bavarian State Library, through the European Foundation. This manuscript may have been written in Tønsberg (NgL IV: 434) for an early fourteenth-century Borgarthing lawman based in Tønsberg, Guðþormr Kolbjarnarson (1304–1320), is linked to letters containing similar linguistic features (BÆK: ii; Grøtvedt 1939: 129); both Storm and Halvorsen & Rindal connected it with Guðþormr's successor Þorvaldr Steinbjarnarson, since a calendar at the front of the manuscript mentions the death of a woman who may have been his wife (NgL IV: 425–7, 434; Halvorsen & Rindal 2008: xxix). The codex seems to have been kept locally in Tønsberg until the end of the sixteenth century (Halvorsen & Rindal 2008: xxix).

Keyser and Munch dated Codex Tunsbergensis to the first quarter of the fourteenth century, and Storm to possibly around 1320–30 or at least the first half of the fourteenth century (NgL I: 338; NgL IV: 434 and 425). Halvorsen & Rindal have found this half-century dating band 'reasonable' (Halvorsen & Rindal 2008: xxix). Its size is around 240 x 200 mm (NgL IV: 434; or 241 x 198 mm according to Kålund 1900: 190–191 nr 546).

Folios 17v – 23r carry the *Older Borgarthing Christian Law*, written in a hand Storm called *d*; note that Storm referred to the folio range of 'Vikens gamle Kristenret' as 18–31 (NgL IV: 428) and Kålund to a range of 18v – 24r (Kålund 1900: 191 nr 546). Both Storm and George Tobias Flom thought of *d* as the 'hand of the Codex proper' (NgL IV: 426; Flom 1925: 9). Apart from the *Older Borgarthing Christian Law*, scribe *d* copied into NKS 1642 4o several legal texts including the local Borgarthing version of the *National Law*, with additional laws and the court text *Hirdskraa* (*Hirðskrá*).

For some reason, although the scribe responsible for *d* wrote in two columns elsewhere in this manuscript, he wrote the Church Law Section of the *Borgarthing Law* without columns (NgL IV: 428). Storm described his script as 'firm, broad and clear, with few abbreviations' (NgL IV: 426) stating that the scribe was 'careful but not perfect'. Storm noted that the rubrics were 'often rather wordy' and that whilst initials were often also red, some were blue or green, and simply drawn; he and his fellow editors of the facsimile edition thought it possible that these were the work of the same scribe responsible for the main text (BÆK: ii). Well-used points were the only form of punctuation. Storm described the orthography associated with hand *d* as 'consistent but with many peculiarities'.

Images of hand *d* in NKS 1642 4o were included in NgL IV (published in 1885) which showed samples from the *National Law* and the court text *Hirdskraa* (NgL IV: Plate VIII). The following year (1886) the Norske Historiske Kildeskriftfond published a photographic facsimile of the part of NKS 1642 4o containing the *Older Borgarthing Christian Law* (BÆK). Nine years later, Storm produced on behalf of the same body a photographic facsimile of *Hirdskraa* in NKS 1642 4o (Storm 1895). An image from *Hirdskraa* was shown by Grøtvedt in his Plate VI (Grøtvedt 1939); Plate V shows an additional, image from the same manuscript. Seip likewise included an image from *Hirdskraa* in Codex Tunsbergensis in *Palæografi B: Norge og Island* (Seip 1954: 109 fig. 37).

An edition of the portion containing the Borgarthing version of Magnús Lawmender's *National Law* was produced by George Tobias Flom in 1925 (Flom 1925). In his introduction, Flom described the appearance of the manuscript in detail, and gave sample images of letters written by the *d* scribe, whose script Flom described as 'a book-hand which has been influenced by the style of the charters' (Flom 1925: 12, 18). In fact, he had previously edited more work of the *d* scribe, namely the *Town Law of Tønsberg*, for the *Journal of English and Germanic Philology*, commenting on the script there also (Flom 1911). Together with the images of the *d* scribe's script in NgL IV and in the facsimile editions of *Hirdskraa* and the Church Law Section of the *Borgarthing Law* (BÆK), these provide much information on that scribe's work in NKS 1642 4o as a whole.

Throughout, NKS 1642 4o features language suggestive of origins in southern Østlandet, around 1300–1350 (Halvorsen & Rindal 2008: xxix); for instance, Grøtvedt gave some examples of vowel (especially /a/) reduction in unstressed word endings and noted frequent use of *a* as svarabhakti vowel (Grøtvedt 1939: 79, 96). East-southeast *mn* appears often in place of western *fn*, by contrast with AM 78 4o and AM 31 8o, which favour the western form (Grøtvedt 1939: 115). On the other hand, *o* also appears relatively often as a negative prefix – despite the fact that this would not usually be associated with either the east or southeast (Grøtvedt 1939: 117).

Grøtvedt drew attention to the fact that, in this manuscript, frequent punctuation, rather free orthography, and recording of svarabhakti vowels tend to give it an air of orality, surmising that this may indicate composition by lawmen (Grøtvedt 1939: 14). Overall, he thought that the language of the manuscript represented a dominant 'chancery norm', overlaid with some markers of a 'free', locally tinged form of expression (Grøtvedt 1939: 129). However, it is at least as likely that some of the features that Grøtvedt saw as signs of an underlying official chancery norm were simply the natural result of scribes from various parts of Norway and Iceland moving around, using a mixture of exemplars, and possibly striving to adopt characteristics they themselves felt were prestigiously Norwegian (Hagland 1984: 78).

AM 68 4o

Due to a binding error, the early fourteenth-century manuscript AM 68 4o includes one leaf (12r-v) carrying part of Version One of the Church Law Section of the *Borgarthing Law*. Keyser and Munch, Storm, and Kålund dated the script in this leaf to the end of the fourteenth century (NgL I: 338; NGL IV: 561–62; Kålund, 1889–94: I, 384 nr 713). Since AM 68 4o also contains the Longer Version of the *Older Eidsivathing Christian Law*, it is described later, along with the other manuscript bearing this text.

Eidsivathing Law: versions and manuscripts

The *Eidsivathing Law* survives in a Long Version and a Short Version. In line with Halvorsen & Rindal, we have based our translation on the Long Version, which is preserved in two manuscripts: AM 68 4o and NB 317 4o (formerly OUB 317 4o). The Short Version is likewise preserved in two manuscripts: AM 58 4o and AM 77 c 4o, which have been described by Halvorsen & Rindal (Halvorsen & Rindal 2008: xxvii–xxviii).

AM 68 4o

This is the principal manuscript of the Long Version of the Church Law Section of the *Older Eidsivathing Law* the *Older Eidsivathing Christian Law*), which is found on fols 8v – 17r of its sixty-six folios (Kålund 1889–94: I, 383–384 nr 713).

(The manuscript also contains one misbound leaf, carrying part of Version One of the Church Law Section of the *Older Borgarthing Law*, as described earlier.) The codex measures 195mm x 145mm. The relevant text has been dated to the beginning of the fourteenth century and contains rubrics and coloured initials (NgL I: 374; NgL IV: 562; Kålund 1889–94: I, 383–384 nr 713).

The whole manuscript, with the exception of some minor additions, was copied by one scribe, who also included in it a copy of the local Eidsivathing version of the *National Law* and some additional laws; the Church Law Section of the *Eidsivathing Law* was in fact interpolated into the *National Law*, immediately after its own Church Law Section (NgL IV: 562; Halvorsen & Rindal 2008: xxv). Storm described the script in question (*a*) as clear but not fine 'half-Gothic', transforming towards the end into a hasty cursive (NgL IV: 562).

Storm noted that the orthography and editing were fairly good (NgL IV: 562). Halvorsen & Rindal reported that a 1970 dissertation by Aud Folkedal found the language of the manuscript to be southeast Norwegian and to reflect origins in the royal chancery in Oslo (Halvorsen & Rindal 2008: xxv), although as we have seen, the existence of a consistent 'chancery style' remains an open question. Possible eastern or southeastern features noted by Folkedal included mostly unmarked *u*-umlaut of */a/* and two uses of *a* as a svarabhakti vowel.

NB 317 4o

This manuscript is now held at Nasjonalbiblioteket, Oslo, but was formerly held at Oslo Universitetsbibliotek, where it was known as OUB 317 4o and before that Chr. Univ. 317 4o (NgL I: 374; NgL IV: 730–34). Still earlier, it had been bound together with two Swedish laws (Halvorsen & Rindal 2008: xxvi). The scribe of the 'codex proper' (labelled *e* by Storm) copied not only the Eidsivathing version of the *National Law*, but also the Church Law Section of the *Eidsivathing Law*. The latter was written onto a set of leaves inserted before the core codex, on pages 95r – 98v. Before this are two further items likewise written by *e*: a contents list for the law and a calendar covering January to October, marking holy days and the anniversary of the death of Bishop Þorsteinn of Hamar, which had taken place in 1304 (Halvorsen & Rindal 2008: xxvi). Storm described *e* as 'a clear, angular Gothic hand from the first half of the fourteenth century (after 1318)'. He also noted that the text was decorated with 'badly drawn' red, green, and multicoloured initials, red – occasionally green – headings, and some individual letters in red. Although Storm remarked that the spelling tended to be careful, he observed that the punctuation of this scribe was sparse and not always accurate.

A 1975 dissertation by Ljubiša Rajić on the language of the manuscript found it to be southeastern rather than eastern as might have been expected from its eastern, Eidsivathing-related contents (Halvorsen & Rindal 2008: xxxvi–xxvii). One trait thought to suggest this was *a* as svarabhakti vowel. A noted tendency to unmarked *u*-umlaut of /a/ is less easy to interpret, since this has been found in both southeastern and eastern sources. Halvorsen & Rindal also drew attention to an article by Halvorsen (Halvorsen 1989) observing that unstressed /a/ was often represented by *æ*, which could point to either eastern or southeastern origin. Halvorsen has agreed with Rajić that, whatever the written dialect of scribe *e*, the manuscript was probably created in Hamar for use by its bishop (Halvorsen & Rindal 2008: xxvii).

Quick guide to probable east and southeast Norwegian dialectal features (early fourteenth century)

a as *æ* in unstr. positions	E/SE (perhaps less at Mariakirken)
vowel harmony	E and other parts of Norway
a as svarabhakti vowel	western parts of SE
æ/e as svarabhakti vowel	rest of SE, E and other parts of Norway
unmarked *u*-umlaut of /a/ (*hafum*)	parts of E (Oppland) and Trøndelag
retention of *v* in initial *vr* (*vreiði*)	only SE
unmarked *i*-umlaut of /e/(*taker*)	SE
ú/u as negative prefix	most of Norway
mn (*namn*)	E (as opposed to W)
ft (*eftir*)	E (as opposed to W)
progressive umlaut *ja> jæ* (*jærn*)	E and Trøndelag after 1200

This simple summary is based on Hagland 2002: 1016–1017.

Part III The Borgarthing Law

Chapter one: here begins the Christian Law:[1] that which shall be valid[2]

1.1 This is first in our law: that we shall bow to the East, and give ourselves to Christ, and attend to churches and clerics.[3]

1.2 Each child born to this world shall be fed, and baptized, and borne to church – except any born with ill marks.[4] These shall be highly visible on anyone to whom a mother may not give food:[5] the heels turn to toes, and toes to heels; the chin (is) between the shoulders; the nape[6] in front, on the chest; the calves in front, on the legs; the eyes at the back, in the nape;[7] he has seal's fins and dog's head. Such shall be taken to a *forvé* and covered with a cairn, where neither men nor livestock will cross it. That is the Evil One's *forvé*.

1.3 Now a *belgborinn* child is different:[8] it has a skin-bag in place of a face. This is clear to all: that such a person could not feed himself, even were he fully-grown. It shall be taken away, and borne to church, and caused to be prime-signed, and laid down, before the church door. The closest relative[9] should attend it, until its breath is gone. It shall be buried in the churchyard, and its soul prayed for as well as may be, and it shall be let be, with the hope willed by God.[10]

1 *cristins doms bolk.*
2 NKS 1642 4o: no heading.
3 NKS 1642 4o: 'clerics and church'.
4 *nema þæt æina er með orkumblum er alet.*
5 *Þau skulu mykil a þæim manne er æighi ma moðer matt gewa.*
6 Alternative translation: 'back of head'.
7 Alternative translation (as previous): 'back of head'.
8 Alternative translation: 'is second'.
9 *hin nanaste niðr.*
10 *lata uerða at þæiri uon er Gud uil.* The precise meaning in this context of the preposition *at* (translated 'with') is unclear. Two possibilities are 'in accordance with' or 'by means of'.

Chapter two: on godparents, and emergency baptism[11]

2.1 Now, such a man and such a woman as one may make spiritual kin to the father and mother of a child shall bear each child for baptism.

2.2 Now, often, a child is overcome, far from home, such that its life lies at risk. They shall unwrap[12] its cloth, and the man shall speak first, and the woman after him, naming the child, saying this, three times: 'I baptize you, in the name of the Father and the Son and the Holy Spirit'. The man shall spit in his palm, and take up his spit with his thumb, and rub it on, in the sign of the cross, in place of chrism: onto the chest and between the shoulders, into the nose[13] and into the ears, and into the crown of the head.[14] If there is enough water for immersion,[15] then he shall dip it in,[16] three times, and, three times, speak these words. But if there is not enough water, then the man shall, with his hand, rub on: water, if there is water; dew, if there is dew; snow, if there is snow; seawater, if there is seawater.

2.3 Now, often, vital sparks[17] remain. The child revives, and is borne, alive, to church. They shall recount its baptism for the priest, and if they have spoken the words prescribed by law,[18] then the priest shall prime-sign the child. Then it has had a full baptism; no-one need be twice immersed. But if they cannot recall them, and repeat them correctly before the priest, then they did not recall them nor speak them correctly over the child. Then the priest shall baptize it, with a full baptism.

2.4 Now, if the child dies, as a result of this loathsomeness, after such a baptism as here prescribed, then one shall bury it in the churchyard, as if the priest had baptized it.

Chapter three: on a woman's labour, and responsibility for her child[19]

3.1 Servant-women and neighbour-women shall stay with each woman in labour, until the child is born, and they shall not leave until they have put it to the mother's breast.[20]

11 NKS 1642 4o: no heading.
12 *rækkia*. NKS 1642 4o: *vefuia*.
13 NKS 1642 4o: 'under the nose'.
14 NKS 1642 4o: 'onto the foot-soles'.
15 *Ef vatn er sua mikit at þau megho barn i hylia.*
16 *døyfa i* . . . oc *i drepa*.
17 *litlar lifs dræggiar* ('small dregs of life').
18 *i rette manna*.
19 NKS 1642 4o: no heading.
20 *at moðor brioste*.

3.2 And if, when people come to her a second time, the child is dead, and they can see upon it hand- or band-marks – it was strangled or choked – and the mother speaks with reason, then she is called a 'murderer of her child'. She has forfeited property and peace, land and chattels. She should travel to heathen land, and should never enter the presence of Christian men. This is why murder of a heathen is worse than that of a Christian: the soul of any man who dies heathen is lost.

3.3 And if, when people come to her, she does not speak with reason, she should make confession to a priest, and pay no fine for this.

3.4 Now if a man lives in isolation, far away from other men, and a birth happens so suddenly that women[21] cannot be brought to his wife in labour, and the couple are alone with each other,[22] and the child is ailing, then the father – and the mother – shall hold and baptize the child, with such a baptism as is here prescribed by law,[23] and the couple shall not dissolve their union.[24] Rather this, than their child die heathen.

3.5 Now, each woman shall breastfeed[25] for no longer than over two (Lenten) fasts and up until the third. And if her husband says that she shall take the[26] child from her breast, and he is subject to such domination by woman that his wife will not yield to his words, then she owes three marks of her own money. But if he cares no more than her, then they together owe three marks of their jointly owned money.[27]

Chapter four: on time limits for baptisms[28]

4.1 Now, annually, there are four[29] legal time limits for baptism of children. Those children born after the First Day of Christmas shall be baptized, Easter Eve. All those born thereafter shall be baptized, St John's Eve. All those born thereafter shall be baptized, Michaelmas. All those born thereafter shall be baptized, the Holy Eve of Christmas. Three marks lie at stake, at each[30] legal time limit.

4.2 And if all legal time limits pass, and any man has not had his child baptized, then that farmer shall, through his child, become a heathen. He has

21 NKS 1642 4o: 'a woman'.
22 *ero þau. ij. æin hiun.*
23 er *nu er talt i rette manna.*
24 NKS 1642 4o: 'shall not dissolve their union afterwards'.
25 *hava barn sit uið briost s*er.
26 *sit.*
27 NKS 1642 4o: final sentence missing.
28 NKS 1642 4o: *Vm laga stefnur* oc *bera born til skirnar.*
29 NKS 1642 4o: 'three additional'.
30 NKS 1642 4o: 'at the first'.

forfeited property and peace, land and chattels. He should go to heathen land. He certainly does not wish to be Christian.

Chapter five: on inedible matter: that which it is forbidden to eat[31]

5.1 Now, men[32] shall eat neither *sveiti* nor *svidda.*[33]

5.2 [34]Any man who eats *sveiti* or *svidda* owes three marks in silver. A fine paid by a farmer covers his wife and children, and his unfree household.

5.3 But if he has a son of eighteen, or older, he shall pay a second fine for himself. If a widowed daughter lives with him, she shall pay a third fine, for herself and her children.[35]

5.4 If a farmer feeds a few guests, and he gives them *svidda* to eat, then he owes three marks for each of them.

5.5 Everything which has died without intervention by human hand is called *svidda.*[36]

5.6 If a man's livestock lies dead on a heath, equally near to all men,[37] neighbours shall be led to it, and allowed to look at it. If they think they see signs of intervention by human hand upon it, then the owner shall have use of it, with the approval of the neighbours. If it seems to them unfit for use, then the owner shall reject it.

5.7 If a man makes use of any livestock[38] which has died in this way, then the bishop's *ármaðr* may prosecute him, leading to a *lýrittr*-oath. If the oath succeeds fully, then he is free of the charge. If that fails, then he is said to be rightly charged. He owes three marks.[39]

5.8 Now, everything which dies in this way, through intervention by human hand, may be eaten and used: it breaks its neck in a cattle-stall; strangles itself in a cattle-fork; twines itself in a tether; lies dead in a still well; falls forward from a board-bridge;[40] walks forward into a human trap; a man leads it onto impassable ice; it swims itself to death;[41] a bear takes it; a

31 NKS 1642 4o: no heading (but see heading preceding 5.2). AM 68: no heading.

32 AM 68 4o: 'Christian men'.

33 *Svidda* is an obscure term, of uncertain etymology. (See commentary.) NKS 1642 4o: 'Now, men are born/brought up/fed (*fodder*) and observe Christianity fully. Now all men need food. They shall eat neither *sveiti* nor *svidda*'.

34 NKS 1642 4o: heading 'On meat-eating, *sveiti* and *svidda*'.

35 NKS 1642 4o /AM 68 4o: 'for herself and her household'.

36 AM 68 4o: 'is called *svídáði*'.

37 *allum monnum iamner*. Halvorsen & Rindal: 'together with other people's livestock' (*sammen med andre folks buskap*).

38 AM 78 4o/ NKS 1642 4o: *smala*. AM 68 4o: *fenad*.

39 NKS 1642 4o: final two sentences missing.

40 *fiolbru*. NKS 1642 4o: *fioll. eða bru* ('small bridge or bridge').

41 Thanks to Ian Crockatt for this solution to the problem of translating the phrase *springr sialft a sundi*.

wolf bites it; it happens through motion of hoof or of horn;[42] dogs bite it to death. All this may be used.[43]

5.9 Now, a man owns one cow. If this becomes *svídauðr*, he may use it. And if he owns two, and both lie *svídauðr*,[44] he shall eat the (one which died) later, but reject the (one which died) earlier. And if he owns three, reject two, but use the third.[45] And if he owns more than three cows, then he shall reject these, and use everything else, if this is lying (on the ground) as *svidda*.

5.10 And if livestock falls from a rock and blood does not gush out, then it shall be rejected. If blood gushes out, then it shall be used.[46]

5.11 Wind fells a tree onto men's livestock. If, due to this tree, blood gushes out, then it shall be used. If blood does not gush out, then it shall be rejected.[47]

5.12 If lightning strikes, then it shall be rejected.[48]

5.13 Now, anything born on a farm may be eaten, except a dog or a cat or a horse. And if a man, without need, eats any one of these, then he has forfeited property and peace, land and chattels. He should travel to heathen land,[49] and he should never enter the presence of Christian men.

5.14 [50]And if a man finds himself at a fjord or a gulf – weather or water so hinder him that he cannot reach habitation – then he shall lie foodless, seven nights, before he eat dog or cat. He shall rather eat dog than dog eat him, and say[51] to the first priest[52] whom he meets that he has, through necessity, eaten inedible matter. He should go to confession, and he need pay no fine for this.

5.15 But if he conceals this and will not tell, and bones are found in his dwelling-place, then the bishop's *ármaðr* may prosecute him. He must undergo a trial by hot iron. If he is clean, according to the trial by hot iron, then he is free of the charge. If he is unclean, then he shall have five-days'[53] grace, following the trial by hot iron, as would a witch.

42 Alternative translation: 'it happens outside the horse- or cow-pasture'.

43 NKS 1642 4o: 'Now all this, which has died in this way, and through intervention by human hand, may be eaten and used'. AM 68 4o: 'All this which has died in this way, as here described, and through intervention by human hand, may be eaten'.

44 NKS 1642 4o: *sialf daudar*. AM 68 4o: *sialf dauder*.

45 AM 68 4o: 'And if a man owns three and/or four, he should reject three but should use the fourth'.

46 NKS 1642 4o: 'And if livestock falls from a fell or rock and blood gushes out, then it shall be used. If blood does not gush out, then it shall be rejected'. AM 68 4o: 'And if livestock falls from a rock, and blood gushes out from the nose, then it may be used – but not otherwise'.

47 NKS 1642 4o /AM 68 4o: lack 5.11.

48 AM 68 4o: 'then it is not fit to be used'.

49 AM 68 4o: 'should leave the land'.

50 NKS 1642 4o: heading: 'On necessity through which meat which is inedible matter is eaten'.

51 NKS 1642 4o: 'before he eats dog or cat or horse, and should say'. AM 68 4o: 'before he eats dog, cat or horse, and should say'.

52 NKS 1642 4o /AM 68 4o: 'cleric'.

53 NKS 1642 4o: 'fifteen nights'.

Chapter six: if men eat meat at improper times[54]

6.1 No man shall eat meat within seven weeks before Easter Day, unless he wishes to pay a fine of three marks.

6.2 If a man eats meat within six weeks before Easter, then he has forfeited property and peace.[55] That is called 'All Men's Fast'.

6.3 If a man eats meat on a Friday, he owes three marks. And if he eats meat on an ember day, he owes three.

6.4 And if a man eats meat on a day on which, it has been announced, a fast should be observed, he should pay a fine, as appropriate to the holiness of the day.

6.5 And if a man errs as to the day and eats meat on a fast day, and a man comes to him suddenly and asks, 'Why do you eat meat, while other men fast?' and he spits out the morsel he has in his mouth, he should make confession to a priest, and need pay no fine for this. If he swallows that which he has in his mouth, and takes another (morsel), he should pay a fine, as appropriate to the holiness of the day.

6.6 Now, if a man finds himself alone, far away, and he errs as to the day, and he eats meat on a Friday, he should go to confession, and need pay no fine for this. If two men are together and both err as to the day, they should make confession to a priest, and need pay no fine for this. If three men are together and they eat meat on a Friday, each of them should pay a fine of three marks. They cannot all have erred as to the day.

Chapter seven: on proper wedding-times[56]

7.1 Now, all this coincides: meat-eating, and marriages of women.

7.2 No man shall take a woman within nine weeks before Easter, unless he wishes to pay a fine of three marks for this.

7.3 And if he takes a woman within six weeks before Easter, then he has forfeited property and peace.

7.4 No man shall take a woman within three weeks before St John's Eve. And none shall take (a woman) within three weeks before Michaelmas, and none within three weeks before Christmas. If he takes (a woman) at any of these times, then he owes three marks to the bishop.[57]

7.5 And if a man takes a woman on a Sunday evening, that is a proper taking-time. Monday in the evening: proper taking-time. A man takes a woman on a Tuesday evening: he owes three ounces. Wednesday evening: proper taking-time. Thursday evening: if a man takes a woman, then he shall pay a fine of three marks for this. Friday evening: proper taking-time.

54 NKS 1642 4o: 'On meat-eating'.
55 NKS 1642 4o: 'land and chattels'.
56 AM 78 4o adds: *Cap*itulum. NKS 1642 4o: 'On marriages of women'.
57 NKS 1642 4o: 'before Christmas, unless he pay a fine of three marks'.

Saturday evening: if a man takes a woman then, then he shall pay a fine of three marks for this.[58]

7.6 If a man takes a woman on an ember day: he owes three marks.

7.7 If a man takes a woman on a feast or a fast night: unless clerics allow this,[59] he should pay a fine, as appropriate to the holiness of the day.

Chapter eight: how a *fylkiskirkja* or *heraðskirkja* or proprietary church shall be restored if it falls into disrepair[60]

8.1 There are six *fylkiskirkjur* in these three *fylki*: one (the outermost) at *Konungahella*;[61] a second at *Svartiborg*;[62] a third at *Túnir*;[63] a fourth at *Akr*[64] in the *herað* of *Ósló*; a fifth at *Sæmr*;[65] a sixth at *Heiðarheimr*.[66]

8.2 If a *fylkiskirkja* falls into disrepair, then a two-year time limit for restoration of the *fylkiskirkja* shall be set, for all the men of the *fylki*. If they let that pass, fifteen marks are owed.

8.3 A second two-year time limit shall be set. If they let that pass, fifteen marks are owed.

8.4 Then the third two-year time limit shall be set for them. If they let that pass, fifteen marks are owed. And that then makes forty-five marks.

8.5 Now the fourth time limit shall be set: four months. Then comes the only raiding which the king may permit[67] within the land, to force men into Christianity through raiding.[68] He shall not kill men, and not burn buildings. He shall take their property and households, and keep them as plunder.

8.6 And as soon as men eat new corn, then the setting of time limits by which they should have restored their *fylkiskirkja* shall be begun anew.

8.7 If a *heraðskirkja* falls into disrepair, a time limit of a year shall be set for restoration of the *heraðskirkja*, for the men of the *herað*. If it is not restored by then, then they owe three marks.

8.8 Then a second twelve-month time limit shall be set for them. If it is not restored by then, three marks are owed.

58 NKS 1642 4o: 'Sunday evening, Monday evening: that is a proper taking-time. But if a man takes a woman on a Tuesday evening, he owes three ounces. Wednesday evening is a proper taking-time. Thursday evening: he owes three marks'.

59 NKS 1642 4o: sentence ends here.

60 NKS 1642 4o: 'On maintenance of all churches'.

61 Kungahälla (Bohuslän, Sweden).

62 Svarteborg (Bohuslän, Sweden).

63 Tune (Østfold, Norway).

64 Aker (Akershus, Norway).

65 Sem (Vestfold, Norway). NKS 1642 4o: '*Sæmr* in Vestfold'.

66 Hedrum (Vestfold, Norway).

67 Alternative translation: 'should permit'.

68 NKS 1642 4o: 'And if it is not then ready, then comes the only raiding permitted to/by the king within the land, to force all men into Christianity through raiding'.

8.9 Again, the third twelve-month time limit shall be set. If it is not restored by then, three marks are owed for this.[69]

8.10 Now a one-month time limit shall be set for them. If it is not restored by then, then each farmer shall pay a fine of three marks.

8.11 A man builds a proprietary church for himself on his land. If that falls into disrepair, he shall be given such time limits as would apply for a *heraðskirkja*. He should pay a fine of three marks for one (passed); six for two; nine for three. The fourth, one-month, time limit shall be set for him. And if it is not restored, then the king owns the farm, and the farmer nothing in it. The king[70] should support the church-building.

8.12 If the church which he[71] mended falls into disrepair, then the farmer – the one who owned the land before, or his heirs[72] – shall call a thing assembly and offer to support the church-building.[73] Then the farmer ought to own the land himself, and this is called 'redemption land'.[74]

8.13 Now, if a man builds a church on another man's land,[75] and it falls into disrepair, he shall be given the same time limits as would apply for a *heraðskirkja*.[76] Three marks are owed for one (passed); six for two; nine for three. If it is not then restored, then a month-long time limit shall be set for him. Then he shall go into outlawry, if it is not then restored, until he has funds with which to support the church-restoration.

Chapter nine: on disrepair of a church enclosure, and on men's graves[77]

9.1 There shall be an enclosure around each church. If it falls into disrepair, then three marks lie at stake for the whole;[78] six ounces for each quarter. Even if only one section is open in a quarter, it is as if the whole quarter is in disrepair.

9.2 A churchyard is divided into quarters for burials.

9.3 *Lendir menn* shall be buried east of the church and in the land to the south, under the eavesdrip. If they do not own a portion of the churchyard, then they shall lie in the burial-place for farmers.

69 NKS 1642 4o combines and rephrases 8.9 and 8.10: 'Now the third month-long time limit shall be set for them. And if it is not restored, then each farmer in that church parish (*sokn*) owes three marks'.

70 NKS 1642 4o: 'And he'.

71 NKS 1642 4o: 'the king'.

72 NKS 1642 4o: 'heir'.

73 NKS 1642 4o: 'maintain the church enclosure' (scribal error).

74 NKS 1642 4o: 'redemption land with king's deed/settlement (*með konongs gerd*)'.

75 NKS 1642 4o: 'property' (*eign*).

76 NKS 1642 4o: 'the lord of the land (*landzðrotten*) should have the same time limits for restoration as would apply for a *heraðskirkja*'.

77 NKS 1642 4o: 'On maintenance of a church enclosure'.

78 NKS 1642 4o: 'and'.

9.4 Then *hǫldar* and the children of *hǫldar* [79] shall be buried.

9.5 Then fully freed slaves and the children of fully freed slaves shall be buried.[80]

9.6 Next, freed slaves and their children shall be buried.[81]

9.7 A slave – and men who have been wrecked on the seashore and have hair cut in northern[82] style – shall be buried nearest to the church enclosure.

9.8 If anyone buries a man (slave) in the burial-place for freed slaves, six ounces are owed.

9.9 If anyone buries a freed slave in the burial-place for fully freed slaves, he should pay a fine of twelve ounces.

9.10 If anyone buries a fully freed slave in the burial-place of a *hǫldr*, he should pay a fine of three marks for this.[83]

9.11 And if a man has unearthed a corpse on which there is flesh or hair, when he inters another, three marks lie at stake.

9.12 If he unearths such, but the limbs cleave together, twelve ounces lie at stake.

9.13 All those bones which he unearths, he shall lay down next to the coffin. As for all those which lie uppermost and the sun reaches, he should pay a fine of six ounces for each bone.

9.14 Now, if a man recognizes someone who has been unearthed as a close relative, then the heirs get the fine which lies at stake. But if no-one recognizes him, then the bishop gets the whole fine which lies at stake. The fine never falls between hands.

Chapter ten: on a bishop's duty and visitation, and on that to which priests should attend[84]

10.1 Now, a bishop is obliged to consecrate all churches: to go to a *fylkiskirkja* with thirty men and remain five nights.

10.2 And he shall go to a *heraðskirkja* with fifteen men and remain three nights.

10.3 Now, the consecration of a church holds for as long as the cornerstones stand, even should it become necessary to repair it. This is called 'church repairs'.

10.4 Now, a bishop shall come to each *graptarkirkja* every year. And if he does not come, then, if farmers wish to use the law against him, he ought to lose the income he would otherwise have taken in the *herað* during that year.

10.5 And he is obliged to confirm men's children every year, and administer penance to those who need it, and obtain chrism for each priest, whether of a *heraðskirkja*, or of a proprietary church.

79 NKS 1642 4o: '*hauldmenn* and their children'.

80 NKS 1642 4o: lacks provision 9.5.

81 NKS 1642 4o: lacks provision 9.6.

82 *norøna*. Alternative translations: 'Norwegian' or 'Nordic'.

83 NKS 1642 4o: '*hauldsmaðr*, he owes one mark'.

84 NKS 1642 4o: 'On all church consecrations'.

10.6 And if men take a child to a proprietary church, and it is near to death, and the priest refuses to baptize it, then he owes six marks – three to the bishop, and three to the father of the child – if it dies heathen.[85]

Chapter eleven: on men's tithe payments[86]

11.1 Now, each man with income is obliged to pay tithe[87] – both *hǫfuðtíund,* and crop tithe – and to divide it into four parts: the bishop takes a quarter; the priest of the *heraðskirkja*[88] takes another; the church takes a third; the farmers themselves take the fourth.[89]

11.2 If a man will not pay his *hǫfuðtíund,* then the bishop's *ármaðr* shall set for him a four-month time limit. If he will not then pay tithe, then he owes three marks. Another four-month time limit shall be set for him. If he lets that pass, then he owes three marks. The third four-month time limit shall be set for him. If he lets that pass, then he owes three marks,[90] and that then makes nine marks. Now a one-month[91] time limit shall be set for him. And if he has not then settled his tithe, then he has forfeited property and peace, land and chattels. He should travel to heathen land. He certainly does not wish to be Christian. The bishop takes up to three marks from his funds, and the king, the surplus.

11.3 A man will not pay crop tithe.[92] The bishop's *ármaðr* shall go to church and set a five-day time limit for all those men who have not paid their crop tithe.[93] Each who has not paid within the five-day time limit owes six ounces. Again, a five-day time limit shall be set for him. He should then pay another six ounces in this way, and so on until he tires of it.

11.4 If he who collects it declares that he – the one from whom he collected it – did not act correctly, then he (the latter) shall personally swear an oath that he has paid tithe as he ought to do. Then the former shall accept this, in accordance with the law.

Chapter twelve: the obligations of a priest to farmers, and farmers to a priest, and on legal oblation[94]

12.1 Now, farmers shall obtain a priest for their *heraðskirkja,*[95] taking whomever they wish. Legally, a bishop has no right to remove him from their

85 NKS 1642 4o: 'then he owes three marks to the father of the child if it dies heathen'.
86 NKS 1642 4o: 'On tithe payment'.
87 NKS 1642 4o: 'his tithe'.
88 NKS 1642 4o: 'the priest'.
89 NKS 1642 4o: 'and the farmers get the fourth, to distribute amongst the poor'.
90 NKS 1642 4o: sentence ends here.
91 NKS 1642 4o: 'A one-month'.
92 NKS 1642 4o: 'And if a man will not pay his crop tithe . . . ' (Sentence ends here.)
93 NKS 1642 4o: omits sentence.
94 NKS 1642 4o: 'On the position (*skipan*) of priests'.
95 NKS 1642 4o: 'their church'.

church, unless he obtains the witness of two church priests – one from nearest him, to the south, and the other from the north[96] – that he is unfit to be a church priest,[97] due to his lack of knowledge.

12.2 [98]This is ancient law: that a priest shall receive a legal oblation. A year's worth of each, butter and meal, from farmers. Half a *sáld* from each full farmer, in *Ólafssáð*. Three *séttungar* from a lone farmer.

12.3 Twelve ells[99] in *legkaup* for a *lendr maðr*, his wife and all those children who hope to possess land.

12.4 Six ells for the son of a *hǫldr*.

12.5 Four ells for the son of a fully freed slave.

12.6 Three for a fully freed slave.[100]

12.7 One and a half ells for a freed slave.

12.8 A weighed penny for a slave and a penny for all those children who are not yet of sufficient age to contribute *gerð*.

12.9 Twelve ells for night watch, during which a priest keeps vigil over a corpse. He is obliged to keep vigil if she (the widow) will pay for this.

12.10 He shall have half a mark – one ounce equalling six ells – for the chrism.

12.11 A man who can answer for his words and his oath shall be sent to fetch a priest, in time of need.

12.12 A priest shall go, day or night, to administer penance and the Eucharist. If he will not go and a man dies without receiving sacrament, then he shall lose the whole oblation due to him within that *herað*, during that year.

12.13 Also, a priest shall visit up to three dead per day, to perform post-mortem rites over them. He shall be obliged to bless three ablutions per day. He shall remain at the third, if he so wishes.

12.14 He is obliged to deliver three readings over each man who wished to have this done, whether[101] in exchange for money or given, as wished (by the priest).[102]

12.15 [103]When men take a corpse to church, then they should have *legkaup* ready for the priest, or provide a pledge, or obtain a warranter as good as the pledge.

12.16 But if they want none of these costs, or things,[104] then he shall forbid them from burying the corpse. They owe three marks if they bury it, despite prohibition by the priest. And in any case, if they bury the corpse, then

96 NKS 1642 4o: 'the witness of two church priests – one from the north, and one from the south – and the witness of those men who are closest'.

97 *kirkiu sætr prestr*.

98 NKS 1642 4o: heading 'On *Ólafssáð* and legal oblations'.

99 NKS 1642 4o: 'ounces'.

100 NKS 1642 4o: 'A fully freed slave: three ells'.

101 NKS 1642 4o suggested translation (meaning unclear): 'done, or he owes three marks; only more if (*þui at eins fleiri nema*)'.

102 Ambiguous phrase: *með fe kaupi eða han vili uæitt hafa*.

103 NKS 1642 4o: heading 'On *Ólafssáð* and legal oblation' (similar to additional heading above).

104 NKS 1642 4o: 'But if they do not offer that thing'.

he shall himself bear witness, with stole around his neck, that they there committed grave robbery against him.[105]

12.17 [106]When such a priest receives tithe from farmers, then he is obliged to perform liturgical services for both the living and the dead, when they have need, and to anoint a farmer and his wife and all those of his children who are old enough to receive this.[107]

12.18 He shall deliver the full service required, in return for tithe,[108] except in the case of night watch. For this, he shall have two ells of payment cloth.[109]

12.19 Now, a priest shall not travel so far from church that its bells are out of earshot, unless he has, with him, everything with which he might perform a service for the living and the dead. If he does not have[110] this, then he owes three marks to the heirs of the one in need of the service.

12.20 Now, a priest shall not travel out of the *herað*, unless he obtains leave from the men of the *herað*, except if he travels to a synod. If he travels elsewhere,[111] then he owes three marks.

12.21 Now, he[112] shall ask for leave at church, on the immediately preceding holy day. They – the men of the *herað* who are at church – shall decide upon leave and should grant leave on behalf of those who remain at home.

Chapter thirteen: on proclamation of ember days and proclamation of feast days[113]

13.1 Now, if a priest misproclaims an ember day, then he owes three marks to the bishop; likewise if he misproclaims a feast day.[114]

13.2 A priest shall stand at the choir door, and there proclaim an ember day or a feast day, and before this carve a cross, and send it along the correct proclamation routes.[115]

13.3 And if they are misproclaimed, then he shall ride or run along the proclamation routes,[116] and attempt to get in front of the cross, so that men do not eat, or work, at improper times.

13.4 And if men eat, or work, at improper times, they should pay such fines for this as are appropriate to the holiness of the day.

105 NKS 1642 4o: 'neck and swear to this: that they committed corpse-grave robbery against him'.

106 NKS 1642 4o: heading 'Obligations of priests in return for tithe'.

107 NKS 1642 4o: 'old enough to receive the full service which he shall perform in return for men's tithe'.

108 NKS 1642 4o: omits the beginning of this sentence, up to this point.

109 NKS 1642 4o: 'two ells or half a weighed *ertog*'.

110 NKS 1642 4o: 'offer'.

111 NKS 1642 4o: 'elsewhere without leave'.

112 NKS 1642 4o: 'And he'.

113 AM 78 4o: adds *Cap*itulum. NKS 1642 4o: 'On proclamation of feast days'.

114 NKS 1642 4o: 'Now if a priest misproclaims a feast day or an ember day, he owes three marks'.

115 NKS 1642 4o: 'correct proclamation route'.

116 NKS 1642 4o: 'correct proclamation route'.

13.5 If a feast day falls on a Monday, then this shall be proclaimed two Sundays beforehand; likewise, if it falls on a Tuesday. But if it falls on a Wednesday, then it must be proclaimed on the immediately preceding Sunday.

Chapter fourteen: on annual feast days and the keeping of holy days[117]

14.1 There are twenty-one of such feast days[118] annually, and each is as holy as a Sunday – each is a six-ounce day: the first four[119] Days of Christmas; the fifth,[120] the Eighth Day (of Christmas); the sixth,[121] the Thirteenth Day (of Christmas: Epiphany); the seventh,[122] Candlemas; eighth,[123] the Last Day of Easter;[124] ninth,[125] Cross Mass (Feast of the Invention of the True Cross); tenth,[126] Hallvarðr Mass; eleventh, Ascension Day;[127] twelfth,[128] St John's Eve;[129] thirteenth,[130] Peter and Paul Mass; fourteenth, that (Mass) of the Saints who rest in Kinn and Selja;[131] fifteenth, Óláfr Mass;[132] sixteenth,[133] Lawrence Mass; seventeenth,[134] the First Marymas (the Assumption of Mary); eighteenth,[135] Michaelmas; nineteenth, Two-Apostle Mass in Autumn (Feast of Saints Simon and Jude)[136]; twentieth,[137] All Saints Mass; (twenty-)one:[138] Andrew Mass.

14.2 The eves of these feast days which have now been mentioned shall become holy on a summer's day when the sun is in the southwest; on a winter's day, when the sun sets.[139]

117 NKS 1642 4o: 'On the calendar of feast days'.
118 NKS 1642 4o: 'Now, there are twenty-two feast days'.
119 NKS 1642 4o: 'the first five'.
120 NKS 1642 4o: 'sixth'.
121 NKS 1642 4o: 'seventh'.
122 NKS 1642 4o: 'eighth'.
123 NKS 1642 4o: 'ninth'.
124 NKS 1642 4o: 'the Fourth Day of Easter'.
125 NKS 1642 4o: 'tenth'.
126 NKS 1642 4o: 'eleventh'.
127 Lit.'Thursday of the *gangdagar*'. NKS 1642 4o: 'twelfth, Holy Thursday'.
128 NKS 1642 4o: 'thirteenth'.
129 Lit. 'the Vigil of St John'.
130 NKS 1642 4o: 'fourteenth'.
131 NKS 1642 4o: 'fifteenth, the Feast of Selja' (lit. 'the Vigil of Selja').
132 NKS 1642 4o: 'sixteenth, the First Vigil of Saint Óláfr'.
133 NKS 1642 4o: 'seventeenth'.
134 NKS 1642 4o: 'eighteenth'.
135 NKS 1642 4o: 'nineteenth'.
136 NKS 1642 4o: 'twentieth (the Feast) of Saints Simon and Jude'.
137 NKS 1642 4o: 'twenty-first'.
138 NKS 1642 4o: 'twenty-second'.
139 Alternative translation: 'The vigils preceding these begin, in summer, when the sun is in the southwest, and in winter, when the sun sets'. NKS 1642 4o: 'The eves of these feast days shall become holy on a Sunday when the sun reaches the south and on a winter's day, when the sun is in descent'.

14.3 [140]If a man is found at work and labouring on a holy day, he should pay such a fine as is appropriate to the holiness of the day.

14.4 If a free man is found at work with unfree men,[141] he should pay a fine; but they go free.

14.5 And if unfree household-members[142] are found at work unaccompanied,[143] and the bishop's *ármaðr* comes to them and asks: 'Why do you work on a holy day?' and they answer thus: 'We[144] would willingly stop. This is our lord's doing: that we work on a holy day,' he shall confirm their reply with witnesses.[145] Then the farmer must pay a fine, on behalf of his household-members. But if the household-members reply in this way: 'This is our own doing: that we work on a holy day. We wish thus to hasten away, from meadow, and from field,' then he should take them – the man's household-members – and convey them back to the owner's house, and demand bail for them. He should call the farmers to a thing assembly for three nights later. He should present the witness of two men, as to the reply of the man's household-members. He must decide on the fine to be imposed on him: three ounces, if he worked on a three-ounce day.[146] And if the farmer is willing to pay the fine for his household-members, then they are free, according to the law. That is called 'hide-ransom'. But if the farmer will not pay the fine, then the bishop's *ármaðr* shall find a man, and all the *heraðsmenn* another, and have that man flogged. He who is most foolish at the assembly thing shall bring about[147] the flogging. And if he dies of the flogging, then all the *heraðsmenn* shall pay him (the owner) *verðaurar*.[148] The only loss to the farmer shall be the fact that he previously owned a greater number of household-members.[149]

14.6 No load requiring cord or rope binding shall be made on a holy day.

14.7 Horse-packs shall not be made on a holy day. That which a man – young or old – rides upon may be carried on a holy day with impunity.

14.8 That which should hang between the roof rafters beside the door shall not be cut on a holy day. Even if only one ham be hung up, a fine (appropriate to) the holiness of the day shall be paid for this.

14.9 No more bread may be baked on a holy day than may be eaten entirely, immediately. Even if only one loaf remains after the holy period has

140 NKS 1642 4o: heading 'On desecration of holy days'.

141 *anauðgum* m*onnum*.

142 *a nauðigh hiun*.

143 NKS 1642 4o: 'found at work after the holy period has begun'.

144 AM 78 4o: *v*er (plural). NKS 1642 4o: *vit* (dual). After this point, NKS 1642 4o uses *v*er in the speech of these characters.

145 *Skirskota skal han vndir vatta suar*um *þæira*. NKS 1642 4o: 'He shall confirm their reply'.

146 NKS 1642 4o: 'three ounces from the funds of anyone who worked on a three-ounce day, and six ounces if he worked on a six-ounce day'.

147 AM 78 4o: *ualda*. NKS 1642 4o: *rada*.

148 NKS 1642 4o: 'shall pay for this with *verðaurar*'.

149 *Bonde missa þæss æins i værði at* han *atte hiuna tall till*. NKS 1642 4o makes less sense: *bøndar missa þess eins i uerdi.* er *han a hiuna tal til*.

ended, a fine (appropriate to) the holiness of the day shall be paid for it, just as if all that was baked had remained uneaten.

14.10 Gruel may be made, whether the day is ordinary or holy. It is so holy that no-one need pay for it.

14.11 Now, if a man sets on a horse-pack before the holy period begins, it may be carried with impunity until evening, if it does not fall off. But if it falls off and needs to be replaced, he should pay such a fine as is appropriate to the holiness of the day.[150]

14.12 Now, if a man moves his household between inhabited areas, and he must travel a great distance, and he travels from home after[151] Wednesday, then he shall refrain from travelling on the first Sunday[152] (of the travel period). Then he may travel on all which follow, with impunity. But if he does not refrain from travelling on the first, he should pay a fine (as appropriate to) the holiness of the day, for each.

14.13 A man shall not unload cargo on a holy day, except in a gale. If he lands cargo needlessly, he should pay a fine as appropriate to the holiness of the day.

14.14 A man should not bear a two-shoulder-strap burden on a holy day, unless he is willing to pay a fine for this[153] (appropriate to) the holiness of the day. A burden is called a 'man's bag' when it has a single shoulder-strap. He may bear such on a holy day with impunity.[154]

14.15 If women hangs cloths[155] out to dry before a holy period begins, and leaves them to hang outside during the holy period, the cloth chest[156] is the worse for it, and no fine need be paid for this. But if she reverses them and turns the second side to the sun, or hangs them out on a holy day, then the bishop's *ármaðr* gets them, unless the (female) owner be willing to pay a fine (appropriate to) the holiness of the day.

14.16 No-one shall hew wood from a stump during the Christmas season, unless he be willing to pay such a fine as is appropriate to the holiness of the day.

Chapter 15: on those women due to whom a man becomes an *úbótamaðr*, in the event of intercourse[157]

15.1 There are seventeen women due to whom a man becomes an *úbótamaðr*, in the event of intercourse[158] or marriage. One is mother. Second is

150 NKS 1642 4o: 'but if it does not fall off and need to be replaced he should pay a fine (appropriate to) the holiness of the day for this'.

151 NKS 1642 4o: 'and he travels a great distance from home before'.

152 NKS 1642 4o: 'on the first holy day'.

153 NKS 1642 4o: 'And if he bears it, he should pay a fine'.

154 NKS 1642 4o: 'He may bear such with impunity, whether (the day) is ordinary or holy'.

155 Alternative translation: 'clothes'.

156 *hirðzla* 'protector'. Halvorsen & Rindal: 'the clothes' (*klærne*).

157 NKS 1642 4o: 'On those women due to whom a man becomes an *úbótamaðr*'. NKS 1642 4o contains only the first two provisions of this chapter.

158 AM 78 4o: *ef han liggr legre*. NKS 1642 4o: *er han liggar með*.

daughter. Third is sister.[159] Fourth is son's daughter. Fifth is daughter's daughter. Sixth is brother's daughter. Seventh is sister's daughter. Eighth is stepmother. Ninth is son's wife. Tenth is brother's wife. Eleventh is stepdaughter. Twelfth is the mother[160] of the man's wife. Thirteenth is the sister of the man's wife. Fourteenth is father's sister. Fifteenth is mother's sister. Sixteenth is father's mother. Seventeenth is mother's mother.

15.2 Any man who lies with any one of these has forfeited property and peace.[161] He should travel to heathen land, and should never enter the presence of Christian men.[162]

15.3 Now, no man shall take to wife a kinswoman more closely related than in the fifth knee, or the widow of a kinsman related in the fifth knee.

15.4 If he takes a more closely related woman to wife, then the bishop's *ármaðr* shall set for them a four-month time limit by which to dissolve their union. If they are not willing to separate, then each of them should pay a fine of three marks.

15.5 A second four-month time limit shall be set for them. If they let this pass, then they should pay a fine of three marks.

15.6 The third four-month time limit shall be set for them. If they let this pass, then they should pay a fine of three marks.

15.7 Now, the fourth four-month time limit shall be set for them. If they are not then willing to dissolve their union, they have forfeited property and peace. They should travel to heathen land, for they do not wish to be Christian.

15.8 Now, a man espouses a woman, and kinship between them is uncovered. Then, the bishop's *ármaðr* shall obtain two kin-counters.[163] He who contracted the marriage shall obtain two more. Their kinship is reckoned collectively. If kinship is found between them, the marriage shall be dissolved with impunity. This was not intentional.[164]

15.9 There are three forms of spiritual kinship, and all are worth as much as ordinary kinship.

15.10 This is one: holding a child during prime-signing.

15.11 Second: holding a child during baptism.

15.12 Third: holding a child whilst a bishop administers confirmation.

15.13 And if a man takes his spiritual kinswoman to wife, such time limits for separation shall apply as if he had married in ordinary kinship. If he lets one of these pass, he should pay a fine of three marks; six for two; nine for three.

15.14 The fourth month-long time limit shall be set for them. If they let that pass, then they forfeit property and peace.

159 NKS 1642 4o: 'the man's sister'.

160 NKS 1642 4o: 'daughter'.

161 NKS 1642 4o: 'property and peace, land and chattels'.

162 NKS 1642 4o: 'men, for he does not wish to be Christian'.

163 *talu* men.

164 *þæt er huaskes uili.*

Chapter sixteen: on episcopal fines, and *úbótaverk*[165]

16.1 The bishop takes all those fines connected with the setting of time limits, up to the point at which a man becomes an *úbótamaðr*. Then he takes up to three marks from the funds of the *úbótamaðr*, and the king, the surplus.

16.2 This is *úbótaverk*: to 'sit out'.

16.3 This is *úbótaverk*: Sámi-seeking:[166] faring to find out the future.

16.4 If a woman bites a finger – or a toe – off her child,[167] for long life, she should pay a fine of three marks.

16.5 And if a woman or farmer raises a child[168] heathen, for long life, s/he should pay three marks for that.

16.6 [169]Such a witch as harms cow or calf, woman or child with magic is worst.

16.7 And if witchcraft-paraphernalia come to be found in men's beds or bolsters – human hair;[170] or frogs' feet; human nails; or[171] such things as seem fit for witchcraft – then legally equal cases[172] may be raised against three women: those who might seem to be likely suspects.[173] Each must undergo trial by hot iron. If she is clean,[174] according to the trial by hot iron, then she is[175] free of the charges. If unclean, according to the trial by hot iron, then she is said to be rightly charged. She has forfeited property and peace,[176] and after five-nights' grace,[177] following the trial by hot iron, whoever can take her: strike and kill!

16.8 If a woman is accused of witchcraft throughout the *herað*, then she must obtain the witness of six women[178] that she is not sorcerous. If that is obtained, she is free of the charges. But if she does not obtain this, she should travel away, out of the *herað*, with her property share. Her being a witch is not within her control.

16.9 Men must trust well in God, and not in heathen cursing, or in heathen practice. And if a man comes to be found guilty of this – that he engages in such heathen practices as are forbidden in book-language – he owes three marks.

165 NKS 1642 4o: 'On fines connected with the setting of time limits'.

166 *at gera finfarar*. NKS 1642 4o: 'to fare to Finnmark'.

167 NKS 1642 4o: 'the child'.

168 NKS 1642 4o: 'her/his child'.

169 NKS 1642 4o: heading 'On witchcraft' (*fordeðo skapp*).

170 NKS 1642 4o: 'hair or nails'.

171 NKS 1642 4o: 'frogs' feet or'.

172 *till iafms rettar*. Halvorsen & Rindal: *med samme bot* ('with the same fine').

173 NKS 1642 4o: 'then the bishop's *ármaðr* may raise a case, with equal right, against three men/ people: those whom, to him, seem to be likely suspects'.

174 NKS 1642 4o: 'If they are clean'.

175 NKS 1642 4o: 'they are'.

176 NKS 1642 4o: 'property and peace, land and chattels'.

177 NKS 1642 4o: 'after fifteen nights' grace'.

178 AM 78 4o: *kuenna*.NKS 1642 4o: *husfrua*.

Chapter seventeen: on separation of a couple, and on adultery, and on those matters which are known throughout the *herað* and which involve fine-payment to the bishop[179]

17.1 And if a couple separate from each other without legal cause,[180] then four month-long[181] time limits shall be set for the one of them responsible for this, so that s/he might return to the household. And if s/he does not return, s/he should pay a fine of three marks per single legal time limit; six for two; nine for three.[182] The fourth month-long time limit should be set. And if s/he will not then return to the household, s/he forfeits property and peace.[183] S/he should go to heathen land, and should never enter the presence of Christian men.

17.2 If a man takes a woman, and already has a wife of his own, he should pay a fine of three marks for this.[184]

17.3 If a woman takes a man other than her husband, she owes three marks to the bishop.

17.4 Whichever one of the couple wrongs the other, they should have done with the matter, and the couple should not dissolve their union.

17.5 [185]Now if cases involving payment of fines to the bishop's *ármaðr*[186] come to be wrongfully conducted[187] in a *herað*, then he[188] shall assemble an assembly thing in the *herað*, and carve summons batons[189] for this assembly thing and cause them to be sent around within the *herað*.

17.6 Every man[190] is obliged to attend[191] the *herað* assembly thing.

17.7 Now, the assembly thing is convened. Then the bishop's *ármaðr* shall stand up:[192] 'I have heard this: that a man has acted wrongfully, in the *herað*,[193] in a case involving fine-payment to the bishop'. He shall report the case accurately. 'Now I wish to know if you have heard of this case before'.

17.8 If a quarter of those men of the *herað* who are there at the assembly thing claim that they have heard of this matter before, then it is said to be 'legally known throughout the *herað*'. Then the bishop's *ármaðr* may pursue that case, for such compensation as lies at stake, by law.

179 *ret.* AM 78 4o: follows heading with *cap*itulum. NKS 1642 4o: 'If a couple wish to separate'.
180 NKS 1642 4o: 'And if a couple wish to separate from each other'.
181 NKS 1642 4o: 'four four-month-long'.
182 NKS 1642 4o: 'And if they will not, they should pay three marks for one and six for two; nine for three'.
183 NKS 1642 4o: 'property and peace, land and chattels'.
184 NKS 1642 4o: 'he owes three marks to the bishop'.
185 NKS 1642 4o: heading: 'On those cases which are conducted within a *herað*'.
186 NKS 1642 4o: 'the bishop'.
187 NKS 1642 4o: 'conducted'.
188 NKS 1642 4o: 'his *ármaðr*'.
189 Alternative translation: 'a summons baton'.
190 NKS 1642 4o: 'farmer'.
191 AM 78 4o: *sœtia*. NKS 1642 4o: *søkia*.
192 NKS 1642 4o: 'stand up and say this'.
193 NKS 1642 4o: 'our *herað*'.

17.9 A *lýrittr*-oath is valid for a case worth three marks, or for those which are lesser.

17.10 But whenever a case is greater, a *hálfrétti*-oath is valid.

17.11 Iron for all *úbótamál.*

17.12 Now, if, on the contrary, fewer than a quarter of the *heraðsmenn*[194] claim that they have heard of the case, then the case collapses, and it is said to be 'his invention'. He may not legally pursue that case.

17.13 He must also pursue all those to which evidence points.

17.14 Now, there must be a single episcopal investigation, in each case.[195] There is no *lǫgfé* payment for this. All men are obliged to defend Christianity.

Chapter eighteen: on violence in a churchyard, or inside a church[196]

18.1 Now, if men fight in a churchyard, and blood touches the churchyard ground, then he who has drawn blood shall pay for consecration of the ground, at a cost of one mark. And if blood touches the exterior of a church, then consecration shall be paid for, at a cost of one mark. It is, then, two for both places.

18.2 And if, through wrath, blood is shed in a church, then consecration shall be paid for with three marks.

18.3 And if men fight outside a churchyard, and a bleeding, injured man runs into the churchyard, and there seeks sanctuary, he who drew blood shall pay for consecration.

18.4 Now, the Christian Law, as we recall it,[197] has been recounted. If anything is lacking, then bishops[198] should mend this, through their legal competence.[199] May Jesus Christ protect us! Amen![200]

Additions

Three of the manuscripts containing Version Two of the *Borgarthing Law* include several additions, translated here. These manuscripts are AM 31 8o, Holm 28 4o,

194 NKS 1642 4o: '*þingmenn*' or 'men of the thing assembly'.

195 *Nu* er *æin sokn* biscu*ps a allum malom*. NKS 1642 4o: *Nu* er *ein sokn a allu*m biskops *malom* ('Now there is a single investigation in all episcopal cases').

196 NKS 1642 4o: no heading. Contains only the final provision in this chapter (18.4), concluding the law.

197 ver *komom minni a*. NKS 1642 4o: *uer hafu*m *minni til*. AM 31 8o (Version Two): *Nv er k*ris*tin domr* var *taldr slikr sæ*m ver *hafu*m *minni t*il.

198 NKS 1642 4o: 'the bishop'.

199 Alternative translations: 'justice' or 'rights'. NKS 1642 4o: 'through commands and legal competence'.

200 NKS 1642 4o: omits 'May Jesus Christ protect us! Amen!'

and Holm 29 4o (from the mid-fourteenth, early to mid-fourteenth, and late fourteenth century, respectively).

The translations of all of the following passages are taken from the Halvorsen & Rindal edition of AM 31 8o, except for Addition 16, which is found in Holm 28 4o only. Several of the other additions are found in Holm 28 4o or Holm 29 4o as well as AM 31 8o, as indicated in the footnotes. Significant variation between manuscripts is also indicated in the footnotes. Note that Halvorsen & Rindal used the NgL edition for most of the AM 31 8o text of Additions 1–4, due to the illegibility of the manuscript in that segment.

1 Now, a man goes to request a marriage agreement.[201] Then he shall seek out the one who is her heir, for the marriage agreement. The man (heir) shall stipulate the marriage conditions for his female relative, and the dowry.[202] They (the couple) shall take each other by the hand and he shall address her by her name: 'I betroth myself to this unmarried woman who shall be my lawful wife, with the stated dowry'. They should confirm this with those who hear this as legal witnesses. The person who brought about the betrothal has the authority to bring their pledges[203] together. This shall be sealed with a handshake and confirmed with legal witnesses. No one may break this agreement, except under one of three conditions. This is only if either partner falls into insanity, or 'fallen flesh',[204] or epilepsy. Whichever one of them [. . .][205] shall decide whether the marriage agreement shall be upheld or broken.

2 [206]A widow for whom marriage-arrangers secure household resources through marriage[207] has authority to decide to marry whichever man she wishes, according to the stated law. Likewise, if she is her father's heir: she has authority to make her own decision, and she may take advice from whomever she wishes.[208] And if her father's relatives or her father's brothers give her in marriage,[209] and make an exchange which is favourable to them, and the person who shall make the betrothal agrees to this, and they enter into a binding agreement with the one who decides this, then this holds until she is married.[210] Then she may set whomever she wishes the task of seeking her full, undiminished inheritance from her father.[211] And the one who made that exchange shall be called a fool.

201 *raðafar*.
202 *hæiman fylgiu*.
203 *abyrgdir*.
204 *harund fall*, meaning either 'leprosy' or 'impotence'.
205 The text is illegible here, reading *e . . . af . . .* Halvorsen & Rindal suggested 'is well' (*er frisk*).
206 This addition is also in Holm 29 4o, from the point indicated later.
207 *gifta til bus*.
208 From this point onwards, this passage is found in Holm 29 4o.
209 Holm 29 4o: 'give the unmarried woman in marriage with lawful betrothal'.
210 Holm 29 4o: 'and no longer'.
211 Holm 29 4o adds 'or that which her father gave her'.

3 And such a woman as lies with a man in secret is called a whore,[212] because she has no decision-making authority in this before her relatives have given her away, as they wish.

4 [213]*Here Bessi's Law is discussed.*[214]

On a marriage agreement for which pledges have been given but which someone wishes to break: Bessi made a law about this which has been valid ever since. If a man does not want to have a woman to whom he has been betrothed, he shall pay her as much as he had agreed for her, and as much as she was to have taken as a dowry. And if a woman – or her marriage-arrangers – does not wish to keep an agreement with a man, then she should pay as much in compensation as she was to have taken, and the marriage agreement is thereby ended. If the agreement has not been guaranteed with pledges, then the person who wishes to break it shall pay three marks in silver.[215] Then it is as if the agreement had never been made, and that is called 'handshake breaking'.[216]

5 . . . raise[217] a case against him according to the same law, he should compensate for the marriage contract as stated in law. Now if a man does not wish to lose his marriage agreement and people argue over this, and pledges have been brought together, then he shall have his betrothed even if the marriage arrangers do not wish to *mol sinn runa*.[218] And if they 'work' at this,[219] then all those who seek legal protection[220] shall have it, and those who stand in the way of this shall be ineligible for protection, either from the king or from relatives, whether they suffer wounding or death from this.

6 *How many sets of legal compensation*[221] *a woman may take*

If a man threatens his wife with keys or locks, then he owes three marks. Likewise, if he takes another woman and lies with her and keeps her in the same house as him or her. That (she) is called a 'hearth woman'.[222] Third: if a man threatens his wife while drinking.[223] Then he owes three marks for each of these. Now if she takes three sets of legal compensation in such a case and he does a fourth thing, then she may do as she pleases: separate from him or be done with it.

7 *On separation*

Now if a couple has separated and the woman has secured land through marriage,[224] then she shall call a *heraðsþing*, giving three nights' notice, and

212 *hor reckia.*
213 This passage is also found in Holm 28 4o.
214 Holm 28 4o: 'On Bessi's law, which he made'.
215 Holm 28 4o omits 'in silver'.
216 AM 31 8o: *handsals rof.*
217 This passage appears to begin in the middle of a sentence.
218 This is unclear. Halvorsen & Rindal suggested 'keep their agreement' (*holde avtalen*).
219 This probably refers to continuation of conflict.
220 *frid hælgir.*
221 *rette.*
222 *aren ælia.*
223 *rædr kono sinni* með *horne* eða *nefa a olbæck.*
224 *til iarða gift.*

bring forward the witness of six men who were at the betrothal meeting or present during the wedding evening. If they all come forward as required, then the *heraðsmenn* shall judge that she shall have everything to which the evidence entitles her. No counter-evidence may be brought against the marriage witnesses of the woman if it is acknowledged that she was properly married.

8 But if a woman has not secured land through marriage then five days' notice shall be given for property division. On the fifth day, the witness of two men shall be brought forward, concerning the marriage land of the woman. She may raise a case wherever she wishes: there or at the assembly thing. And if the man will not divide the property on the fifth day, then he owes three marks in silver.

9 Now if a couple has lived together for thirty years or longer, and all the witnesses to the marriage have died, but she (the woman) has been in charge of the latches and locks throughout the home, and sat according to her age with the other housewives, and been called his proper wife by all, then she shall have six men's witness that their marriage has been this way for thirty years or longer. Then she is entitled to legal married status with a share in the man's farm: a third of the property in land and chattels, and up to three marks in bride price.[225] And if a woman says that she has been legally married but the opposing party denies that this is so – she invokes witnesses but he names others opposing this who say that she was never legally married – then the group of witnesses which is largest shall win, unless the others wish to undergo trial by iron; if they do, the outcome of the case shall be decided as the trial by iron indicates. Anyone who brings forward false evidence owes six marks in silver and three marks for each person who offers such evidence, and he shall never again be eligible to sit on a *dómr* panel, or eligible as a legal witness.

10 *On legal right to compensation for a woman when she has been laid down for unlawful sex*[226]

When a woman has been laid down for unlawful sex, then she is most expensive regarding legal right to compensation[227] if she has a husband, and if her father is alive, and a son which she had by another man: she is a twelve-mark woman regarding legal right to compensation. Six marks are allotted to her husband, and three marks to her father and three marks to a son she has had by another man. Likewise, a man is allotted six marks for his betrothed. There are three gifts[228] which shall be given for lying with a woman: a six-ounce gift, and a three-ounce, and a one and a half-ounce gift. The largest two gifts

225 *mundi*.
226 *legen*.
227 *at rette*.
228 *Giafar*.

shall go to the father's family, the smallest to the mother's, and the nearest relative (on each side) shall receive these.

11 If a man travels abroad, away from his wife, then she shall sit and wait for her husband for three years, but longer only if she wishes.

12 [229]*If a man takes a woman against her will*[230]

Now if a woman is travelling between farms along with an accompanying child of at least three years old, known as a *kvennaleiðir*,[231] and a man comes to her and commits a misdeed against her, and she goes to a farm and tells people, and raises a case against the one responsible for the misdeed, and the child stands by her and confirms what she says, and says that the one against whom she has raised a case committed the misdeed, those whom she made witnesses to her ill fortune ought to bear witness to this at the thing assembly. Her use of witnesses, along with the confirmation of the truth by the child, gives her full rights to compensation in the case she has raised.[232]

13 [233]Now if a woman travels between farms without anyone accompanying her, and a man comes to her and violates her,[234] and if he strikes her or binds her, and she is bruised or bloody, then he owes three marks for the binding and six for the wounding, and six more for the intercourse. Now if there are no eye-witnesses and she makes the first people she comes across witnesses, then she makes them witnesses for a *halfrétti* oath and a *halfrétti* payment[235] as befits the case. But if she passes the first farm, then she takes witnesses for the same kind of oath and twelve ounces in *trygðakaup*. If she passes two and goes to the third, then there is an oath but no payment.[236] Now if she is woundless and makes the first people (she meets) witnesses to this, then there is a *halfrétti* oath and twelve ounces in *trygðakaup*. If she passes the first (farm), the oath is the same and the *trygðakaup* is six ounces. If she passes two and goes on to the third, then there is an oath but no payment. If she passes three and goes to the fourth, there is neither word nor oath. That is called a 'white strike'.

14 [237]*Evidence on paternity, and childbed*[238]

And if a woman is pregnant with a child conceived in secret and her labour pains begin, the person taking care of her affairs shall go and fetch people and bring them to the door of the place where the woman is lying. He shall ask her who she says the father is before the child is born. And if she tells

229 This passage is also in Holm 28 4o.

230 AM 31 8o: *Ef* maðr *tæk kono navdiga*. Holm 28 4o: 'On a woman's rights and use of witnesses to uphold her rights' (*Vm ret kuænna oc skirskotta till rettar sins*).

231 'Someone accompanying a woman'.

232 Holm 28 4o: 'as befits the case'.

233 The first part of this passage is also in Holm 28 4o.

234 AM 31 8o: *bry(tr) hena* til *suæfnis*.

235 Holm 28 4o: omits 'and a *halfrétti* payment'.

236 Holm 28 4o omits the second part of this passage, from this point onwards.

237 The first part of this passage is also in Holm 28 4o.

238 Holm 28 4o: 'How a woman shall declare the father of a child conceived in secret, and on payment due to a woman' (*ret a kono*).

this, and her words can be heard through the door,[239] then her oral testimony shall be confirmed by witnesses.[240] Women are as eligible as men to be witnesses in this case. And if there is a woman in the *herað* who has gained a reputation[241] as being more likely than other women to behave in a helpful way,[242] then she shall bring forward the witness of two people and be called a 'help woman'.[243] Then the man ought to swear a *halfrétti* oath and pay a half payment[244] and be called 'half father' to the child,[245] and provide half maintenance payment[246] during the first twelve months. And if the woman does not say who the father is before the child is born, but says this within nine nights of childbed, then the oath is the same and the *trygðakaup* is twelve ounces. And if she says this within a month after the birth, then the oath is the same but there is no payment. But if she does not say it within a month of the birth, then it is said that the child's father is a *þræll*, and she has to pay a fornication fine[247] to the king of three marks. The child does not need to be freed: it could be the child of a distinguished man or a near relative of the mother. Six marks is the legal fine[248] for the wife of a *hauldr*, four marks for the daughter of a fully freed slave, three marks if she herself is a fully freed slave, twelve ounces for a freed slave.

15 *That a man may be killed without compensation when another man catches him in the act*

Now a man has the right to kill if he comes across a man with his wife, mother, daughter or sister, stepmother or son's wife or brother's wife, wife's mother or sister, his stepdaughter, son's daughter, brother's daughter, or sister's daughter. And that is thirteen (women) altogether. A man can be killed over any of the women from whom a man can inherit, without any compensation being due, if he is caught in the act. Witnesses shall bear witness to this if there are any. If there is blood on her clothes – going-out clothes or bed clothes – this is additional evidence. This shall all be confirmed with witnesses at an 'arrow' thing assembly. Then neither the king nor relatives can demand compensation for him. And a fully freed slave and a fully freed slave's son and a freed slave: each has the right to kill for four women: wife, mother, daughter, and sister. A *þræll* has the right to kill for his wife and his

239 Holm 28 4o: omits 'through the door'.

240 Holm 28 4o: 'then he shall confirm with witnesses her oral testimony as to the father of the child'.

241 Holm 28 4o: omits the next part: 'as being more likely than other women to behave in a helpful way, then she shall bring forward the witness of two people and be called a "help woman"'.

242 AM 31 8o: *ordlagh hefir fenget at haeldr verdr bot at hennar nauist en annara kuenna.*

243 AM 31 8o: *biarghryghr*.

244 *rette*.

245 Holm 28 4o ends the passage at this point.

246 *fulghu*.

247 *leghet sæckt*.

248 *rette*.

daughter. If he finds a man with her, then he shall go to a well and take a pail of water and pour it over them and bid his in-law sleep well.

16 [249]After (collection), cod tithe shall go the fish racks, and corn to store.

17 [250]It is *úbotaverk* if someone kills himself.

18 [251]The bishop shall visit every *fylki* once a year to provide services, if there are no compelling reasons he cannot do so. And the farmers shall provide horse transport – every horse which has been under saddle or harness – wherever the bishop wishes to go, if the *ármaðr* does not make an alternative arrangement. And anyone who does not shall pay three ounces[252] for each horse, and six ounces for the failure to provide horse transport. And if a man comes to the meeting for sharing out horse transport and conceals it, and does not provide it for sharing, then it is as if it was not done.

249 In Holm 28 4o only.

250 Also in Holm 28 4o.

251 The first part of this addition is also in Holm 28 4o. There, it has the heading 'On animal transport for the bishop'.

252 Holm 28 4o ends here.

Part IV Notes on the text

Chapter one: here begins the Christian Law: that which shall be valid

1.1

This paragraph functions as a preamble, briefly summing up the purpose of the law. The Old Norwegian term *uphaf*, which could be translated as 'first point', 'origin', or 'beginning', indicates that the Church Law Section constituted the first section of the law, and was followed by several other sections of secular law material, which, save for a few fragments, are now lost. This positioning is regarded by some scholars as an argument for Anglo-Saxon influence, since the same order is found in Anglo-Saxon law (Taranger 1890: 209–210; Helle 2001: 180–181).

The reference to bowing to the east and giving ourselves to Christ is nearly identical with the opening phrase of the *Gulathing Law* (Gul. 1). The east was established as the 'Christian direction of prayer' by the Early Church (Lang 2009: 35), as mentioned by many of the Church Fathers, including Clement of Alexandria, Origen, and Augustine (Lang 2009: 48–56). Thomas Aquinas summed up the various reasons for turning to the east while praying, with biblical references to John 8:12, Zechariah 6:12, Psalms 67:34, and Matthew 24:27: 'To adore facing east is fitting, first because the movement of the heavens which manifest the divine majesty is from the east. Secondly, paradise was situated in the east according to the Septuagint version of Genesis, and we seek to return to paradise. Thirdly, because of Christ who is *the light of the world* and is called *the Orient, who mounteth above the heaven of heaven to the east*, and is expected to come from the east according to Matthew, *as lightning comes out of the east, and shines even to the west, so also will the coming of the Son of Man be*' (quotation including the italics taken from Lang 2009: 60).

One could also speculate whether the term *uphaf* 'beginning' has theological connotations in this particular context and participates in a play on words together with *austr* (east). As mentioned earlier, one of the reasons Thomas Aquinas gave for turning towards the east was the fact that paradise was located there. The Septuagint version uses the term *mikedem*, 'towards the east', and according to Corin Braga, '[t]he fathers of the Church freely interpreted *mikedem* as signifying either . . . *a principio*, at the beginning (hence the deduction that the biblical text wanted to say that God created the Paradise before the rest of the world) . . . or *contra orientem*, *ad orientem*, towards the Orient (the rising sun suggesting the beginning both of time and space)' (Braga 2008: 141–142). Thus, *uphaf*, *austr* and *Kristi*, 'who is called the Orient', all have interrelated connotations.

1.2–1.3

The vivid and detailed descriptions of these monstrous births are quite unique in European legal history and no parallels have yet been found. Jenny Jochens somewhat surprisingly argued for a literal interpretation of the depictions and suggested 'constant inbreeding' as the cause of the physical deformities: 'The narrow confines of the deep Norwegian valleys had compelled local communities to live together and to intermarry for centuries. With insufficient differentiation in their genetic makeup, closely related couples may have produced biological enormities that were routinely exterminated' (Jochens 1998: 2). In such circumstances, the Church had compromised and accepted child exposure under these specific terms. However, it is more likely that at least some of the depictions are of mythological-theological origin, and should be read in connection with medieval ideas about possible consequences of violation of abstinence regulations. The paragraph seems to deal with two different cases of monstrous birth. The last category (1.3), skin-bag-born children, were allowed to be prime-signed (*prima signatio*), an initial act of the baptismal rite during which the candidate was marked with the sign of the cross and buried alive in the churchyard. By contrast, the children in the first case (1.2) were to be placed at the Evil One's *forvé*. The Old Norwegian term *forvé* consists of two morphemes: -*vé*, which means 'holy/consecrated place' and the negative prefix *for-* (NgL V: 204 s.v. *forvé*). (The same term is used in the later *National Code* from 1274 (L IX 2), denoting an executing place.) The Evil One's *forvé* thus seems to be the Devil's place. The most prominent features of these children were their reversed limbs, and this fits well with the medieval conception of the Devil having backward-pointing feet (Crawford Cree 1906: nr 1; Landro 2010: 214). There are several claims in ecclesiastical sources that conception during certain forbidden time periods, determined by the liturgical year, leads to physical deformities (Metzler 2006: 88; Landro 2010: 215). Bishop Thietmar of Merseburg, for instance, in his Chronicle, written down between 1012 and 1018, refers to two different cases, in each of which a child is conceived at a forbidden time period and the Devil is involved (Hamilton 2001: 230). In the first case the Devil appears and claims the child as his own. In the other case the child is conceived during Holy Innocents' Day (December 28), and is born with reversed toes (*pareret infantem in pedibus digitos habentem retortos*) (Holzmann 1935: 30, 32).

Chapter two: on godparents, and emergency baptism

2.1

This phrase reflects the medieval Church's conception of the spiritual kinship that arose out of the baptismal ceremony. Baptism was regarded as the child's second and spiritual birth, and created a spiritual kinship between the actors involved in the ceremony, with significant consequences: 'They were literally "coparents" of their common child and as such were forbidden to marry one another in order to prevent sexual relations among spiritual kin, which were regarded as a kind of incest' (Lynch 1998: 17). The concept of spiritual kinship originated in the Eastern Church and was introduced to the western parts of Europe in the early Middle Ages. Bishop Boniface (d. 754), for instance, encountered the idea of 'spiritual incest' for the first time with surprise during one of his missionary journeys, and asked Archbishop Nothelm of Canterbury (d. 739) for clarification about it (Tangl 1916: 57–58; Lynch 1998: 92–93; Landro 2010: 70).

2.2–2.4

This part of the text describes a baptismal rite for emergency situations, which is only a shortened version of the ritual used under normal circumstances. Due to the extraordinary situation, the chrism is replaced by spittle. The paragraph is, however, quite ambiguous when it comes to the chronological order of the rite, and two different interpretations have been proposed. From a western point of view, it would have been usual to perform pre-baptismal rites, in which an anointing ceremony played an important part, *before* baptism by immersion. The main purpose of these pre-baptismal rites was exorcism, driving the Devil out and making the candidate ready to receive the Holy Spirit (Winkler 1995: 58; Landro 2010: 53). However, three of the manuscripts also mention anointing the *hiarsa* 'crown of the head', which was abnormal in western pre-baptismal rites. Anointing the head belonged to the postbaptismal rites, alluding to the new status of the candidate, bearing a diadem as a member of the 'royal priesthood'. The *hiarsa* does not fit in with the other body parts mentioned. Furthermore, manuscript NKS 1642 4o has replaced the Old Norwegian term *hiarsa* with *illiar* 'foot soles'. Anointing these was another rarity in western baptismal practice, although it was more commonly used in Eastern baptismal rites. The Gallican *pedilavium*, 'washing of the feet', was admittedly in use in the early Middle Ages and could have been a source of inspiration, but this ceremony took place *after* baptism in the same way as anointing the head (Levesque 1995; Landro 2010: 59). The presence of these rather unusual features could lead to another interpretation of this text. It is possible that the author of this part started out with the chronological order of the rite and then moved on to deal with practicalities, such as limited access to water, before turning to ways in which this issue affected the question of immersion versus sprinkling of water. Such a two-part composition, matching that in Iceland, would imply that the whole anointing ceremony was postbaptismal, more in line with baptismal rites in the Eastern Church (Landro 2010: 43–68).

Chapter three: on a woman's labour, and responsibility for her child

3.2–3.3

These paragraphs deal with infanticide. However, while the corresponding paragraph in the *Eidsivathing Law* (Eid. I 3) mainly focuses on use of oaths and ordeal to throw light on the case, the paragraphs in the *Borgarthing Law* emphasize first, examination of the evidence ('hand- or band-marks'); and second, the question of whether or not the woman speaks with reason. If the woman 'does not speak with reason' she is not to blame for the crime. The focus on reason seems to reveal acquaintance with the concept of personal guilt. In contrast to the *Eidsivathing Law*, the *Borgarthing Law* thus seems to reflect a 'procedure not based on fire and water, but on evidence and arguments' (Pennington 1993: 135; see also Landro 2010: 170).

3.4

This paragraph deals with an application of the regulations outlined in paragraph 2.1. Husband and wife could not under normal circumstances sponsor the same child, since acting as godparents in a baptismal ceremony created a kinship of spiritual character which barred the participants from marriage and sexual relations. (See comments on Chapter 2.1, with references.) However, a life of isolation, combined with urgency to get the child baptized, has in this case created an exception to the rule.

3.5

This paragraph does not explain why the period of breastfeeding should be limited, but one possible interpretation is that the paragraph reflects the medieval regulations on sexual abstinence, as explained by James Brundage: 'Once pregnancy was over, the child was born, and the postpartum continence period had passed, couples were still forbidden to have sexual intercourse, according to the Responsa Gregorii, until after the child had been weaned' (Brundage 1987: 157). Perhaps the limitation of the period of breastfeeding was motivated by the fact that sexual intercourse was forbidden during this period. The fact that the husband takes the role of the 'accuser' might suggest that it was in his interests to bring an end to his wife's breastfeeding, to resume their sexual relations (Landro 2010: 216, nr 707).

Chapter four: on time limits for baptisms

4.1

stefnur, from *stefna, stæmna* ('time limit'): This word is believed to derive from Proto-Germanic (Hellquist 1980: 1106, s.v. *stämma*). The Old Norwegian term has several meanings, including ‘meeting’, ‘gathering’, ‘set day’, ‘time limit within which something must be done’, and ‘deadline’. In Norway, time limits of this type could vary in length from three days to five days (*fimt* or *fimtarstefna*, the time limit found most commonly in the laws) to several months, a year, or (in some cases) several generations (Langseth 1974: 210–213).

4.1–4.2

With some minor variations, all of the Norwegian Church laws divide the year into several different baptismal terms, with Christmas Day, Easter Eve, St John’s Eve, and Michaelmas each functioning as the terminus of such a period. This arrangement is quite unusual in a European context. In 385, Pope Siricius (384–399) prescribed Easter and Pentecost as the only legitimate dates for baptism, with exceptions for emergency situations – a provision which is also commonly found in canonical collections from the tenth and eleventh centuries (Nilsson, Bertil 2012: 138–141). However, the fact that large parts of Europe had been converted to Christianity at the same time the Augustinian notion of original sin was spreading created ‘the demand that infants be baptized “as soon as possible” (*quamprimum*) after birth’ (Johnson 1999: 213; Landro 2010: 76). For this reason, Anglo-Saxon sources such as the writings of Aelfric, the Canons of Edgar, or the Northumbrian Priests’ Law required baptism as soon as possible, or within seven or nine days after baptism (Fehr 1966: 53; Lynch 1998: 101, nr 8).

The Norwegian baptismal terms do not reflect any of these traditions, and two different suggestions could be made as to their origins. One possibility is that the Norwegian arrangement served non-liturgical, practical purposes, without links to any of the previously mentioned traditions: these termini divided the year into four more or less equal time periods, with each terminus placed in the middle of a season. In support of this, it might be remarked that the same deadlines are found in the *Frostathing Law* in the section concerning farming activities: both Christmas Eve and Michaelmas are used as deadlines in a couple of chapters (Frost. XII 2, F XII 6) which deal with selling and buying of land (Landro 2010: 77–81).

Another and more likely possibility is that the baptismal terms follow the *gagnfǫstur* (singular *gagnfasta*), which were to be observed during the three weeks before the Feast of St John, Michaelmas, and Christmas, and during the two weeks before the Lenten fast. The *gagnfǫstur* are not a part of the general liturgical year, and were found only in Norway, on Iceland, and in the Swedish *Uppland Law* (Maurer 1881; Rafnsson 1985: 24). They were removed from the later Norwegian and Icelandic Church laws from the late thirteenth century.

The exact reason for linking baptismal terms with fasts is not easy to establish, but the underlying rationale seems to be that a child born before or during a fast should for some unknown reason be baptized before that particular fast expired. This seems to be confirmed by the baptismal terms in the *Eidsivathing Law*. That law also mentions four particular eves and prescribes that children born on the eve of either Easter, Pentecost, the Feast of St John, or Christmas should be baptized the very same night, before mass the following morning (Eid. 8). The evidence seems conclusive: it was of importance that the child born during a fast was baptized before the prevailing fast expired (Landro 2010: 77–78).

Chapter five: on inedible matter: that which it is forbidden to eat

5.1–5.12

Three different canon law traditions are mixed in this text, which makes parts mutually inconsistent and thus incomprehensible to the reader or listener.

The penitential handbooks from the early Middle Ages and the more comprehensive canon law collections from the eleventh century onwards contain many dietary regulations inspired by Mosaic law from the Old Testament. This issue was dealt with at the so-called Council of Jerusalem, mentioned in Acts 15, during which the Old Testament regulations were confirmed as still valid. As a consequence, a wide array of meat sources was regulated: animals which had been strangled, drowned, or killed by dogs, wolves, or bears, as well as animals which had died without bloodshed, were all forbidden as food (Meens 1995; Lutterbach 1998; Meens 2002; Landro 2010: 83–91).

The Old Norwegian term *suæitra* (*sveita*) referred to animals which had died without the blood being shed, reflecting biblical principle (NgL V: 620 s.v. *sveita*). The case chosen to illustrate the regulation, in 5.10 ('and if livestock falls from a rock and blood does not gush out, then it shall be rejected') is nearly the same as Canon 2 from the Irish *Canones Adomnani*: *Pecora de rupe cadentia, si sanguis eorum effusus sit, recipienda; sin vero, sed fracta sunt ossa eorum et sanguis foras non fluxerit, refutanda sunt ut morticina* (Wasserschleben 1958: 120).

The term *suida* or *sviðða* is, more problematic, however. Etymologically, the term can be translated 'self-dead', which probably indicates 'dead through disease' (de Vries, 2000: 569; NgL V: 621 s.v. *svidái*). However, the paragraph actually contains a definition of *suida*, and more important than the original etymological meaning is the expression used in this definition: *manz handa verk* 'works of the human hand' or 'intervention by human hand'. This means that anything killed by 'works of the human hand' may be eaten, and vice versa: anything not killed by 'works of the human hand' is defined as *suida*, and consequently forbidden as food.

The expression *manz handa verk* must be considered a leitmotif in the fifth chapter of the *Borgarthing Law*, and is of great importance for two reasons. Firstly, this expression reveals acquaintance with an alternative canonical interpretation of the dietary regulations, originating in the kingdom of East-Francia in the middle of the ninth century, which deviates from the previously-mentioned biblical notion (Landro 2010: 99–105, 2011, 2019). Based on the idea of man's God-given right to hunt (*venatio hominis*), granted first to Noah, an anonymous cleric introduced a new interpretation of the dietary regulations, which is echoed in the *Borgarthing Law*. According to this, under certain conditions, an animal which one would be forbidden to eat, according to biblically inspired canon law standards, could be eaten, if a man had caused the animal's death in any way (*homo in causa*). The principle of *homo in causa* is more or less equivalent with the Old Norwegian *manz handa verk* which later in the paragraph (5.8) introduces a series of cases, inserted to illustrate the governing principle: 'breaks its neck in a cattle-stall, strangles itself in a cattle-fork, twines itself in a tether', and so on.

Secondly, the presence of the expression *manz handa verk* provides a glimpse of the ways in which foreign legal concepts and material were received, modified, and adapted to Norwegian conditions. *Manz handa verk* is in all probability a legal concept taken from the secular sections of the *Borgarthing Law* (Landro 2010: 105–106). Although the secular parts of the East Norwegian provincial laws are admittedly lost save for a few fragments, the expression is used in the Swedish *Older Västgöta Law*, valid in a legal province neighbouring the Borgarthing area, in a completely different context: 'If a creature falls into a well or a ditch through works of the human hand and meets its death as a result of this, a fine should be paid: six ounces for a horse, half a mark for an ox, and the same for a cow and a mare' (VgL I R 9). The well mentioned in the Swedish law is also present in the *Borgarthing Law*: 'lies dead in a still well'. The author or authors in charge of formulating this chapter found it convenient to make use of a familiar and already established legal concept from secular law to express the canonical concept of *homo in causa*. It is possible that several of the cases in the *Borgarthing Law* listed to exemplify the principle of *manz handa verk* were copied from secular law.

The second half of this series of cases, starting with 'it swims itself to death', does not reflect the principle of *manz handa verk* found in the first half, since animals killed by bears, wolves, or dogs do not fit into the category 'animals killed by works of the human hand'. This is a later addition and represents the third interpretation of the medieval dietary regulations, for which Augustine was the authoritative source. Augustine regarded the decision by the Council in Jerusalem as a temporary regulation, with no binding force for later generations of Christians. The only matter of importance was simply *knowing* the cause of the animal's death, to prevent eating animals killed by disease (Landro 2010: 109–115). This interpretation is found both in the *Gulathing Law* and in the Icelandic *Grágás*, which explicitly states that anything may be eaten 'whatever causes its death, as long as the cause of its death is known' (Gr. 16). In the *Gulathing Law* this principle is formulated in the following way: '*Sviðða* we are also forbidden to eat. If a man is accused and convicted of having eaten the flesh of animals that have died of themselves, he shall pay a fine of three ounces to the bishop and shall go to confession and do penance. We speak of those animals as having died of themselves whose death is not known to men. But men may eat what *wolves* rend and deprive of life; and men may eat the flesh of a beast attacked by *bears* or bitten by *dogs*. Men may also eat the flesh of a beast that is drowned in running water or falls out over a cliff or is choked by the halter' (Gul. 31).

The illustrative cases in the *Gulathing Law* have at some point been inserted into the *Borgarthing Law*, in which this material represents a later stratum, probably as a result of an attempt to harmonize the dietary regulations in the Norwegian laws. This addition is probably also the reason why the manuscripts of the *Borgarthing Law* differ from each other in their concluding remarks. Whereas

AM 68 4o and NKS 1642 4o add versions of the sentence, 'Now all this, which has died in this way, and through intervention by human hand, may be eaten and used', the other manuscripts leave out 'through intervention by human hand'. This comment made no sense after the second layer was inserted, and has presumably been removed, at least in some of the manuscripts.

5.13

This part of the text deals with dietary regulations belonging to a slightly different category, namely those involving animals which are unclean *per se*, irrespective of the cause of death. The prohibitions against the eating of cats, dogs, and horses have traditionally been interpreted as reactions to pre-Christian, heathen cultic rituals, in which the eating of horsemeat was customary. This theory has been supported by discoveries of bones belonging to horses and dogs in pre-Christian human graves (Gräslund 2004; Sanmark 2005). Rob Meens has challenged this theory, inspired by Mary Douglas's concepts of purity, pollution, and taboos (Douglas 1996), and argued that the impurity of these animals had to do with their special relationships to human beings, as 'anomalous or ambiguous creatures . . . which lived around human dwellings, in the marginal area between house and forest, culture and nature' (Meens 2002: 16; Landro 2010: 131).

5.14–5.15

Here some traces of the procedural revision mentioned in the introduction (see pp. 6–7) come into view. To eat dogs, cats, or horses intentionally was considered the severest crime, with exile as punishment. But if a man faces an emergency, the principle of necessity might be applied: 'He shall rather eat dog than dog eat him'. Under such circumstances, the crime was considered unintentional and led only to confession before a priest. The bishop's *ármaðr* in the role of the prosecutor is another hallmark of the revision, in addition to the final sentence of the chapter, 'then he has five-days' grace, following the trial by hot iron, as would a witch'. Here the revisionist points to a parallel case in chapter sixteen, thereby revealing his knowledge of the entire law (Landro 2010: 154–170).

The proverb-like phrase, 'He shall rather eat dog than dog eat him', is found in nearly the same wording in both the *Eidsivathing Law* (Eid. 29): *þa skal hann fyrr eta hunnden en hunndren ete hann*, and the *Gulathing Law* (Gul. 20): *helldr scal hann hund eta helldr en hundr ete hann*. This strongly indicates either a common origin or a later exchange of regulations between the provincial laws (Landro 2010: 207–208).

Chapter six: if men eat meat at improper times

6.1–6.2

Lent, the fast undertaken in preparation for Easter, has its roots in the Early Church. An initial two-day fast was soon extended to a week, and further extended to forty days by the time of the Council of Nicaea in 325. The period of forty days was inspired by the fasting of Jesus, Moses, and Elijah, who all, on certain occasions, fasted for forty days. This resulted in a six-week fast, but included only thirty-six days of fasting, since no fasting took place on Sundays. To reach the number of forty, the *caput ieiunii* was finally made four days earlier, with Ash Wednesday as the starting point (Adam 1979: 91–92).

By the time of the conversion of Scandinavia, the actual duration of Lent was not yet fully settled, and the Scandinavian laws witness acquaintance with fasting periods of six, seven, and nine weeks (Taranger 1890: 374). The *Gulathing Law*, for instance, states that 'if he takes himself a wife during Lent, those nine weeks when the bishop observes the fast . . .' (Gul. 27), which shows that a longer fasting period was prescribed for the clergy. Both the *Eidsivathing Law* (Eid. I 21) and the Icelandic *Grágás* (§ 15) seem to operate with a general fasting period of seven weeks, while the paragraphs 6.1 and 6.2 in the *Borgarthing Law* make a distinction between six and seven weeks of fasting. It was forbidden to eat meat 'within seven weeks before Easter Day', but the punishment was increased if the eating of meat took place 'within six weeks before Easter'. The term *alra manna fasta* 'All Men's Fast' is used of a six-week period in the *Borgarthing Law*, and, as the term implies, applied to the laity as well as the clergy.

6.3

The ember days was a period of three fasting days, which occurred four times (lat. *quattuor tempora*) during the liturgical year (see 13.1). The *Gulathing Law* is lacking these fast days, and thus gives a glimpse of the gradual development and implementation of the liturgical year.

6.5

The vivid scene of a man caught in the act of eating meat on a fast day is rendered in more or less the same manner in both the *Eidsivathing Law* (Eid. 21) and the *Gulathing Law* (Gul. 20), and has been used as evidence for the theory that the Norwegian Church laws originally had a common core of shared paragraphs (Meißner 1941: 42; Landro 2010: 207). At the same time, this is also one of the chapters where the revision of the *Borgarthing Law* comes into view.

6.5–6.6

Here there is a careful distinction between intentional and unintentional crimes, in line with the procedural standards of the thirteenth-century revision, mentioned in the introduction (see pp. 6–7). A leitmotif throughout the entire law is a contrast between unintentional crime, which could be atoned for through confession with the priest, and intentional violation, for which fines had to be paid. Thus, the distinction between two or three men mistaking the day was presumably inserted to illustrate where the line between an intentional and unintentional violation should be drawn. This probably required both an elaboration and a rearrangement of the original content (Landro 2010: 156–160).

Chapter seven: on proper wedding times

7.1

During the early Middle Ages and up until the middle of the twelfth century, there was a dominant belief that sexual union was the visible element of marriage. Marriage was viewed as having been instituted in paradise for the purpose of bringing about childbirth, and was also seen as a form of cure for sin, after the Fall. The linkage of entry into marriage with sex was thus grounded in theological beliefs about Creation. Whilst the Church defended marriage and its sexual aspects, some lines of thinking emphasized the character of marriage as a spiritual institution – particularly from the beginning of the eleventh century onwards. According to allegorical interpretations of marriage, it was like the union of Christ and the Church. In this way, emphasis came to be laid on asceticism in marriage: abstention from sex (Brundage 1987: 136–137, 188–189, 235–237; Christensen-Nugues 2003: 102–106; Korpiola 2004: 88–96). Limitations on rights to enter into marriage on days and at times which also required fasting should be understood in this context.

The detailed passages in chapter seven listing times when entry into marriage was forbidden have parallels in the oldest surviving Norwegian legislation (Gul. 27; Frost. III 9; Eid. 21). Similar regulations were found in canon law, defined in the broadest terms – that is, in penitential handbooks as well as early medieval law collections. These regulations related partly to women's biological rhythms, and partly to the liturgical year, and included express prohibitions against holding weddings during fasts (Brundage 1987: 154–164, 191 with tables 4.4., 4.5., 5.2.). The regulations of the *Borgarthing Law* here are thus in harmony with the demands of canon law, particularly as this was laid out during the Church reform movement from the middle of the eleventh century onwards.

7.2–7.3 (see also 6.1–6.2)

The time which covered the three Sundays preceding Lent was called the 'pre-Lenten season' (*Septuagesima*, Shrovetide) and can be evidenced from the seventh century onwards (Lindberg 1937: 72–75; Auf der Mauer 1983: 147). This season did not have the same status as that which began with Ash Wednesday, which signalled the beginning of the 'forty-day fast' or 'all men's fast' before Easter: Lent. The penalty for breaches of the prohibitions against weddings and sexual activity was therefore significantly higher during Lent itself, which stood out from other fast periods in this respect.

7.4

Three-week fasts were ordained before the Feast of John the Baptist (24th June), Michaelmas (29th September), and Christmas.

7.5

As is outlined here, the day was reckoned to begin the preceding evening, as in Jewish tradition. For this reason, prohibitions applied on Tuesday and Thursday evenings, since Wednesdays and Fridays were fast days (see Lindberg 1937: 53–58; Morgenroth 2004: 265–266). Saturday evening, when the Sabbath began, was also considered an unsuitable time for sexual activity.

7.6

On ember days, see 13.1.

7.7

The prohibition is here summarized and generalized to apply to all nights followed by fast days or mass days. The detail that a priest could grant dispensation from this is not found in comparable regulations in the other Old Norwegian laws and seems not to have been normal in Church legislation more generally. However, in *Archbishop Jón's Christian Law* (J 28) there is one example of a priest's power to grant dispensation from such fast regulations.

Chapter eight: how a *fylkiskirkja* or *heraðskirkja* or proprietary church shall be restored if it falls into disrepair

8.1

fylkis kirkiur (from *fylkiskirkja*): In the oldest Norwegian laws, *fylkiskirkjur* ('*fylki* churches') are labelled explicitly as such only here and in the *Frostathing Law* (Frost. II 7; Brendalsmo 2001: 138–153). The term also appears in the *Older Town Law (Bjarkeyjarréttr)* (Bj. 56); in *Archbishop Jón's Church Law* of 1273 (J 9, 13); and in *Archbishop Eiríkr's Statute* of 1189x90. In the *Gulathing Law*, the corresponding term is *hǫfuðkirkjur* (Gul. 10; Smedberg 1973: 45; Skre 1995: 184–188, 1996: 105–108). Investigation of the corpus of early Norwegian laws as a whole reveals that their ecclesiastical terminology was strikingly complex (Smedberg 1973: 34–63).

8.2

Similar (although not identical) regulations concerning the obligations of farmers towards a church owner if his church fell into ruin, or was destroyed by fire, and concerning its restoration, are also found in the *Gulathing Law* (Gul. 12) and the

Frostathing Law (Frost. II: 12, 13), and in *Archbishop Jón's Church Law* (J 11), along with the *Older Västgöta Law*, the *Younger Västgöta Law*, and the *Uppland Law* (VgL I Kk 6; VgL II Kk 9; UL Kk 7§4).

8.7

heraz kirkia (heraðskirkja): This term is found in the margins of the *Borgarthing Law* (although it is missing from Version One in NKS 1642 4o and Version Two in AM 31 8o), but otherwise only in the *Gulathing Law* (Gul. 12; see also *Archbishop Jón's Statute* of 1280 and *Archbishop Jǫrundr's First Statute* of 1290). However, there it has a completely different meaning, with no reference to any specific territorial division: simply 'rural church' or 'village church' (Smedberg 1973: 46–47). By contrast, in the *Borgarthing Law*, the *heraðskirkja* had a direct relationship with the *herað* as an administrative unit (Smedberg 1973: 42–44).

8.11

høgenda kirkiu (from *hægenðiskirkja*): This term is also found in the *Eidsivathing Law* (Eid. 39.1), the *Gulathing Law* (Gul. 12), and the *Frostathing Law* (Frost. II:13) (see also Skre 1996: 109–112; Brendalsmo 2001: 153–165), as well as in the so-called *King Sverrir's Christian Law* (Sv. 21) and in *Archbishop Jón's Church Law* (J 8). In all probability, this was the same type of church to which the *Guta Law* referred (GL 3§3; Peel 2009: 73–74, 2015: 96). *Hægenðiskirkja*, which is translated here as 'proprietary church', could alternatively have been translated as 'private church' (Brendalsmo 2001: 153, nr 758), just as the *Borgarthing Law* indicates, since a church of this kind had been built by a private individual on his own land (see Wood 2006: 729–921).

8.12

lausnar iorð ('redemption land'): This concept is linked to rights to redeem pledged, sold, or forfeited land. The situation described by the *Borgarthing Law* is clear. A king had the right to intervene if a proprietary church was poorly maintained, but the landowner or his heirs could reclaim the land, if they committed themselves to caring for the church in the future. An obligation to care for a proprietary church is set forth quite explicitly in canon law: namely, in the *Decretum Gratiani*, where Gratian quoted the ninth Council of Toledo in 655 (C. 16 q. 7 c. 32; see Friedberg 1879). This was later cited in King Sverrir's Latin *Speech Against the Bishops* (*En tale mot biskopene*) of 1196x1197, along with its translation into Norwegian, modified to fit the situation in Norway at that time (Holtsmark 1961: 277 nr 28; Brendalsmo 2001: 164).

8.13

a annars manz iorðu ('on another man's land'): This refers to land which a church owner had leased.

fara utlægr ('go into outlawry'): Opinions are divided as to the original meaning of *útlægr* (NgL V: 676–677 s.v. *útlagr, útlægr*; Breisch 1994: 132–133; Riisøy 2014) but there is consensus that, in Norwegian legal language, it refers to an individual lacking entitlement to peace. The fact that, in the *Borgarthing Law*, this term is used alongside the verb *fara* means that *utlægr* must here be linked to banishment from a particular space. It therefore concerns something more than a person 'outside the law' in the sense of lacking legal protection (compare Old English *ūtlah*; Middle Low German *uutlagh*).

Chapter nine: on disrepair of a church enclosure, and on men's graves

9.1

garðr ('enclosure'): This word derives from a Proto-Germanic term meaning 'fence', 'enclosure', or 'enclosed area'. It could therefore denote both a boundary itself and the area within this. *Kirkjugarðr* could thus have a double meaning, as was clearly the case in Norwegian legal language. Regulations on fencing or enclosure of a specific area around a church building are found in various Nordic provincial laws (Eid. 38, 50; Gul. 11, 13; Frost. II 7; Sv. 12; J 7; A 13; VgL I Kk 13, 20pr, J 9; UL Kk 19pr; SdmL Kk 18§1). There are no corresponding regulations in canon law, as represented by *Corpus Iuris Canonici.*

According to the liturgical handbooks which would have guided a bishop, when founding a church he had to mark out not only the site of the church but also an area around it: the 'church plot'. There is a regulation touching upon this in *Decretum Gratiani* (De con. D.1 c.9). The origin of this is unknown, but it is included in the legal compilations created by Burchard of Worms and Ivo of Chartres, and dated to the beginning and the end of the eleventh century, respectively. The same episcopal act is suggested by *Archbishop Jón's Church Law* (J 8), in which the expression 'mark a plot' (*marka tuft*) is used in place of the Latin *designare* (Smedberg 1973: 157). The regulation here in the *Borgarthing Law* has been interpreted as meaning that all church buildings had to have some form of enclosure or boundary around them, whether or not the church plot was used for burial, and that this was related to both pre-Christian and medieval concepts of peace and asylum (Nilsson, Bertil 1989: 126).

The material to be used for the church enclosure was not regulated by legislation, but rules in the *Gulathing Law* (Gul. 13) and the *Frostathing Law* (Frost. II 7) indicate that such structures were wooden, by stating that the farmers had obligations to provide wood for these. (On church plot boundaries in the Swedish *Västgöta Laws*, see Pellijeff 1967: 24–46; Nilsson, Göran B. 2012: 224–229.)

The stipulation that the fence should be kept intact, and the fact that fines are specified as penalties for neglect, derive both from a need to prevent animals from entering the churchyard and rooting amongst the graves, and from a view that such an area was holy and should be kept separate from the profane. As soon as burials were carried out, the churchyard became a *locus religiosus*. When the bishop consecrated it, it became a *locus sacer* (Nilsson, Bertil 1989: 61–64, 70).

9.2

Division into quarters was probably mainly related to the quadrilateral shape of the enclosure as a whole. But round or oval churchyards were also found in Scandinavia in the Middle Ages, and early on, in Iceland and Greenland. When it comes to these, there is much that remains to be explained (Brendalsmo & Stylegar 2003).

Division of the churchyard into distinct burial areas, used for different social classes, is mentioned in no Norwegian law other than the *Borgarthing Law* and the *Eidsivathing Law* (Eid. 50.1–6) (Riisøy 2005: 61–64; Jonsson 2009: 51–53). Equally, such regulation is absent from canon law.

9.3

lenda men (from *lendr maðr* 'landed man'): This term originates in a participle, used as an adjective, deriving from the verb *lenda*, meaning 'give land'. *Lendir menn* were thus men who held land granted by the king. The term designated the most important dignitaries in the kingdom, outwith royal circles. Landed men are named in several places in various early Norwegian laws, and later also in Magnús Lawmender Hákonarson's *National Law* (1274), and his *Town Law* (1276), in addition to *Hirðskrá* (1274–77), *Jónsbók* (1280), and a number of 'additional laws' (*réttarbætr*). (On social hierarchies in the Norwegian laws, see the comparisons in Lindkvist 1979: 140; Riisøy 2005: 64–65.) People of probably comparable status are described as *lændæ maþer* in the Land Section of the *Older* and *Younger Västgöta Law* respectively (VgL I J 5; VgL II J 13), but these are found in no other provincial Swedish laws (Nilsson, Göran B. 2011: 57, 2012: 207–209).

austan at kirkiu ('east of the church'): The most prestigious burial location in the churchyard was the area reserved for the graves of landed men with ownership rights. According to folk belief, proximity to the choir, in the eastern part of the church with the altar and relics, was thought to yield rewards on Judgement Day for those who had been buried there. It was also widely believed that burial under the eaves-drip (*sub stillicidio*) was significant. This was because water which had been in contact with the roof of the church was seen as blessed; dripping from the roof was thus a kind of extension of the blessing of the grave with holy water done during the burial itself (Nilsson, Bertil 1989: 134–135).

Ef þæir æigu æigi lut i kirkiugarðe ('if they do not own a portion of the churchyard'): This phrase reflects the fact that landed men often (although not always) contributed their private funds to church building and maintenance. Often, in cases like this, the churches concerned were those designated as *hægendiskirkjur* in the Norwegian Church laws (Smedberg 1973: 129; Brendalsmo 2001: 244, 259–260).

bonda legho (from *bóndalega* 'burial-place for farmers'): The area of the churchyard in which the farmers were buried. This term occurs exclusively in the *Borgarthing Law*.

9.4

haulda (from *hauldr*): *Hauldr* (*hǫldr*) is related to the noun *halr*, meaning 'man'. According to the *Borgarthing Law* and the *Eidsivathing Law*, a *hauldr* was a free farmer. In both laws, the word is found in compounds such as *hauldmaðr, haulsmaðr* and *hauldborinn*, meaning 'free-born (person)'. In earlier research it was maintained that there was a difference with regard to the status of the *hauldr* between the west and north of Norway on the one hand, and the eastern parts on the other (NgL V: 269 s.v. *hauldr*). In modern research, it has been pointed out that the *hauldr* was something more than just a free farmer with odal rights in eastern areas too (Riisøy 2005: 70–72; Ugulen 2006). Odal land was property held with full ownership rights, and often preserved within a single family, through inheritance, over several generations (see Gul. 88, 270; Frost. XII 4; L VI 2). *Hauldr* was used in the same sense later, in Magnús Lawmender Hákonarson's *National Law* (1274).

9.5

løysingia (*leysingi* 'fully freed slave'): A *leysingi* was a slave who had been fully freed, either after holding a freedom ale ceremony (*frælsisǫl*) or in some other way. People of this kind are mentioned in all four of the provincial laws (for example, Eid. 50; Gul. 63; Frost. IX 10), as well as in the *Older Town Law* (Bj. 162).

9.6

frials giafa (*frjálsgjafi* 'freed slaves'): A *frjálsgjafi* was a freed slave who had not yet held a freedom ale ceremony. The term is only found in the early laws (Eid. 50; Frost. IX 13) and does not even occur in the *Gulathing Law*. (On thralls and emancipation, see Nevéus 1974; Iversen 1994: 354–457; Iversen 2003; on the terminology regarding thralls in different types of source material, see Brink 2012: 111–168.) In Denmark, thralldom seems to have been in decline around 1240 (Skyum-Nielsen 1975: 21) and in Iceland, during the twelfth century (Foote 1975: 18). In Norway, thralldom was probably disappearing in the second half of the thirteenth century (Iversen 1994: 458–464). In Sweden, thralldom was abolished after an official royal statute was issued in 1335 (Nevéus 1974: 158).

9.7

The stipulation that a person washed up as a corpse in Norway must have had his hair cut in a 'northern' or 'Norwegian' style to be eligible for burial is linked to the fact that unbaptized people had no right to burial in a churchyard. Here, the assumption was that anyone who could be identified as Norwegian must have been baptized. This particular regulation must therefore date from a period during which it was viewed as obvious that all Norwegians had been baptized.

9.7–9.10

Five categories of person are named, but the churchyard is said to be divided into four parts. Judging by the fines mentioned, the explanation for this is that the lairs of the landed men were situated in the area for the farmers, in a part which was seen as particularly prestigious. The number of landed men was lower than the number of farmers or of people belonging to the other categories, so this group did not need a full quarter of the total area (Nilsson, Bertil 1989: 134–135).

The ranking of the social classes mentioned is reflected in the fines demanded when people were buried in the wrong areas: in other words, buried above their social stations. The regulations thus seem to show that it must have been clear where the boundaries between the areas were located. However, there is no other textual or archaeological evidence which gives any hint of whether or how the quarters of a churchyard might have been marked.

9.11–9.12

No equivalent of the modern Scandinavian legal term *griftefrid* ('peace of the tomb') is to be found in medieval Nordic legislation, nor in contemporary canon law. However, evidence for the existence of related ideas can be found. Protection of graves and human remains have left some traces in legislation, as here in the *Borgarthing Law*, and similar, although not identical, regulations are found in the *Eidsivathing Law* (Eid. 50.7) and the Swedish *Church Law Section of Tiohärad* (TiL 17§1). The *griftefrid* was in inverse proportion to the time which had passed since the burial had taken place. This was because the proportion of the deceased which remained intact normally depended on the time elapsed since burial. The more that remained, the higher the fine for desecration, at least as long as the various parts of the corpse remained joined: that is, as long as soft tissue remained. It was seen as a breach of *griftefrid* to disturb one corpse during burial of another. This regulation might imply that it was not always clear exactly where individual graves were to be found within the churchyard (Nilsson, Bertil 1989: 174–178).

9.13

After the soft tissue had rotted away from a corpse completely, disturbing it no longer led to a fine, as long as any bones which had been unearthed were not allowed to lie exposed to the sun; in this way, the person, once buried, was allowed to remain buried. The principle that no bone should be removed from the grave had been emphasized by Church councils during the Carolingian period, motivated by a belief that God had prepared a grave for each and every one, so that a dead person could wait there for his judgement (Nilsson, Bertil 2010: 47). The gravedigger therefore had to cover any bones which had been accidentally unearthed with soil, whilst the new grave was being prepared for the more recent corpse, and then lay them to rest after the fresh burial had taken place. It is presumed in this particular legal text that a coffin is used, but archaeological evidence shows that this was not always the case. Rather, it is thought that use of coffins varied over time and between regions (Nordeide & Gulliksen 2007: 11–13).

9.14

The requirement for fines to be paid must be understood in the light of the fact that *griftefrid* primarily concerned the deceased, whether or not he or she had any living relatives who might consider themselves injured by the unearthing of the remains of a relative.

Chapter ten: on a bishop's duty and visitation, and on that to which priests should attend

10.1–2

Similar, but not identical, provisions on church consecration are found in a number of Nordic laws, besides those from Norway (Eid. 34, 40; Gul. 14; F II 8; Sv. 11, 16; J 11). These include Swedish laws (VgL I Kk 3; VgL II Kk 3; ÖgL Kk 2; UL Kk 4; SdmL Kk 5pr; HL Kk 4) and laws from Denmark (SkKk 1; SjKk 2). (For a bishop's obligation to consecrate church buildings, see Smedberg 1973: 154–158 on the Norwegian laws.)

The size of a bishop's retinue during church consecrations and visitations was also regulated by canon law in the *Decretum Gratiani* (C.10 q.1 c.9; C.10 q.3 cc.1, 6; Inger 1961: 124, 128–129). Since church consecration as well as visitation entailed economic burdens for the men of the parish, conflicts could arise over the rights of the bishop versus the obligations of the farmers (Inger 1961: 415–443 on the Swedish church province; Nilsson, Bertil 2014: 169–174 on the Church Law of Scania).

10.3

horn steinar (from *hornsteinn* 'cornerstone'): This phrase meaning 'cornerstones' appears to be a scribal error for *hornstafr* 'corner stave' (compare Gul. 10, 12), since this provision applied to wooden churches. If a church lost its consecrated status, it had to be consecrated anew in order to fulfil its function as a space for divine service; according to canon law in the *Decretum Gratiani*, mass could only be celebrated in a church which had been consecrated by a bishop (De con. D.1 cc.1, 2, 11, 14), although that was not obeyed everywhere (see Smedberg 1973: 102–105). In canon law, the term *reconsecratio* ('reconsecration') was used, showing that the liturgical act carried out in this case differed not at all from that carried out when a church built on previously unconsecrated ground was consecrated. (On the form of the act of church consecration in the early Middle Ages, see Ström 1997).

kirkiu bøtr (*kirkjubætr* 'church repairs'): Amongst the early Norwegian laws, this term means 'repairs' only here. This remark in the *Borgarthing Law* must be understood in light of the fact that church repairs did not require fresh consecration (compare VgL I Kk 6). This was stipulated in canon law, in both *Decretum Gratiani* (De con. D.1 cc.20, 24) and the *Liber Extra* (X 3.40.6 = decretal issued by Pope Innocent III the year 1212).

10.4

græftar kirkiu (from *graptarkirkja*): This word occurs only here, in the early Norwegian laws. There have been various opinions as to what exactly might have been meant by 'burial church'. In the *Borgarthing Law*, it must concern *fylkiskirkjur* – perhaps exclusively. In *Archbishop Jón's Church Law* and *Archbishop Eilífr's Fifth Statute* (1327), it probably meant any church with burial rights (Smedberg 1973: 42–44; Nilsson, Bertil 1989, 52–54).

A bishop's visitation duties were regulated by canon law through decisions made by Church councils in the sixth and seventh centuries, which were included in *Decrteum Gratiani*. A bishop was bound to visit each parish in his diocese once a year, unless he was prevented from doing so by ill health or by a demand that he carry out some duty; what sort of duty is not specified (C.10 q.1 cc.10, 11; C.10 q.1 d.p.c.10; Inger 1961: 122).

The next part of the paragraph in the *Borgarthing Law* was probably connected with a specific bishop's neglect of his visitation duties, or failure for some reason (for example, through illness) to fulfil them. The farmers could therefore keep their annual oblations. Probably what is meant here is the bishop's tithe. According to the manuscript Holm 28 4o, the bishop had a duty to visit every third year. This should be seen as a modification of the law to reflect contemporary local circumstances. This manuscript must therefore represent a later stage in legal development in the Borgarthing area.

10.5

færma (*ferma* 'confirm'): from Latin *confirmare*/*confirmatio*. The verb *ferma* is also found in the *Eidsivathing Law* (Eid. 32) as well as in more recent Church laws (J 6; A 10) and statutes (*Archbishop Páll's Third Statue* 1336x1346); *Archbishop Árni's Statute* 1346x1349).

In the early Church, confirmation was defined as a special rite, along with baptism, which it affirmed. In the Western Church, towards the end of the sixth century, the administration of this rite came to be reserved for bishops (Andrén 1957: 17–27). This situation was reflected in the language of medieval Norway, in which the noun *biskupan* (J 6; A 10), and the verb *biskupa* (*Archbishop Páll's Third Statute*) referred to this rite, which was viewed as a sacrament from the twelfth century onwards. In practice, administration of confirmation tended to happen during a bishop's visitations – although this was not compulsory. This is why a regulation in the manuscript Holm 28 4o states that the bishop had a duty to carry out confirmations of children every third year, rather than annually.

uæita . . . skript (*veita skrift* 'administer penance'): The original meaning behind these words seems to have been 'impose penance'. This led to their double meaning, applying both to confession before a bishop or priest and to the actual performance of penance (Thors 1957: 222–223; SAOB 26: 4838 s.v. *skrift*; Söderwall 2: 393 s.v. *skript*).

þæim . . . er þurfu (*þeim er þurfu* 'to those who need it'): The meaning of this expression is not entirely clear, but it probably concerns people who had committed sins for which only a bishop could provide forgiveness: that is, *casus episcopales*. According to later statutes, these included murder, sacrilege, unnatural acts, incest, and violence towards clerics (Gummerus 1902: 61–62; Inger 1961: 379–382).

krismu (*krisma* 'chrism'): Chrism was consecrated oil which was mixed with fragrant herbs and used during various liturgical acts. The consecration was normally carried out by a bishop, in a cathedral, on Maundy Thursday. Parish priests used the consecrated oil during baptism and Anointing of the Sick (extreme unction).

10.6

morkum.vi ('six marks'): Three marks was usually the highest fine demanded for an offence, according to the *Borgarthing Law*. The severity of this fine underlines the seriousness of the offence, both with respect to the breach of duty committed by the cleric and to the injury suffered by the father of the child.

Chapter eleven: on men's tithe payments

11.1

The regulations on tithe, which ultimately derive from rules in the Old Testament (Genesis 14:20; Deuteronomy 14:22), had been in existence since at least the fifth century. A large number of these, based partly on early medieval decisions by councils, are found scattered throughout *Decretum Gratiani*, and particularly in *Causa* 16. Regulation of tithing is mentioned in a variety of places in each of the Nordic provincial laws. Tithes could be divided in various ways – into three or four shares – but a fundamental principle was that one share should go to the priest's table (*mensa*), one to the church building itself (*fabrica*), and one to the bishop. Where the tithe was divided into quarters, the poor were usually named as the recipients of the final share (Plöchl 1962: 431–434).

The farmers are here named as recipients of a quarter because they had obligations to distribute the share reserved for the poor to those who needed it, as is explicitly stated in NKS 1642 4o.

hafuð tiund (*họfuðtíund*): This payment was given only once in the lifetime of any person, either after death and inheritance by heirs, or upon marriage. It was drawn from the total assets of the giver. It is only found in Norwegian legislation (Eid. 48.9; Frost. II:17) (Hamre 1974: 280–281) and in the *Västgöta Laws* (VgL I Kk 3, 4; VgL II Kk 2) according to which this form of tithe also had to be paid on the consecration of a church and by those who had committed grave sins (*hovoþsynd*) (Nilsson, Göran B. 2012: 98–99; Runer 2012).

avaxstar tiund (*ávaxtartíund* 'crop tithe'): This word related to growth and fertility, and denoted a tithe which was paid from anything which had been cultivated: a so-called 'corn tithe' or 'crop tithe'.

Judging by statements made in saga literature, tithes were introduced into Norway during the first half of the twelfth century. However, the emergence of this form of taxation must have been a gradual process which happened with varying speed in different regions (Skre 1996: 122–145; Brendalsmo 2001: 177–180; Riisøy 2005: 62 nr 11).

11.2

biscups armaðr (*biskups ármaðr*): The office of *ármaðr* had roots in secular society. In secular contexts, an *ármaðr* could function as a steward on a royal estate (see Orning & Poulsen 2019: 215). In the *Borgarthing Law*, the bishop has an *ármaðr* 'bishop's emissary'. He had authority to carry out various tasks on behalf of the bishop. According to Norwegian legal sources, his duties were an extension of some of the bishop's functions when it came to the administration of justice and recovery of fines (Landro 2010: 155–156).

a land hæiðit (*á land heiðit* 'to heathen land'): This punishment is peculiar, given that there were no heathen territories near Norway at this period, except for areas in which Sámi people lived. However, it has been suggested that it could refer to parts of Sweden (Olavsson 1914a: 11, nr 1).

æigi kristin uera (*eigi vera kristinn* 'does not wish to be Christian'): If any baptized person came to be regarded as 'heathen', this could have been due to a failure to bow to the authority of the Church, showing disobedience, or rebellion. Alternatively, it could mean that he fell to practising activities viewed as idolatry or superstitious behaviour (Janson 2010).

11.4

æin æiði (*eineiði* or *einseiði* 'personal oath'): Oath-making was a fundamental means through which a person could clear himself following an accusation. In most cases, this required compurgators (oath-helpers), who supported an oath. One, two, five, or eleven of these were possible. According to the Norwegian laws, individual oaths sufficed when it came to minor offences: economic crimes with values of less than one ounce (Gul. 37; Frost. V: 42; Bj. 154) or minor lapses, as here (compare Frost. II:15, 28, 29, 32, 35, 46; Bj. 61) (Hamre 1958: 492–493).

Chapter twelve: the obligations of a priest to farmers, and farmers to a priest, and on legal oblation

12.1

How and by whom priests were appointed varied in the Middle Ages (see Nilsson, Bertil 2014: 177–181). The appointment of a parish priest and his status often reflected tensions and conflicts between the bishop and the farmers of the parish. According to the *Borgarthing Law*, the farmers themselves decided who they would take as their parish priest, but they also had an obligation to provide a priest for each church. Here, the farmers were obviously in a strong position in relation to the bishop, in terms of both appointment procedures and possible dismissal of priests. In order for dismissal to be legal, evidence was required from two priests also appointed by the farmers: priests from neighbouring parishes. What sort of lack of knowledge on the part of a priest would lead to dismissal is not specified, and potential justifications for dismissing priests are found nowhere else in the Nordic provincial laws.

This provision has been mentioned as an example of a compromise between the church and the laity. While the bishop is given the responsibility of hiring the local priest in the other Norwegian – and Swedish – laws, the farmers in the *Borgarthing Law* had allegedly shown more resistance and claimed this right for themselves (Helle 2001: 177–178). This provision could, however, very well be explained by the lack of modernisation of the material content in the *Borgarthing Law*. The other Norwegian laws are more influenced by the Magnús-revision from the 1160s, during which it is probable that the right of hiring the local priest was handed over to the bishop. Consequently, it is likely that the *Borgarthing Law* reveals the original arrangement, from a time when a small number of missionary bishops did not have the capacity to supervise local church conditions (Landro 2010: 211–213).

12.2

forn log (*forn lǫg*)

Several cases in the secular parts of the Norwegian provincial laws use similar expressions, like *at forno fare* ('according to ancient customs') or *at forno/i fyrnsku* ('in ancient times'), (NgL V: 202 s.v. *forn*; Helle 2001: 43; Landro 2010: 195). It might be that the *Ólafssáð* referred to in this particular chapter was a long-established custom at the time when the laws were committed to writing. In general, however, references to ancient customs should not always be taken literally. During the twelfth and thirteenth centuries both ecclesiastical and royal authorities employed a strategy of presenting certain paragraphs as reinventions of divine law, and attaching them to St Óláfr's name to enhance their authority (Helle 1999: 14–20; Bagge 2010: 201–204).

gift (*gipt* 'gift, oblation'): This word is found as a simplex only in the *Borgarthing Law*, amongst the Norwegian laws. (Compare, however, the *Older*

Västgöta Law (VgL I Kk 19), which also uses this term.) It reflects circumstances before the introduction of tithing. In the *Gulathing Law* (G 22) this oblation is called *prestreiða*. It was paid by the parishioners, sometimes each time a priest performed one of his clerical duties (Compare *tiðakaup* in Gul. 1 variant; A 22, and Grágás 1A§6, 1B§258; VgL II Kk 43; DL Kk 3§4) (Smedberg 1973: 196–197).

saald (*sáld*): This was a unit of volume measurement, for grain.

fullum bonda (*fullr bóndi* 'full farmer'): A *fullr bóndi* was a person who had a fully-grown worker to help him on his farm. An *einvirki* looked after his farm without such help (Frost. II 33; Bj. 63).

Olafs saað (*Óláfssáð*): This was a name for a grain oblation. It does not occur anywhere else in the Norwegian laws (Rindal 2004: 132–133).

settonga (*séttungar*): A *séttungr* was a smaller unit of volume measurement than the *sáld*. According to Magnús Lawmender Hákonarson's *National Law*, this was equal to one thirty-sixth of a *sáld* (NgL V: 550–551 s.v. *séttungr*; Bjørkvik 1970, 164–165).

12.3–12.8

leghkaup (*legkaup, legrkaup*): According to the *Gulathing Law* (Gul. 23), this term covered the totality of offices performed by a priest 'when a corpse arrived at church'. According to the *Eidsivathing Law* (Eid. 47), it also covered the blessing of the corpse and the night watch at home which preceded these. Here in the *Borgarthing Law*, too, it is likely that all of these activities are covered by the term. Halvorsen & Rindal translate the term as 'payment for the burial plot' (see 12.15), but this expression is too limited in scope (Nilsson, Bertil 1989: 188–191).

From at least the end of the sixth century, the Church had, through Pope Gregory the Great (590–604), explicitly opposed demands for payment for burial and lair purchase. Making such demands was equated with 'selling God's mercy'. The Church could only accept a gift, voluntarily given out of gratefulness for the salvation of the soul of the deceased, as expressed by the Council of Tribur in 895 (Nilsson, Bertil 2010: 47–48). Various regulations forbidding payments were included by Gratian in his *Decretum* (C.13 q.2 cc.12, 13, 14, 15; see Friedberg 1879), after they had been cited by Burchard of Worms and Ivo of Chartres in their own legal compilations. However, this ban was not completely successful in practice, as we see here. Payment could be motivated by either personal wish or custom. However, the Fourth Lateran Council in 1215 made a decision which was decisive for the future of this question, and which in practice meant that priests could force laymen to observe customs concerning payment, where these existed (can. 66, conc. Lat. IV; Nilsson, Bertil 1989: 179–186). The regulation in the *Borgarthing Law* reflects a contrast between a salary system for priests, based on tithing, and a system in which priests were paid for performance of specific ecclesiastical tasks. Judging by the *Borgarthing Law*, two parallel payment systems operated in this legal province.

alnar (*ǫln* 'ell'): The payment was given in *alnar*: ells of payment cloth (*vaðmál*). An ell of *vaðmál* was a standard unit of currency.

æigi ero til gærðar komen (*eigi eru til gerðar komin* 'not yet of sufficient age to contribute to *gerð*'): This expression refers to military service and to children who had not yet reached an age at which they would be counted when the size of the *leiðangr* was calculated (NgL V: 234–235 s.v. *gerð*).

The same social classes are mentioned here as in the section on the division of the churchyard into quarters, except that the son of a slave is mentioned explicitly, with a payment higher than that for his father. This was probably due to the fact that the son would have been further removed than his father from slave status and would therefore have had a higher social standing.

12.9

A priest could also be hired to take part in a vigil, or night watch. This was not one of the offices he had to perform to be entitled to his tithe share. (Compare 12.14).

12.10

Anointing of the Sick can be traced back to Biblical models in the New Testament (Mark 6:12–13; James 5:14–15). It was counted amongst the Seven Sacraments from the beginning of the twelfth century, despite the fact that neither the number seven nor any clear definition of the meaning of 'sacrament' became fixed until the flowering of High Scholasticism in the thirteenth century, particularly through Thomas Aquinas. From the end of the twelfth century, anointing began to be seen primarily as a preparation for death: extreme unction (Andrén 1963: 43–57; Sundmark 2008: 15–17).

olian, related to the verb *olia* ('administer unction'): This name for the sacrament is found in various other places in Norwegian legislation and in Church statutes (Gul. 23; Eid. 47; Frost. II 17; Sv 81; King Magnús Hákonarson's additional law on the rights and duties of the clergy (1308x09); *Archbishop Jǫrundr's First Statute* (1290); *Archbishop Eilífr's Third Statute* (1320); *Archbishop Páll's Third Statute* (1336x1346); *Archbishop Árni's Statute* (1346x1349)). In the *Gulathing Law*, the word *olianarkaup* is used for the payment made when a person receives extreme unction.

12.11

A priest's obligations towards his parishioners when they found themselves in extreme need (*nauðsyn*) were stipulated in various places. In practice, these concerned preparation for death. A priest had to hear the confession of the dying person, and then administer the Sacrament of Eucharist to him or to her (Sundmark 2008: 61–68).

hyggia kan firi orðe oc æiði (*hyggja kan fyrir orði ok eiði* 'who can answer for his words and his oath'): This expression referred to people who had reached the age of legal maturity (Gul. 24, 28, 135; Frost. IV 8, XV 11, Bj. 23): fifteen years old. Canon law operated with various age limits, depending on context.

Sometimes, it was simply stated that a certain maturity had to have been reached (Metz 1976: 11–23).

12.12

þionosto (from *þjónusta* 'the Eucharist): The fundamental meaning of this word is 'service', but in ecclesiastical language, it almost exclusively refers to services rendered by a priest to his parishioners. In some cases, the term had a more specific meaning, referring solely to the Sacrament of Eucharist. An example of this is the phrase 'take Communion on Easter Sunday' (*taka tjónustu a paskadag*) (Frost. II 40 variant; J 63; A 38). Apart from here in the *Borgarthing Law*, the word seems to occur in this sense in later legal language only, and not in the older versions of the provincial laws (NgL V: 743 s.v. *þjónusta*).

The penalty laid down for priests who failed to participate in preparations for death in such cases might appear excessively harsh, but this must be understood in the context of the risks presented to the eternal soul of the dying parishioner. According to medieval theology, in principle a person who died without confession would go to hell (Sundmark 2008: 156–157). The question is what exactly the term *gift*/*gipt* (payment, 'oblation') actually stood for. If a priest lost his *gipt* from the *herað* for a year, it is difficult to imagine that he would retain his office.

12.13

There is no explicit explanation for the limit of three corpses per day. However, the number three does occur in other contexts related to the obligations of priests (for example Borg. 12.14).

lik song (*liksǫngr* 'post-mortem rites'): This term occurs in a number of Nordic regulations (Gul. 23; Sv. 81; J 16; A 18; *Archbishop Jǫrundr's First Statute* (1290); *Grágás* I:9, 238, II:133, 262). It was an inclusive term, covering various liturgical acts which a priest was obliged to perform in connexion with a death. In this particular case, the act of intercession corresponded to the liturgical rite *commendatio animae*, which could take place either at the home of the deceased or at the place to which the deceased was conveyed (Nilsson, Bertil 1987: 134).

iij laughar (*iij laugar* 'three ablutions'): The statement that a priest should consecrate three *laughar* probably meant that he blessed the water which was to be used to wash the corpse. No corresponding rule is found anywhere in Nordic legislation. However, in the Eddic verse *Sigrdrífumál* 34, it is stated quite straightforwardly that '[a] warm bath shall be made for those who are departed;/hands and head be washed,/combed, and dried before they go in the coffin,/and bid them sleep blessedly' (Larrington 1996: 171; see also Nilsson, Bertil 1987: 134). It is not particularly surprising that a blessing (*benedictio*) of the water was carried out. Broadly speaking, a blessing could be directed at almost anything in medieval Christianity (Franz 1909).

If a priest stayed at the third home, this was a vigil, or night watch. Halvorsen & Rindal add the term *gravølet* in parentheses in their translation, but such an event was held several days after the whole burial process had been completed (Bø 1960: 450–451; Rodríguez 2007: 235–256).

12.14

This duty was compulsory only if the priest had been paid (see 12.9 on the Vigil).

iij boklester, (from *bóklest* 'book-reading'): This word is thought to occur only in the *Borgarthing Law*, and denoted reading of 'the priest's blessing, or something similar, from a brevarium' (NgL V: 107 s.v. *bóklest*) or 'reading from a legend of the saints' (Cleasby 1957: 74 s.v. *bóklest*) or 'reading from a holy book or holy lectionary' (Degnbol 2: 565 s.v. *bóklest*). Nowhere do we find any very clear formulation of what exactly this might have meant in practice. Probably, it was the ritual itself – the act of reading from a book – which was important, and which went beyond the obligations of the priest connected with illness and deaths. The book from which the priest read may have been of lesser importance. The manuscripts of the *Borgarthing Law* show variation in their handling of matters connected with these priestly obligations. According to NKS 1642 4o and AM 31 8o, the priest's obligations included unpaid performance of three readings for those who desired this, and he was to be fined three marks in silver if he failed to deliver these. By contrast, if more than three readings were requested, the priest had to be paid, unless he voluntarily decided to provide these without payment. (Compare VgL I Kk 16; VgL II Kk 35.)

12.15

There do not seem to be any parallels for this in other Nordic provincial laws. Here, it is clear that payment should be made or at least guaranteed in advance. This contrasted with the principle expressed in canon law, which stated that nothing should be requested in advance (see 12.3–12.8).

12.16

Prohibitions against churchyard interments could arise for a variety of reasons, but most often related to lack of eligibility for such burial. In practice, this was due to lack of baptism, or to excommunication, or dying without repentance (Nilsson, Bertil 1989: 242–296). Here, the basis for such a prohibition seems somewhat strange: namely, that those who had brought the problematic corpse in question to the church had not been aware that the burial would cost money nor how much it would cost. The situation described is also unusual in that it solely concerns interment; no requiem mass, which would have taken place beforehand, is mentioned, and nor are any of the priest's other duties – despite the fact that he could presumably also refuse to perform those, if he were not paid.

hava a stola a halse ser (*hafa stóla a halsi sér* 'with stole around his neck'): The stole was the outward sign of a priest's ministry: a band of cloth, worn around the neck then allowed to hang, either straight or crossed, over his chest. From the ninth and tenth centuries, there are various indications that priests were required to wear stoles, so they could be recognized as such. At the Council of Tribur in 895, it was decreed that anyone who killed a priest wearing a stole should be punished three times as severely as otherwise (Eisenhofer I 1932: 455).

greftar raan (*graptarrán* 'grave robbery'): This word seems to be used to denote burial in the face of prohibition by a priest only in the *Borgarthing Law*. The element *–rán* ('robbery') here points to refusal to pay the priest the required fee.

12.17

This rule partially contradicts previous information in the chapter on payment for the various duties carried out by priests. Here, there is an assumption that their income came from tithes, rather than fees. Nevertheless, the phrase 'such a priest' (*sa prestr*) could suggest that certain priests had rights to payment from tithes, but others did not.

sua . . . gomul at við megho taka (*svá gǫmul at við megu taka* 'old enough to receive this'): No specific age is mentioned here, but according to the rules of the Church on 'canonical age', children under seven years could not reason (*usus rationis*), and were therefore not allowed to receive the Church's sacraments. Children had to have reached 'the age of discernment' (*anni discretionis*), at which point they were believed to be able to differentiate between the Holy Sacrament and an ordinary meal, for example (Gallén 1963: 226–228; Metz 1976: 61–63).

12.18

natvaku (from *náttvaka* 'night watch'): This refers to a vigil or night watch over the deceased (comparable with Old English *nihtwæcce*) leading up to the burial. Usually, the burial took place the day after the death. This word seems only to occur in the *Borgarthing Law*, amongst the Norwegian provincial laws. Priests had no obligation to be present during such night watches, so people had to pay for these. Here, the cost was two ells of payment cloth (*vaðmál*), but in 12.9, it was twelve ells. According to Version One in NKS 1642 4o, the fee was two ells or half a weighed *ertog*, and according to Version Two in Holm 28 4o, it cost one ounce. According to the same manuscript, the priest also required two weighed ounces for extreme unction; unlike in the other versions, payment was thus required for administering a sacrament.

12.19

In effect, this regulation concerns requests for parish visits (despite the fact that the term is not used here): in other words, requests made to a priest to venture out into his parish to perform liturgical and other pastoral services for the sick and dying. For this reason, whenever he was out of earshot of church bells, he needed to have with him a liturgical handbook and the liturgical implements required to perform such services. When he was within earshot, he was required to make his way to the church immediately to find out why the bells had been rung. Amongst the objects he was obliged to carry were a container for the consecrated Host, a vessel of oil for anointment of the sick, and a tool for sprinkling holy water (*aspergillum*) (Sundmark 2008: 69–88).

12.20–12.21

A priest had a duty to be resident in his parish: to live in his parish and remain there, unless extenuating circumstances called him away. This obligation, which had roots traceable to the Early Church, was specified by councils during the Carolingian period and underscored by the Third Lateran Council of 1179 (can. 130). The decisions made by this council were incorporated into the *Liber Extra* (X 3.4.3). The decision that a priest should be allowed to leave his parish was made by the parishioners present at mass on the preceding holy day; no further arrangement was needed (Landro 2010: 211).

presta motz (from *prestamót/prestastefna* similar to 'meeting or gathering of priests', 'synod'): This phenomenon is mentioned in the laws by either of these names only in the *Borgarthing Law* and *Bishop Árni's Christian Law for Iceland* (A 20). However, it also occurs in a couple of church statutes (*Archbishop Eilífr's Third Statute* (1320), *Archbishop Páll's First Statute* (1334)). The earliest general legal regulation of meetings of priests (which were also called 'diocesan synods'), occurred during the Fourth Lateran Council (can. 6), at which it was stipulated that these should be held annually in each diocese. This regulation was included in the *Liber Extra* (X 5.1.25). Nevertheless, such clerical meetings had taken place earlier, without having been legally regulated in this way (Kroon 1948: 26–29).

Chapter thirteen: on proclamation of ember days and proclamation of feast days

13.1

imbru dagha (from *ymbrudagr* 'ember day'): The origin of this word appears to be unclear, but it has been linked to Old English *ymbrendæg* from *ymb-ryne* 'cycle, go round'. This might in turn have been a corruption of Latin *quattor tempora*. Ember days were three consecutive, strictly imposed days of penance and fasting (Wednesday, Thursday (or Friday), and Saturday) which were observed four times a year, during the ember weeks at the beginning of each season (Thors 1957: 331–332; Gjerløw 1962: 361–363). After centuries with regional variations, the dates were fixed in 1078 by Pope Gregory VII (1073–1085). The ember days followed the four seasons and were placed in the week after Pentecost, the Exaltation of the Holy Cross (September 14), the Feast of St Lucy (December 13), and in the week after the first Sunday of Lent (Adam 1979: 186–189). In the older Norwegian provincial laws, there is no mention of which specific days are meant, but this issue is regulated in detail in the younger versions.

messodagha (*messudagr* 'mass day'): The name for any day on which High Mass was sung, apart from a Sunday.

13.2

skera up kross (*skera upp kross* 'carve a cross'): This expression refers to a summons baton in the shape of a cross which was circulated along with announcements pertaining to Church law. This phenomenon was common and also prescribed in the other old Norwegian laws (Eid. 10, 11, 27; Gul. 19; Frost. II 22, 23) (Grieg 1957: 338–340).

13.4

eta a vtiðum (*eta á utíðum* 'eat at improper times'): Medieval prescriptions about fasting could be tremendously detailed. Several of these, varying in scope, were found in all the Nordic provincial laws (Bøe 1959: 189–190).

Chapter fourteen: on annual feast days and the keeping of holy days

14.1

Regulations on the keeping of holy days are found in all four of the early Norwegian Church Law Sections (Eid. 9; Frost. II 24; Gul. 17, 18). These differ on various specific points. The list in the *Borgarthing Law* contains only Norwegian holy days and the traditional holy days established before the Carolingian period (Gjerløw 1963: 98–99). This regulation contains an inconsistency in that four days of Christmas are mentioned, but only the fourth day of Easter (see Version One in NKS 1642 4o). The first of the specifically Norwegian saints' days is Hallvarðr's Mass, honouring St Hallvarðr, who was killed, according to legend, on the Drammensfjord in 1043. His relics were later translated, very likely in the 1120s, to the high altar of the cathedral in Oslo (Antonsson 2007: 121–126). The holy day honouring 'the saints who rest in Kinn and Selja' refers to Sunnifa and her companions (see articles in Rindal 1997). St Óláfr's Mass honours Óláfr Haraldsson, king of Norway, who fell in battle in Stiklastaðir in 1030.

vi aura daghr (*vi aura dagr* 'six-ounce day'): Anyone who worked illegally on such a Sunday or holy day had to pay six ounces; the holy days which were not considered equivalent to Sundays attracted three-ounce fines for the same offence.

14.2

Each major holy day was preceded by an eve, during which the period of holiness began and prohibitions against work had to be respected. In ecclesiastical terms, the eve began with *non* (compare Gul. 17; Frost. II 24): the office which a priest performed at the ninth canonical hour, around three o'clock in the afternoon. This agrees well with the information provided here in terms of the sun's position in the east of Norway.

14.5

This passage differs from all others in the *Borgarthing Law* in that it reproduces an imagined dialogue important to the decision of which punishment should be meted out for *helgabrot* ('breaking, desecration of a holy day') as this is called in the heading found in NKS 1642 4o.

huðar lausn (*húðarlausn* 'hide-ransom'): This term occurs here only amongst the Norwegian laws, but is equivalent to Old English *hydgild* (NgL V: 296 s.v. *húðarlausn*) and means that money was paid to prevent the offender from being killed by flogging. A similar expression is *Hǫfuðlausn, 'Head Ransom'*, the title of a skaldic verse attributed to Egill Skallagrímsson.

hyða (*húð* 'flay, whip'): This punishment is also mentioned in the *Gulathing Law* (Gul. 22, 259) and the *Frostathing Law* (Frost. II 2, X 40).

14.10

graut . . . hæilagr (from *grautr . . . heilagr* 'gruel . . . holy'): The implication that gruel is holy probably comes from the fact that this was a subsistence foodstuff essential to life (Olsson 1960: 524).

14.6–14.16

Regulations prohibiting work, and stating the consequences of disobedience, are found in a number of places in the early Norwegian laws (Eid. 12; Gul. 16, 17, 18; Frost. II 24, 25, 28) (see also Bøe 1961: 385–388). In comparison with other medieval legislation from outside Norway, these regulations are strikingly detailed. It has therefore been suggested that some of these regulations were not expected to be used in practice, but were descriptions of hypothetical cases, intended to be read by people interested in formulating laws (see Landro 2010: 198–202).

Chapter fifteen: on those women due to whom a man becomes an *úbótamaðr*, in the event of intercourse

15

During the Middle Ages, the Church developed the so-called 'incest prohibition': that is, a prohibition against sexual relations – and therefore against marriage – between people who were perceived to be related. As a result of this, biological kinship (*consanguinitas*), familial relationship through marriage (*affinitas*), and spiritual kinship (*cognatio spiritualis*) all constituted barriers to marriage (Plöchl 1962: 321–323; Brundage 1987: 140–141, 191–195; Christensen-Nugues 2003: 145, 151–153). Dealing with sex which was forbidden either due to the relationship between the participants or to the time at which it took place (see chapter seven) kept people trained in Church law extremely busy, especially from the beginning of the tenth century onwards (see Payer 1984: 88–114). This chapter should be viewed as part of the Church's attempt to bring marriage legislation under ecclesiastical jurisdiction – one aim of the Gregorian reform movement (Korpiola 2004: 57–63). Similar regulations can be found in the other early Norwegian laws (Gul. 24–26; Frost. III 3, 6, 8; Eid. 52, 53; Hagland 2004; also, for instance, Sv. 61–62; J 49–50; Archbishop Páll's Third Statute: 288–289; Archbishop Árni's Statute: 297–298).

15.1–15.2

These paragraphs concern the closest female relatives, related either by blood or through marriage. The first seven in the list refer to *consanguinitas*; the eighth to the thirteenth, *affinitas*; and those remaining, *consanguinitas* again. The distinction between the two classes of relationship was of no consequence for the severity of the punishments they attracted: these were implemented immediately and were of the harshest possible kind.

15.3–15.7

These paragraphs likewise concern both *consanguinitas* and *affinitas*, but probably in more distant relatives than those named in 15.1, in which a culprit became an *úbótamaðr*. This passage is about people who knowingly enter into marriage despite being aware that they are related, and that such marriage is prohibited. Punishment for this was relatively mild – at least during the first year – and consisted of fines taken by the bishop and separation of the couple. (On divorce and separation, see Brundage 1987: 200–201, 370–376.)

15.8

Given that marriage prohibitions applied up to and including the fifth degree, as in 15.3, it is perhaps unsurprising that people entered into marriage without knowing they were significantly related (on the term for 'degree', *kné*, see Hagland 2004: 213–216). Due to the fact that, according to the ideals of the reform movement, the incest prohibition by the Church should apply up to and including the seventh degree, this became impossible to enforce. The Fourth Lateran Council (1215) limited the prohibition to the fourth degree (can. 50 conc. Lat. IV). One might ask whether prohibition up to and including the fifth degree, as mentioned here in the *Borgarthing Law*, was really possible in small, fairly static communities (see also Christensen-Nugues 2003: 152–153).

15.9–15.13

Cognatio spiritualis was signified in Norwegian by the term *guðsifjar* 'relationship through God', and breach of the prohibition against entering into sexual relations despite such a relationship as *guðsifjaspell* (NgL V: 252). If a marriage of this kind was contracted, the penalty was the same as that for people related by blood to fairly distant but still forbidden degrees. Here, three sources of spiritual kinship are mentioned; in the *Gulathing Law*, six (Gul. 26). In the *Borgarthing Law*, the issue was solely liturgical participation in the sacraments of baptism and confirmation.

Chapter sixteen: on episcopal fines, and *úbótaverk*

Chapter sixteen deals with different kinds of sorcery and superstitious customs, each classified as *ubota værk*, which means that the violation was regarded as so severe a crime that it was not possible to atone for it. Among the prohibited customs is 'Sámi-seeking', which refers to Sámi people living in the northernmost parts of Norway, Sweden, and Finland. Sámi people also appear in saga literature, pictured as 'highly skilled wizards and sorcerers' (Pálsson 1999: 29). In this particular case it is obvious that the law material reflects local customs and conditions. The other examples of sorcery, however, are probably copied from literary, ecclesiastical sources. The last paragraph (16.9) refers to *bok male* (lit. 'the book language') as an authoritative source. This is an Old Norwegian term which refers to the Latin language as an allusion to canon law in general (Halvorsen & Rindal 2008: 157; NgL V: 107 s.v. *bókmál*). Rob Meens has discussed why identical descriptions of magic, sorcery, and superstition appear in a wide variety of ecclesiastical sources from different geographical regions, and concludes thus: 'While the repetition of superstitious behavior is an indication that magic was important, it does not mean that the description of a magical rite corresponds with actual behavior. The description often derives from a literary tradition, though the fact that it is repeated tells us about the enduring need for such legislation' (Meens 1998: 286; Landro 2010: 217). Several of the prohibited customs mentioned in the *Borgarthing Law* have parallels in other written sources, in line with this assertion by Meens (Landro 2010: 218).

16.4

The phrase 'If a woman bites a finger – or a toe – off her child, for long life' echoes an ecclesiastical source written by the Carolingian bishop Theodulf of Orleans (ca. 760–820): *truncare membrum hominis, ut non moriatur* (Brommer 1984: 177).

16.6

'Such a witch as harms cow or calf, woman or child . . .' is found in nearly the same wording in the Swedish *Younger Västgöta Law* (VgL II R 10).

16.7

The text on witchcraft paraphernalia concretized to human hair, nails, and frog feet, is another example of a Norwegian-Swedish parallel. A chapter in the Swedish *Dala Law* also regulates sorcery, and refers to a woman caught with hairs and nails (DL Kk 11).

Chapter seventeen: on separation of spouses, and on adultery, and on those matters which are known throughout the *herað* and which involve fine-payment to the bishop

The first part of chapter seventeen regulates dissolution of marriage, while the second part (from 17.5) deals with procedural matters.

17.5–17.13

The procedure described in these paragraphs is quite reminiscent of the inquisitorial procedure which was established by Pope Innocent III at Lateran IV in 1215 (Trusen 1988; Brundage 1996; Landro 2010: 172–181). The bishop responds to a rumour circulating in the *herað*; if the rumour turns out to be credible, a second stage can be initiated, and the bishop's *ármaðr* may pursue the case himself. This paragraph thus seems to contain both the *inquisitio famae* and the *inquisitio veritatis*: the two stages which characterize the inquisitorial procedure: 'Winfried Trusen has convincingly argued that the inquisitorial procedure was modeled on the infamatory procedure, in which an inquest (*inquisitio*) was conducted to establish whether the public outcry (*publica fama*) that a crime had been committed was true. In order to avoid public scandal in the community (*scandalum publicum*), the alleged perpetrator was expected to exonerate himself by taking a public oath (*purgatio canonica*). The crime itself was not investigated. *In inquisitorial procedures, however, the judicial activity was not confined to establishing the truth of the report* (inquisitio famae) *but also concerned an investigation of the alleged crime* (inquisitio veritatis). In canonistic practice the distinction between the establishment of the notoriety of a crime, constituted by *fama*, and the crime itself was not always sharply drawn. *But in theory the fame or public outcry had to be proved first before a judge could proceed to investigate the truth of the crime*' (Thijssen 1996: 53–54; our emphasis. See also Landro 2010: 175). Although there is a striking similarity between chapter seventeen and the inquisitorial procedure regarding the distinction between *inquisitio famae* and *inquisitio veritatis*, it is still questionable whether the regulations in the *Borgarthing Law* render the inquisitorial procedure in its purest form. In the inquisitorial procedure 'the judge carried on the investigation and presented the charges' (Thijssen 1996: 53), which implies that the judge and the investigator were identical. The *Eidsivathing Law* explicitly states that the farmers were to serve as judges at the thing (Eid. 25). It is not clear whether this was the case in the *Borgarthing Law* as well, as late as the early thirteenth century. If so, however, the role of the judge and the investigator were kept separate, and one of the hallmarks of the inquisitorial procedure was lacking.

17.14

The sentence *Nu* er *œin sokn b*iscu*ps a allum malom* is given various interpretations by scholars. Eyvind Fjeld Halvorsen translates: 'The same procedural regulations apply to all episcopal cases' (Halvorsen & Rindal 2008: 159); the historian

Jens Arup Seip translated: 'Now there is a single investigation in all episcopal cases' (Seip 1942: 17). From a legal point of view, Seip's interpretation makes more sense, since it corresponds to the prohibition against double jeopardy (*Non bis in idem*), which should prevent a person from being prosecuted for the same crime more than once (Helmholz 1996: 286–290; Pennington 1997: 1108; Landro 2010: 178–179). This principle has deep roots, both in Roman and canon law, and was referenced by Burchard of Worms and Ivo of Chartres, amongst others (Pennington 1997: 1108; Landro 2010: 178–179).

Chapter eighteen: on violence in a churchyard, or inside a church

bardagha (from *bardagi* derived from the verb *berja* 'to fight, brawl'): The term is rare in legal language, and occurs only here in the *Borgarthing Law*, in the *Hirðskrá* (H 28, 38, 53), the *Gulathing Law* (Gul. 212), and the *Older Town Law* (Bj. 15, 74). In the last three texts, a 'full assault' is defined as an assault in which one person hits another three times or more.

18:1–2

Canon law clearly stated that churches and churchyards could be desecrated in various ways, causing them to become deconsecrated and therefore useless (Nilsson, Bertil 1989: 87–106). When it came to questions of battle and blood loss, Gratian (C.17 q.4 c.7; see Friedberg 1879) quoted partly from the Council of Tribur in 895 (can. 4) which had been disseminated by Burchard of Worms and Ivo of Chartres, but also from another decree of unknown provenance (D.68 c.3; De con. D.1 c.20; see Friedberg 1879). Any fight resulting in blood loss in a churchyard meant that the churchyard had to be reconsecrated (*reconsecratio cimeterii*). This was an act reserved for bishops, but it was clearly simpler in form than a fresh act of church consecration (*consecratio ecclesiae*). This explains the differences in the sizes of the fines mentioned in 18.1 and 18.2. During the latter part of the twelfth century and the beginning of the thirteenth century, developments in liturgy and ecclesiastical law meant that a fresh consecration of a churchyard or church could be replaced by a liturgical act of cleansing (*reconciliatio*), which was shorter and simpler than a consecration. When it came to church buildings, *reconciliatio* was mentioned for the first time by Pope Innocent III in 1207; for churchyards, it was mentioned by the same pope in 1213. Amongst the Norwegian laws, it is only *Archbishop Jón's Christian Law* (J 11; see also A 12) which shows any trace of this change (Nilsson, Bertil 1989: 107–117; see also VgL I Kk 21; Nilsson, Bertil 1989: 117–121). The legislation here in the *Borgarthing Law* reflects a layer of ecclesiastical law laid down before the first decades of the thirteenth century.

As we can see here, distinctions were also made between the inside and outside of church buildings, reflecting a belief that, inside and around church buildings, there were differing degrees of holiness (see HL Kk 21§2).

18.3

In the situation outlined, it is assumed that blood entered the churchyard, despite the fact that the offence did not take place there. Blood could in itself cause a churchyard to become desecrated. It is possible that folk and perhaps also pre-Christian beliefs could have contributed to such thinking (Nilsson, Bertil 1989: 96–97).

Part V The Eidsivathing Law

The Eidsivathing Christian Law[1]

Chapter one: here it is said that every child shall be baptized[2]

1.1 Now, this is next: that men shall be Christians,[3] and reject heathendom.

1.2 Each child which is born and has a human head shall be nurtured, even should any ill marks be upon it,[4] and none shall lose its life.[5]

1.3 Each woman shall make known her labour, and have her child taken to church and baptized.[6] A woman shall accompany it, and a man, and they shall be its godparents.[7]

Chapter two: on lay baptism[8]

2.1 And if illness ails the child out on the road,[9] and no priest can be reached, then those travelling with the child ought to do this: make the sign of the

1 At an earlier point in NB 317 4o (92r), the manuscript contains a list of the openings of the chapters in the Eidsivathing Law, introduced by the words 'There are many chapters (*capitula*) in the Christian Law and also in the king list. Hálfdan svarti. Haraldr hárfagr . . .' (Halvorsen & Rindal 2008 note that the black script which begins each listed chapter opening in this section is legible, whereas the red script which follows is not.) Then, immediately before the start of the text of the *Eidsivathing Law* (on 95r), there is a list of kings of Norway, ending: 'The very wise and brave and victorious son of King Sverrir was called King Hákon inn góði. His son was King Hákon the Crowned. King Magnús, his son, who is crowned with many good things, should strengthen his kingdom with law and righteousness, and gladden his thegns with other good things, and with legal amendments, with kingly mercy'. This is followed by a separate heading reading: 'Here our old Christianity is discussed, and how it begins, and the first chapter tells how a child must be baptized in an emergency and how that must be done, according to the law'.

2 NB 317 4o: *Primum capitulum*. Otherwise, the headings of NB 317 4o contain numbers rather than words (although these are different from the numbers used by the modern editors). Both manuscripts containing the short version of the law do include descriptive headings.

3 *kristnir uera*. NB 317 4o: 'accept Christianity'.

4 NB 317 4o: omits 'and has a human head . . . even should any ill marks be upon it'.

5 *ængu spilla*.

6 NB 317 4o: omits 'and baptized'.

7 *uæita þui guðciuiar*.

8 *skiring læikmanna*.

9 *a ueg uti*.

cross on its back and on its chest, and in every place where chrism should be put; and take water, and make the sign of the cross in it, and say this: 'I bless you, water, in the name of the Father and the Son and the Holy Spirit,'[10] and dip the child into water three times,[11] and speak these words: 'I baptize you in the name of the Father and the Son and the Holy Spirit,' and give the child a name.[12]

2.2 And if the child dies later, out on the road, then, afterwards, they should continue their journey, and find a priest, and, before the priest, speak those words which they spoke when they baptized the child.[13] And if they speak them correctly before the priest, then they must have spoken them correctly before, and then the child is buried in the churchyard.[14] But if they do not speak them correctly before the priest, then they must not have spoken them correctly before. Then the child is not buried in the churchyard. It shall be covered and buried in unconsecrated ground, such that dogs cannot eat it,[15] nor ravens, nor men's livestock. And if they do, then six ounces are owed to the bishop by the one who should have protected the child.

Chapter three: on a woman's labour[16]

3.1 If a woman is in need at the time of her labour and only one woman is nearby, and she gives birth to a dead child, then she shall show that to a man, as second witness.[17] And if no woman is near her during her labour,[18] then she shall show two men that the child is neither blue nor bloody, and there is no drawn cord around its neck, and no hand-mark[19] on it.

3.2 And if she does not do this, then the bishop or *ármaðr*[20] may accuse her of murder of a heathen.[21] She shall deny this with a *lýrittr*-oath, with two[22] free

10 NB 317 4o: omits 'and in every place where chrism should be put; and take water, and make the sign of the cross in it, and say this: "I bless you, water, in the name of the Father and the Son and the Holy Spirit" '. However, the phrase 'in every place where chrism should be put' does appear in Addition One to the manuscript, just here.

11 NB 317 4o: instead of 'three times' reads 'if this is possible'.

12 NB 317 4o: 'and give it a name, and name it'. In the same manuscript, this is followed by Addition One: 'And if water cannot be found in any way, then the one travelling with the child, whether a man or a woman, shall make a cross on its back and its chest and in every place where chrism should be put, and speak the same words which were told before'.

13 *skirðu barnet*. NB 317 4o: *cristnaðo þatt barn*.

14 *kirkiugarðe*. NB 317 4o: *uigðæ iorð*.

15 NB 317 4o: 'reach it'.

16 *sengfor kono*.

17 *aðrum uætte*.

18 NB 317 4o: omits 'during her labour'.

19 NB 317 4o: adds 'or blemish (*uom*)'.

20 NB 317 4o: 'the bishop's *ármaðr*'.

21 *morð hæiðit*.

22 NB 317 4o: omits 'two'.

women. And people must be painstaking in oath-taking, then, so that men know that they will be reliable, with truthful oaths and witness-bearing.[23]

3.3 And if she fails to do this, then it falls to her to undergo trial by hot iron.[24] And if she is not clean, according to the trial by hot iron,[25] then she is an outlaw, and the bishop shall impose on her this penance: that she shall leave the land,[26] and she shall remain away for as long as he requires.

3.4 And if she returns to the land, and wishes to remain in the land, then she shall pay three marks to the bishop, and half a *mannsgildi*[27] to the king, and that is called 'heathen *mannsgjǫld*'.[28]

Chapter four: on baptism by a couple[29]

And it may come to pass that a lone couple[30] go with their child to church[31] to baptize it, because they do not have the choice of having others (go with it), due to a scarcity of men. And, on the way, such great illness ails the child that since they can reach neither a priest, nor any other men, they must baptize it themselves, in the way told before, rather than let it die heathen. And they shall refrain from conjugal relations[32] until they find the bishop. And then he may permit them conjugal relations, and not part them.

Chapter five: on deformity[33]

And if it should happen that a child is born with ill marks[34] – the calves in front, on the legs; the eyes at the back, in the nape, and with ungodly shape, but with human head and human voice[35] – it shall be nurtured, and brought to church, and baptized, and fed.[36] And then it shall be taken to a meeting with the bishop,[37] and the child shall be shown to him, and whatever he advises shall be done.

23 *þæir uilia i sannum æiðum uera stadder eða uitnisburðum.*
24 *iarnburðar.*
25 *skir at iarne.*
26 *skal biscup scrifta henne af lannde brot.*
27 NB 317 4o: *þægngilldi.*
28 *hæiðins mannz giolld.* NB 317 4o: *hæiðins morðz giolld* 'heathen murder payment'.
29 *hiuna skirn.*
30 *hion. ij.*
31 NB 317 4o: omits 'to church'.
32 *hiunskap.*
33 AM 68 4°: *oukt liki.* The word *oukt* represents *ǫfugt, afugt,* found in the rule following the heading. NgL V: s.v. *ǫfugr, afugr* suggested this meant 'backwards, distorted figure'. Likewise, Cleasby-Vigfusson, s.v. *ǫfigr, ǫfugr* derived this from *af-vegr*, meaning something like 'turning the wrong way'.
34 *orkymblum.*
35 Short version in AM 58 4o and AM 77 c 4o: 'dog's head and human voice'.
36 NB 317 4o: omits 'and fed'.
37 *funnd* biscupc.

Chapter six: on monstrous[38] form

But if the child is born with monstrous form – it has no human head and no human voice – then one may take it to a church, if one wishes, and have a priest baptize[39] it, if he will; and dig a grave in the churchyard, and lay the child there in it,[40] and lay a flat stone over it there, as best one can, so that neither dogs nor foxes may reach it; but let no earth fall on it before it is dead, and let it live as long as it may.

Chapter seven: on the labour of a bondwoman[41]

If a bondwoman[42] goes into labour, and she bears a dead child[43] and does not show it to witnesses,[44] then the bishop's *ármaðr* may accuse her of murder of a heathen.[45] Then she shall swear an oath, with two (other) women,[46] that she did not murder her child. And if that oath fails, then it befalls her to go into outlawry.[47]

Chapter eight: on baptism[48] of children

8.1 All those children born before Christmas shall be baptized before Christmas Eve. And those born on the night before Christmas shall be baptized on Christmas Day, before mass. And those children born before Lent shall all be baptized on the Saturday, before men begin the Seven-Week-Fast (Lent), the following morning. And those born during the night before that Sunday[49] shall be baptized in the morning, before mass. And those born during Lent shall be baptized on Easter Eve.[50] And if they are born the night before Easter Day, they shall be baptized on Easter Day before mass. And if they are born on[51] Pentecost Eve, they shall be baptized on that same Eve. And if they are born during the night before Pentecost,

38 *hærliki*. This word for 'monstrous form' seems to be a corruption of *ferlíki*, related to Old English *fǽr*. See NgL V: s.v. *hærlíki*.
39 NB 317 4o: 'see and baptize'.
40 NB 317 4o: omits 'and lay the child there in it'.
41 *sengfor ambottar*.
42 *ambot*. NB 317 4o: *ambot manz*.
43 NB 317 4o adds 'at home'.
44 *uattom*. NB 317 4o: 'does not take (*ter*) it to lawful witnesses'.
45 *morð hæiðit*.
46 NB 317 4o: 'deny this with two witnesses (to show)'.
47 NB 317 4o: 'what was mentioned before befalls her'.
48 *skiring*.
49 *a sunnu not*. NB 317 4o: 'born during the "summer night" (*sumarnottena*)'.
50 Also known as Holy Saturday.
51 *En ef alen ero a huita sunnu æftan*. Judging by the pattern of this paragraph, this should read 'before', as indicated by NB 317 4°: 'And (as for) those children who are born between Easter Sunday and Pentecost Eve . . .'

they shall be baptized in the morning before mass. And those children who are born before the Feast of St John: they shall be baptized on the evening of St John's Eve.[52] And if they are born during the night before the Feast of St John, they shall be baptized in the morning,[53] before mass.

8.2 Now if a man has a heathen child in his home on any one of these five nights which have been mentioned here, then he owes six ounces to the bishop, and he should have it baptized within a five-day time limit.[54]

8.3 And if he keeps it inside all of these five nights,[55] then he owes three marks to the bishop, and he should have it baptized within a five-day time limit – or else the one who should look after the child owes everything he owns.[56] And this shall be divided in three. The bishop takes a third; the king, the second (third); and the farmers, the third (third).[57]

Chapter nine: on holy days

9.1 One is the First Day of Christmas. Second, the Feast of St Stephen.[58] Third is the Feast of St John (the Evangelist).[59] Fourth is Childermas.[60] Five is the Feast of St Thomas (Becket).[61] Six is the Eighth Day of Christmas.[62] Seven is the Thirteenth Day of Christmas.[63] Eight is Candlemas.[64] Ninth is the Cross Mass.[65] Ten: Hallvarðr Mass.[66] Eleven: Holy Thursday.[67] Twelve is the Feast of St John (the Baptist).[68] Thirteen: Peter and Paul Mass.[69] Fourteen is the Feast of Those who Rest in Kinn and Selja.[70] Fifteen is the First Feast of St Óláfr (Óláfr Mass).[71] Sixteen is Lawrence

52 *Jons uaku æftan*. NB 317 4o: adds 'before mass'.
53 NB 317 4o: 'on the Feast of St John'.
54 NB 317 4o: omits 'and he should have it baptized within a five-day time limit'.
55 NB 317 4o: omits 'inside . . . these five nights'.
56 NB 317 4o: 'is outlawed (*utlægr*), along with everything he owns'.
57 In NB 317 4o, the king is mentioned before the bishop.
58 26th December.
59 27th December.
60 28th December. Also known as the Feast of the Holy Innocents. This is erroneously placed after the next Feast in NB 317 4o.
61 29th December.
62 1st January. Also known as the Octave of the Nativity.
63 6th January. Also known as Epiphany.
64 2nd February.
65 3rd May. Also known as the Feast of the Invention (Finding) of the Cross (Crouchmas, Roodmas). NB 317 4o also adds 'Cross Mass in the spring' at the end of the list, with the additional detail that this was legally adopted by the Eidsivathing.
66 15th May.
67 Ascension Day.
68 24th June.
69 29th June. NB 317 4o mentions Peter only.
70 8th July.
71 29th July. NB 317 4o: 'Óláfr Mass'.

Mass.[72] Seventeen: the First Marymas.[73] Eighteen: Michaelmas.[74] Nineteen: All Hallows.[75] Twenty: the Feast of St Nicholas.[76]

9.2 And although the Feast of St Mary in the (Lenten) Fast[77] is not ordered in its place,[78] we should keep it like a Sunday,[79] and also the Later Feast of St Mary,[80] and also the Feast of St Magnús in the spring.

9.3 As for each of the six days which is not preceded by a vigil,[81] they are as holy as Sundays. And if any man works on those days, then he owes six ounces to the bishop.

Chapter ten: on cross-carving[82]

10.1 *Hǫfuðprestar* shall make crosses (as summons batons), and carve them before all feast days – as far in advance as is necessary for (timely use of each) proclamation route.[83] And if they do not carve them in this way, or if they misproclaim feast days or ember days, then they owe three marks to the bishop.

10.2 Now the bishop shall go to the Eidsivathing assembly each summer,[84] and listen to (recitation from) the law-book there,[85] and perform liturgical services there,[86] and speak publicly there.[87]

10.3 All priests shall come to meet the bishop there, unless prevented from doing so by some necessity. And each of those who does not come to the bishop there then owes three marks in silver to the bishop.

10.4 There, the bishop shall see their books, and all their work, in full,[88] to find out whether they are able to perform services[89] for the living and the

72 10th August.
73 15th August. Also known as the Assumption of Mary. This was the 'First Marymas' because it came before the Later Feast of St. Mary (Nativity of Mary) on the 8th September (mentioned in the next rule). NB 317 4° mentions Martinmas (11th November) here instead, then misses out Michaelmas and All Hallows.
74 29th September.
75 1st November. Also known as Hallowmas.
76 6th December. NB 317 4o: adds 'Twenty is Cross Mass in spring after Easter. It is as holy as a Sunday, since it was legally adopted at the Eidsivathing'.
77 25th March. Also known as the Feast of the Annunciation (Lady Day). NB 317 4° does not specify which Feast of St Mary it means here.
78 NB 317 4o: 'not mentioned here'.
79 NB 317 4o adds: 'but it is not preceded by a vigil' and omits the rest of the sentence.
80 8th September. Also known as the Nativity of Mary. It came after the 'First Marymas' in August.
81 NB 317 4o: 'all of the feast days which have been mentioned'.
82 *krosskurð*.
83 *sua myklu fyr* sem *þæir uitu at boðlæið er til*.
84 NB 317 4o: omits 'each summer'.
85 *høyra þar logbok*. NB 317 4o: 'listen to recital of the law there (*høyra þar loghtalu*)'.
86 *uæita þar tiðir*.
87 *tælia þar fi*ri *mannu*m. NB 317 4o: 'speak publicly of the Christian faith (*tælia tru fi*rir *mo*nnu*m*)'.
88 *allt æmbætti at fullu*.
89 *uæita þionosto*. NB 317 4o: adds 'fully'.

dead.[90] And (the bishop shall) correct matters, if they (priests) have misproclaimed feast days or ember days, or (made mistakes with) the crosses which the priests carve.[91]

10.5 Each farmer shall carry (such a cross) to others.

10.6 The one who is foremost on the farm shall carry a cross to them.[92]

Chapter eleven: on failure in the passing-on of a (summons baton) cross[93]

11.1 And if a (summons baton) cross[94] has failed to be passed on, and a man says that it has not come to him, he shall swear to this with a *lýrittr*-oath. If the bearer has one witness[95] with him, then the summons baton is a second witness.[96] And if he arrives, then the oath from the one towards whom the summons baton was carried is void.[97] Then he owes such a fine[98] as is appropriate to the day.

11.2 Now, if it so happens that a man misremembers which night it is,[99] and the summons baton remains in his hand, then he shall run or ride[100] and go to all the places where the summons baton should have gone, and warn men, so that they do not eat wrongfully, or work wrongfully.[101]

11.3 And if he does not go to all those places where the summons baton should go, then he owes as much as is appropriate to the day. But if he goes to all those places, then he owes nothing.[102]

11.4 Now if a farm for which a man has summons baton duty[103] becomes deserted, and the buildings are moved from the odal plot,[104] and taken away from the proclamation route,[105] then he shall take it (the summons baton) there, where he took it before: to the odal plot. And if he does not take it in this way, then he owes as much as is appropriate to the day.[106]

90 *kuikum oc dauðum*.

91 *krossa þa er prestar skera*. The last part of this sentence seems somewhat awkward. It would probably make more sense as the first part of the following rule, as it is in NB 317 4º: 'The crosses which priests carve, each farmer shall carry to the next'.

92 NB 317 4o: adds 'ok *sæigi hanum till*' which may be a mistake.

93 *krosfall*.

94 *kross*. NB 317 4o: *boð*.

95 Scribal error: *æina not* ('a net'). The phrase is correct in NB 317 4o: *ein uatt*.

96 *anner uattr*.

97 *firiskotet*. NB 317 4o: 'ought to be quashed' (*eigi æiði firirkoma*)'.

98 *uiti*.

99 NB 317 4o: omits 'which night it is'.

100 NB 317 4o: 'ride or walk'.

101 NB 317 4o: omits 'eat wrongfully, or'.

102 *er hann orsæckr*. NB 317 4o: adds a chapter division at the end of this rule.

103 *boðburð*.

104 *aðal tuftum*.

105 *boðlæið*.

106 NB 317 4o: 'owes as much as if it has not been taken at all'.

11.5 And if a man removes a building from the proclamation route or from the odal plot,[107] then he (the baton bearer) shall carry it once, with two witnesses,[108] to the odal plot. And after that it is his responsibility (the responsibility of the one who moved the building), for all summons batons,[109] to take them away (to the next point on the proclamation route), for as long as he makes use of the field or meadow.[110]

11.6 But as soon as he fails to enclose it, and it becomes cattle-trodden grazing land,[111] and animals[112] cross it, then he (the bearer) shall carry it (the summons baton) to the farm to which the other one (who moved the buildings) carried it before, and thereby earn himself grazing land.[113]

Chapter twelve: on the holy period of Sunday[114]

12.1 Now, the holy period of Sunday begins at nones[115] on Saturday, and lasts until daylight is in the sky on Monday.

12.2 And if a farmer is at work[116] with his servants,[117] then he owes six ounces for his servants.[118]

12.3 Now, if his servants are caught working unaccompanied, then the farmer shall release them with six ounces for the bishop,[119] or he should offer them to the bishop's *ármaðr* for flogging.[120]

12.4 And every free man should release himself from (guilt or punishment for such) a deed with six ounces for the bishop.[121]

12.5 The *ármaðr*[122] shall have evidence[123] that they worked wrongfully, but not demand oath-taking.

12.6 Now a man may begin his journey, with a burden which he bears with a single strap on one shoulder, on a Sunday. But if he bears (a burden) with two straps, then he owes six ounces to the bishop.

107 NB 317 4o: omits 'or from the odal plot'.

108 *uatto. ij.*

109 *abyrð a allum boðom*. The manuscript has been corrected here, by striking out an extra letter *n* (from *bonðom*).

110 *akrs eða ænngs*. This is a variant of a stock phrase.

111 *fællr i nauta troð. oc hofn*. NB 317 4o: 'cattle-grazing land'.

112 *fe. eða fole*. Literally: 'cattle or foals'. NB 317 4o: *fenaðr*.

113 *kaupi þui ser ofn.*

114 *sunnu dags hælgi.*

115 *none.*

116 NB 317 4o: 'caught working'.

117 *hionom sinum*. The first *-o-* has been written above the line.

118 NB 317 4o: 'he owes six ounces to the bishop and six ounces to the others for his servants'.

119 NB 317 4o: omits 'for the bishop'.

120 *bioðe hann huð þæira fram firi biscups armanne.*

121 NB 317 4o: 'should release himself with six ounces'.

122 NB 317 4o: 'The bishop's *ármaðr*'.

123 *uitni*. Alternative translation: 'witness evidence'.

12.7 A man may travel on a Sunday with impunity, with a packhorse which he rides, and with a load which he does not tie with ropes.

Chapter thirteen: on men's traps

13.1 A man may go to his trap,[124] and take out anything which has entered it, and set it again, with impunity – but not do anything more with it.[125]

13.2 A man may go fishing[126] on a Sunday, and if he tears his net, then he may repair it with bast,[127] but not with yarn.

13.3 And if a man lays his net, then he may take fish from it, but not carry the net up to dry, nor put it on poles, nor sticks.[128] And if he does any of this[129] then he owes six ounces to the bishop.[130]

Chapter fourteen: on guests

14. If four or more guests come to a man, and if he has meal, then he may, with impunity, have whatever he will eat with the guests[131] baked, on a Sunday as on a working day,[132] and have (an animal) slaughtered and hung up between the rafters by the door – but not take it out into the storehouse.

Chapter fifteen: on isolated land[133]

15.1 And those who inhabit isolated land should obtain all crosses and all summons batons[134] themselves, so that they do not eat wrongfully, or work wrongfully. If they eat wrongfully or work wrongfully,[135] they owe three marks to the bishop.

15.2 But they are not obliged to go to the thing assembly, unless the bishop's *ármaðr* sends them a summons baton, in their settlement district.[136]

124 *ganga um gilldri.*
125 *gera æcki nyt uið.*
126 *fara a fiski.*
127 *bøta mæð bastum.* Bast is coarse fibre, made from bark or similar material.
128 *a stanger eða a sprota.* NB 317 4o: 'carry the net up to land, or poles or sticks, to dry'.
129 NB 317 4o: 'any of this which is forbidden'.
130 The last sentence is numbered separately as 13.4 in the edition of NB 317 4o.
131 NB 317 4o: 'whatever they will eat'.
132 *syknan dag.* NB 317 4o: omits 'as on a working day'.
133 *stoklond.*
134 *boð.*
135 NB 317 4o: 'If they do either'.
136 *bygð.* NB 317 4o: 'summons them, or has a summons baton sent to their settlement district'.

Chapter sixteen: on holy periods[137]

16.1 Now, if a man begins his journey on a Saturday before nones,[138] with a packhorse or strapped burden,[139] he should travel when it is a working day,[140] and he should rest when it is a holy period.[141]

16.2 And if he travels during a holy period, then six ounces in silver[142] lie at stake.

16.3 And if he makes his journey home on a Friday, or earlier in the week, then he may travel with impunity, with however much he takes.

16.4 And if a man sails his ship[143] on a Saturday, then he may go to land[144] as he wishes, and throw baggage up over the high-tide mark,[145] and then travel whilst it is a working day.[146]

16.5 And if he travels during a holy period, then he owes[147] six ounces to the bishop.[148]

16.6 And if he travels with his baggage on a Friday[149] or earlier in the week, then he may travel during a holy period as he wishes, with impunity.[150]

Chapter seventeen: work which may be done during a holy period

17.1 And if a bear carries a man's livestock into a wood[151] or wild animals attack, then he (the man) may flay it,[152] and take the meat home from the wood,[153] whichever day it is.

17.2 If a man comes from a little-converted area[154] and calls himself a Christian, and if he can[155] name the priest who baptized him, and his godfather and godmother, that supports his position.[156]

137 *hælgi.*
138 *non.* NB 317 4o: 'before the holy period'.
139 NB 317 4o: 'with a load or burden'.
140 *synkt.*
141 *hæilagt.*
142 NB 317 4o: omits 'in silver'.
143 NB 317 4o: *kiænnir skipp sitt*, possibly 'reaches land with his ship'.
144 NB 317 4o: 'to a landing-place'.
145 *fløðar male.*
146 NB 317 4o: 'and travel as soon as he wishes'.
147 Written, later, in abbreviated form: *sæ* (for *sæckr*).
148 This rule is included at the end of 16.4 in the edition of NB 317 4o.
149 *fær mæð fatum sinum a friadægi.* NB 317 4o: 'with his group (*for*) on a Friday'.
150 This rule is numbered 16.5 in the edition of NB 317 4o.
151 *ef biorn bær smala mannz. i skoge.* NB 317 4o replaces *skoge* with *toge*, making it nonsensical: 'carries a man's livestock in tow'.
152 Presumably it is the prey which is found and flayed – not the bear.
153 NB 317 4o: omits 'from the wood'.
154 *lannde þui. er lit er kristit.*
155 NB 317 4o: 'then he should'.
156 *þat hæildar honum.*

17.3 But if he fails in this, then a five-day time limit shall be set for those who have him in their house, for him to be baptized within the five-day time limit. And if he is not baptized,[157] three marks belonging to the farmer lie at stake, and he (the unbaptized man) should go into outlawry.

Chapter eighteen: on holy days

18.1 On all holy days, people shall (be allowed to) tend to the dead[158] – except Christmas Day, and Good Friday, and Easter Eve before nones,[159] and the First Day of Easter (Easter Sunday).

18.2 But if anyone carries out a burial on (any of) these aforementioned days, then he owes six ounces to the bishop.

Chapter nineteen

If one of a man's stock animals dies (without being slaughtered),[160] then it shall be flayed, and the flesh cut up, on Sunday as on a working day.[161]

Chapter twenty

20.1 If washing is hung up before a holy period, then it shall hang undisturbed.

20.2 If it is dipped in water, and later hung up, then the one[162] who does that owes six ounces to the bishop.

20.3 But if it falls down, then it should be carried inside and put away, with impunity.[163]

20.4 And if linen lies, bleaching, and it has been laid out before a holy period, then it may lie undisturbed during the holy period.

20.5 But if it is dipped in water during a holy period and later laid out for bleaching, then she (who has done this) owes six ounces to the bishop.[164]

20.6 The night before Sunday and the night before Friday and those nights which are as holy as the night before Sunday, with six-ounce days

157 NB 317 4o: adds 'within the five-day time limit'.

158 *hialpa likum. dauðra manna*. According to NgL V: s.v. *hjálpa*, this refers to burial, specifically. However, this rule is the sole witness listed for this phrase.

159 *firi ringinga tima*. For the interpretation as nones, see NgL V: s.v. *rininga(r)tími*.

160 *(E)f fall kømr i bu mannz*. The initial *E* was omitted from AM 68 4o.

161 NB 317 4o: 'any other day'.

162 *han*. The gender of the person to whom this pronoun refers is unclear. A woman does have to pay her own fine for a similar offence in 20.5, and it is perhaps most likely that the person imagined here is a woman also.

163 This rule is missing from NB 317 4o.

164 NB 317 4o: 'then six ounces for the bishop lie at stake'.

following them: if a man takes a woman, then, then she[165] owes six ounces to the bishop for each such night.[166]

Chapter twenty-one

21.1 No-one shall take a woman during the three weeks[167] immediately before Christmas, nor before the Eighth Day (of Christmas) – or the Thirteenth Day (Epiphany)[168] – and not in the three weeks before the Feast of St John, and not in the three weeks before Michaelmas.

21.2 And no-one shall take a woman in the two weeks[169] immediately before the Seven Week Fast (Lent).

21.3 And if a man takes a woman during these aforementioned times, then he owes six ounces to the bishop.

21.4 If a man takes a woman during the Long Fast (Lent), three marks[170] lie at stake.

21.5 And if a man takes a woman[171] when the morning after is a three-ounce day, then a three-ounce fine[172] for him lies at stake. That belongs to the bishop.[173]

Chapter twenty-two

22.1 (When it comes to) a marriage which comes about blamelessly,[174] according to God's rightful law,[175] and according to the will of each of those who have come together,[176] and other relatives, neither man nor woman shall separate them, even if they change their minds.[177]

165 *hon*. NB 317 4°: 'he' (*han*), if Halvorsen & Rindal 2008 are correct in assuming that the missing central letter was *a*. This requires further consideration, as any difference between the manuscripts here has the potential to shed light on when and where women paid fines for sexual offences like this. Perhaps there was some link with the previous rule, on wet linen lying out.

166 In NB 317 4o, this rule is separated from those which precede it by a chapter heading. The content is essentially the same as in AM 68 4o (except for the possible pronoun difference mentioned earlier), although the word order is slightly different (as in many of the rules) and the detail 'for each such night' is missing.

167 NB 317 4o: 'month'.

168 NB 317 4°: omits: 'or the Thirteenth Day (Epiphany)'. Short version in AM 58 4°: 'nor before the eighth day after the Thirteenth Day'.

169 NB 317 4o: 'in the whole month'.

170 NB 317 4o: 'three marks for the bishop'.

171 NB 317 4o: 'takes a woman during a night'.

172 *uiti*. The phrase *at uiti* was repeated erroneously in AM 68 4°, before being struck out.

173 NB 317 4o: 'then he owes three ounces to the bishop'.

174 *mæinlaus*.

175 NB 317 4o: 'according to the rightful law of the land' (*at retto*m *landzlagum*).

176 NB 317 4o: 'their will'.

177 *brøyting gange a skaplyndi þæira*.

22.2 And even if he (the husband)[178] announces that they have separated from each other,[179] neither of them may take another spouse[180] as long as they are both alive,[181] neither according to the law of God, nor that of man.

22.3 And if he marries[182] (again) whilst his first wife[183] is still living, then the children he then has by this (second) woman are not entitled to any inheritance,[184] neither according to the law of God, nor that of man. And in the same way, if she (the first wife) marries another man, then the children she has by this (second) man[185] are not eligible to inherit anything.

22.4 And (as for) whichever one of a couple[186] causes a separation,[187] then that one owes six ounces to the bishop.

22.5 And a marriage is rightful, and rightfully brought about, when it is no closer[188] than is counted (to be allowed) by our[189] laws – neither as regards relationship through marriage of relatives (affinity),[190] nor as regards blood relationship (consanguinity).[191]

22.6 And if a man wishes to seek marriage, then he shall seek approval from her nearest relatives, to gain permission to marry,[192] according to rightful law. And next he shall find out what she desires.

22.7 Now, they arrange a meeting, and he (the suitor) comes to the betrothal meeting.[193] Then two highly esteemed[194] men who are at this meeting,[195] – one from his party,[196] and the other from amongst her relatives – shall be taken and sent to her, and they shall hear[197] whether she says no to this decision, or yes. And if she says yes to it, or stays silent, then a marriage bond may be made,[198] according to both the law of God and that of man.

178 There is an interesting later addition here: *hiun* 'the couple'.
179 *skilit millim sin*. NB 317 4o: 'And even if they separate'.
180 *til forræða læita*. See NgL V: s.v. *forræði* and 22.6.
181 NB 317 4o: instead of 'as long as they are both alive' has 'neither he for marriage (*kuænfangs*) nor she for marriage (*giptingar*)'.
182 *kuangez*.
183 *henne* [. . .] *er fyr atte hann*.
184 *arfgeng*.
185 NB 317 4o: omits 'by this (second) man'.
186 NB 317 4o: omits 'of a couple'.
187 *skilnade uællðr*.
188 'Closer' (*nermæir*) was added here later, to make sense of this rule, and it also appears in NB 317 4o.
189 NB 317 4o: omits 'our'.
190 *syfskaper*.
191 *frenndsæmi*. NB 317 4o has a chapter division after this rule.
192 *forræða*. See NgL V: s.v. *forræði* and 22.2.
193 *fæstingar stæfnu*.
194 *uiliaster*. NB 317 4o: 'highly reliable' (*skillrikæzster*).
195 *fyndi*. NB 317 4o: *stæmfnu*.
196 *stæfnu liði*.
197 NB 317 4o: omits 'sent to her, and they shall hear'.
198 *hiunskapr bindazst*.

And if a marriage bond is made, then it may never be broken[199] whilst they are both living.

22.8 And if she says no to him, then that marriage bond may not be made[200] according to the law.

Chapter twenty-three

23.1 And if a woman is married under compulsion, then she may announce her separation[201] from her husband on whichever day she wishes, within twelve months.

23.2 But if she stays with him for twelve months, or one month longer, then she never has any possibility of separation.[202]

Chapter twenty-four

24.1 No man shall have in his building staff (stave) or stand (heathen altar),[203] figure or offering,[204] or anything which could be used for heathen practices.[205]

24.2 And if he has (such a thing), and is named as guilty[206] of this, then he is an outlaw, and unholy, along with every penny[207] he owns.

24.3 Now if an offering is found in an unlocked building – a food offering, or a 'clay offering'[208] in human form, made from clay or from dough[209] – then he (the owner or occupier) shall clear himself with a *lýrittr*-oath. If the oath fails, he owes three marks.[210]

24.4 But if it is found locked away,[211] in a vessel or chest, in a kist or in a coffer,[212] then the keeper of the key which fits (the lock of the container) is outlawed.[213]

24.5 But if it is in a man's storehouse,[214] and it (the storehouse) has windows, and (the offering) lies on (top of) sedge or straw,[215] then that is called a

199 NB 317 4o: 'no man may break it'.

200 *saman binnda*. NB 317 4o: 'that marriage may not stand' (*halldæzst*).

201 *sægia skilit*. NB 317 4o: 'separate'.

202 *uon til nikuæðes*. NB 317 4o: 'she may never separate from him'.

203 *staf eða stalla*. *Stafr* could mean 'pole, stave' or 'staff, stick'.

204 *vit eða blot*. NB 317 4o: 'figure, offering, or root'.

205 *þat er til hæiðins siðar uæit*.

206 *kunnr eða sannr*.

207 *pæningr*.

208 *læirblot*.

209 NB 317 4o adds 'or *hamfrær*'. This term is open to interpretation. For comments, see NgL V, s.v. *hamfrer*.

210 NB 317 4o adds 'to the bishop'.

211 NB 317 4o: 'found under stores/stalls' (*basom*).

212 *i kerom. eða kistum. i byrðum. eða i orkom*.

213 NB 317 4o adds 'along with all his property'.

214 *buri*. NB 317 4o: 'the owner's storehouse'.

215 *a starru. eða stræ*.

'plant'.[216] Then the farmer[217] may clear himself with a *lýrittr*-oath. He owes three marks if the oath fails.

24.6 But if it is found under sedge or straw, and it could not have been put under there from outside the building,[218] then the keeper of the key is outlawed, along with all his property.

Chapter twenty-five

25. (As for) the property of people who have been outlawed in legal cases pursued by a bishop: he (the bishop) takes a third; the king, another third; the farmers who were involved in the judgement,[219] a third.

Chapter twenty-six

26.1 Everything which dies in this way, through intervention by human hand, is edible: that which strangles itself in a cattle-fork, or falls at a bridge[220] or which a man knocks over with a boat,[221] or a man drives onto unpassable ice, or is killed by a falling tree which a man has chopped, or is killed by a falling tree to which a man has set fire; or it died because[222] it got stuck in a stream,[223] or fell in a well. All that is edible, then. It is permitted to eat anything which has a clear cause of death.

26.2 But (as for) anything which is killed by 'frenzy sickness'[224] or which is struck by lightning or by falling sickness,[225] that is *svidda*.[226] That is not edible.

Chapter twenty-seven

27.1 Four times in a twelve-month period, there are ember days. Then, priests should ask every man who is twelve years old or older to fast throughout, if he is well.

216 *stunga fole*.
217 NB 317 4o: 'the farmer who owns the storehouse'.
218 *oc mætte æigi unndan læggia i hus þar undir*.
219 *bøndr . . . er um døma*.
220 *i bru*.
221 *uælltir* maðr *skipi*. NB 317 4o: *i skipi*.
222 NB 317 4o: omits 'which a man has chopped, or is killed by a falling tree to which a man has set fire; or it died because'.
223 *bæcki*. Halvorsen & Rindal 2008 prefer the reading *bælki* in NB 317 4° and in the short version of this law in AM 58 4o, which they interpret as 'stall' in this context (from *bǫlkr, bolkr, bálkr*, which can mean 'wall between stalls in a byre' as well as 'law section').
224 *ørsla sot*.
225 *braða sot*.
226 NB 317 4o: *kuæisa*. The meaning is unclear. See NgL V: s.v. *kveisa*.

27.2 And (as for) anyone who does not fast, or eats meat or dairy foods[227] during the ember days,[228] he owes six ounces to the bishop.

27.3 And if a man comes in[229] (to a place) where a man is eating meat on a Friday, and asks him 'Why are you eating meat now, on a Friday?'[230] and he answers 'I have erred as to the day' and gets rid of the bit which he has in his mouth, then there is no fine[231] for this, and he should go to confession.

27.4 But if he answers, '*Nu gengr æi skiall a skia*!'[232] and swallows down the bit, then that bit would be called 'the costly one'. He should pay[233] three marks to the bishop,[234] and he should go to confession.

27.5 And if he continues to eat, and will not stop and will not go to confession, then he is a heathen man, and commits (the offence of carrying out) heathen practice,[235] and he is an outlaw and unholy, along with every penny[236] of his property.

27.6 And if a man eats meat during the Long Fast (Lent) or[237] during ember days, and a (summons baton) cross has come to his farm, then he owes three marks to the bishop.

Chapter twenty-eight

28.1 And if a man eats (the wrong foods)[238] during the Long Fast (Lent), it may not be said that he has erred as to the day. He is an outlaw, along with all the property in his ownership.

28.2 And if a man's servant eats meat[239] during the Long Fast (Lent), then he is an outlaw, and it shall be in the hands of his lawful master, who owns him,[240] whether he (the owner) wants to release him from that debt – half

227 *huit*. NB 317 4°: 'eats dairy foods'.

228 NB 317 4°: 'on a Friday during the ember-days . . .'

229 NB 317 4o: 'comes in suddenly'.

230 NB 317 4o: omits 'on a Friday'.

231 *sækt*.

232 *nu gengr æi skiall a skia*. This is an obscure phrase, with the literal meaning 'Now the membrane doesn't go across the window!' Halvorsen & Rindal 2008 have translated this as 'I don't bother about that!' ('Det bryr jeg meg ikke om'), probably reflecting NgL V: s.v. *skjall*: 'en ironisk tilkjendgivelse af, at man er ligeglad med, om det ikke netop gaar, som det skulde'.

233 *gialldi*.

234 NB 317 4o: omits 'to the bishop'.

235 *drygir hæiðin sið*.

236 *pæningr*.

237 NB 317 4° and the short version of this law in AM 58 4°: omit 'during the Long Fast (Lent) or . . .'

238 NB 317 4o: 'meat'.

239 NB 317 4o: 'men's meat' or 'meat of men' (*mannæ kiot*).

240 *i uallde skapdrottens hans er a*.

a *þegngildi* to the king – and so buy him the right to remain in the land;[241] or, alternatively, whether (the master wants) him to leave the land.[242]

Chapter twenty-nine

29.1 And if a man goes astray out in the wilderness,[243] and if he has been gone for seven days and seven nights,[244] and if a dog should follow him, then he shall eat the dog, rather than the dog eat him.

29.2 And if he should come upon a horse, then he shall eat that, rather than starve any longer.

29.3 And when he comes to a settlement, then he shall tell people about his wrongful eating,[245] and go to confession. Then no fine[246] lies at stake for this.

29.4 But if he hides this, and it emerges later, and he is found guilty of it, then he is an outlaw, along with all his property.

Chapter thirty

30.1 It is also forbidden that any man[247] should take his kinswoman to wife, or his kinsman's widow, or his spiritual kinswoman. All are separated, except for the woman whom a man takes to church by his own choice.[248]

30.2 Now, their kinship shall be counted to the fifth knee, and he may marry at the seventh.[249]

30.3 But when it comes to the widow of a relative, kinship shall be counted to the third knee, and he may marry at the fifth.[250]

30.4 If he takes a more closely related woman to wife, then he may not have her, according to the law.[251]

241 *la*nn*zuist.*
242 NB 317 4o: 'go into outlawry'.
243 *i mork uti.*
244 NB 317 4o: 'fourteen twelve-hour periods (*døgr*), seven days and seven nights'.
245 NB 317 4o: 'tell someone'.
246 *sækt.*
247 NB 317 4o: 'It is stated in the law that no man'.
248 *Allar ero u*nn*dan skildar. nema su æin kona æi. er maðr læiðir i* kirk*iu. þui at þat er æcki nema kosgirni æi*nn. This rule is difficult to interpret. Halvorsen & Rindal 2008 suggested: 'alle er skilt ut, uten den kvinnen som en mann fører inn i kirken, for det er bare noe han gjerne vil gjøre (men fører ikke til "religiøst slektskap")'. Perhaps this is an awkward interpolation on the subject of consent to marriage, rather than on the main theme: avoidance of incest.
249 This rule is also hard to interpret. The translation of Halvorsen & Rindal 2008 suggests that it means marriage is possible at the seventh knee: 'og gifte seg i sjuende' but this leaves the link to the first part of the rule obscure. NB 317 4o: 'Now, their kinship shall be counted from the father. It shall be counted from the sixth knee and he may marry at the seventh.'
250 NB 317 4o and short version: 'shall be counted to the fourth knee, and he may marry at the fifth'.
251 *at lagu*m. NB 317 4o: *at logmale.*

30.5 And if the bishop's *ármaðr* gets a kin-counter[252] to reckon up their kinship,[253] whether he counts well or badly, then kinship between them must be disproved[254] with eight witnesses: two from his paternal kin and two from his maternal kin, and two from her paternal kin, and two from her maternal kin.[255]

30.6 And if they stay as they are for three months, or longer than three months, from the time when the bishop's *ármaðr* gives them a time limit (for separation), then they owe three marks.[256]

30.7 And if they bring forward witnesses in their favour[257] during those three months, they shall let that evidence[258] be brought forward at a thing assembly – whether they arrange that thing assembly, or someone else – on a working day.[259] But if they (witnesses) are not brought forward, (such) evidence can never be called upon again (in that case).

30.8 Now he (the bishop's *ármaðr*) shall set another three-month time limit, before which he (the man in the couple) should separate from[260] her. But if he stays as he is over two three-month time limits, then they owe six marks.[261]

30.9 Again, a three-month time limit shall be set, before which they should separate.[262] But if he stays as he is past the third three-month time limit, then they owe nine marks to the bishop.

30.10 Then the bishop's *ármaðr* should again set (a time limit)[263] before which they (the couple) should be separated. If they are not separated (by then), they are both outlawed, along with all their property.

30.11 Then, the bishop shall first take nine marks, if he has brought a case[264] against him (the man in the couple) for this.[265] Then the outlawed property shall be divided in three. The bishop takes a third, the king another, the lawman the third.[266]

252 *talu mann.*

253 *tælia frenndsæmi þæira.*

254 *skal føra sunndr frenndsæmi þæira.*

255 NB 317 4o: omits 'and two from her paternal kin, and two from her maternal kin'.

256 NB 317 4o: 'two marks'. Note that the contents of this rule and the following one are presented slightly differently in AM 68 4o and NB 317 4o, so both should be consulted together, when comparing the manuscripts.

257 *læiða vitni sin.*

258 *þat vitni.*

259 *a søknom dagum.* NB 317 4o: *a suornom dægi.* This has essentially the same meaning. See NgL V, s.v. *særr, sværr.*

260 *skiliz uið.*

261 NB 317 4o: omits 'But if he stays as he is over two three-month time limits, then they owe six marks'.

262 NB 317 4o omits this sentence.

263 AM 68 4o erroneously omits 'a time limit' (*fimt*) but this is supplied by NB 317 4o and the short version of the law.

264 *sottan hann til.*

265 Halvorsen and Rindal 2008 include this sentence at the end of the previous rule in their edition of NB 317 4o.

266 NB 317 4o: 'the person who brings the case (*sakærabære*) and the lawman the third'.

Chapter thirty-one: on the bishop's seat[267]

31.1 The one whom the king wishes, and who has been correctly chosen,[268] and consecrated here *til starfs oc stols,*[269] shall be the bishop in this seat.[270]

31.2 We shall give him resources.[271] And he shall perform services at the canonical hours[272] for us, and all (other) services which go along with his position.[273]

31.3 And we shall give[274] him a quarter of the tithe.

31.4 He shall obtain for us clerics[275] whom he knows to have the knowledge (needful) to baptize children, and hear our confessions,[276] and take proper care of our churches, and perform all the services befitting our Christian faith.[277]

31.5 And we shall give him our resources, as described here: a tithe of all kinds of grain, both beardless corn (rye or wheat)[278] and barley.[279]

Chapter thirty-two[280]

32.1 And a tithe shall be collected from the crop,[281] and divided into four lots. The bishop shall take one third,[282] the church another, the priest the third, poor men the fourth. And the farmers themselves should deal with that lot (for the poor), and divide it in a way defensible before God.[283]

32.2 And a farmer shall take care of the whole tithe, until the whole tithe is taken.

32.3 And anyone who keeps the tithe (without passing it on) for twelve months, and will not do what has been described here, owes three marks to the bishop, and he should pass on the tithe as before.[284]

267 Heading added later: *Vm biscups stooll.*
268 *retkosen.*
269 *uigðr til starfs. oc stols*: an alliterative phrase. NB 317 4°: *till stafs* ok *till stolls.*
270 *at stole*. NB 317 4o: *at lande.*
271 *fe.*
272 *tiðir uæita.*
273 *þionosto* er *til hans æmbættis høyrir.*
274 *gefa*: added later. NB 317 4°: *fa.*
275 *kænni menn.*
276 *scrifta malom uarom at lyða.*
277 *æmbætti þat allt uæita* er *cristni uare boger*. The last word in this phrase in NB 317 4° is *byriar*, which NgL V: s.v. *boger*, viewed as probably correct, with *boger* being a scribal error.
278 *hamal kyrni.*
279 This rule is clearer in NB 317 4°. Here in AM 68 4°, *sua* appears as *sinu* in error.
280 Later addition: 'Here it is said' (*Her sæghr*), with 'it is said' (*sæghr*) struck out.
281 *a akre.*
282 NB 317 4° and the short version of the law: 'a quarter'.
283 *sem hann uill suara firi Guði*. An awkward singular pronoun (hann) is used here, in AM 68 4°, but not in the other manuscripts.
284 NB 317 4o combines 32.3 and 32.4, making the penalty for the first year six marks (instead of three) and omitting mention of the two-year penalty. This seems less logical and may be an error.

32.4 And if he keeps it another year, then he owes six marks.

32.5 If he keeps it for a third year, then he owes nine marks. And the bishop owns those resources.

32.6 And the bishop's *ármaðr* shall create a five-day time limit before which both the fine[285] and the tithe must be paid. And if he does not pay[286] before the five-day time limit, then he is an outlaw, along with all his property. But first the bishop shall take the nine marks for which he was pursuing the other man (who kept the tithe).[287] And then (the rest) shall be divided in three: the bishop shall take a third, the king another, and the farmers a third.

32.7 Now the bishop shall come to each third,[288] every twelve months, and perform services in the *hǫfuðkirkja* there, and confirm[289] men's children. Then he has the right to receive[290] men's property, if he does that.

32.8 If he does not come in this way to offer men liturgical services,[291] and he has not been prevented by any adverse circumstances, then he loses his *reiða* payment[292] for the year when he does not come.

32.9 And these are the adverse circumstances (which might prevent a bishop from performing the duties mentioned earlier): he lies sick or wounded;[293] or the king sends for him, or the archbishop, and he is performing the duties they require (of him). Then he has the right to have his *reiða* payment, even though he does not come (to the *hǫfuðkirkja*). Now the adverse circumstances (which could prevent him from performing his annual duties at the *hǫfuðkirkja*) have been listed.[294]

32.10 All those priests who are at the *hǫfuðkirkja* should send a summons baton,[295] and have that summons baton passed on, when the bishop is to come and perform services for men.

32.11 Now the priest who is at the *hǫfuðkirkja* shall (offer)[296] four nights of hospitality (procuration)[297] for his bishop, along with ten men and six[298] horses in winter, and in summer, ten (riding) horses and a packhorse. The priest shall obtain enough food and ale for the bishop and his retinue.[299] He shall give food for his (the bishop's) packhorse, and the one he rides.

285 *sæktenne.*
286 *lykr.*
287 NB 317 4o: omits this sentence.
288 *þriðiung.*
289 *færma.*
290 *oðlaz.*
291 *tiðir.*
292 *ræiðu.*
293 *siukr. eða sar.*
294 NB 317 4o adds 'and no more' and a chapter division.
295 *boð.*
296 The missing verb (*uæita*) was added later.
297 *uist.*
298 NB 317 4o: fifteen.
299 *lax mannum.*

Chapter thirty-three

33.1 Now the one arranged to carry out the task by the bishop shall have his (the bishop's) *reiða* payment collected. And he shall begin (the circulation of) a meeting summons baton[300] throughout the *herað*, and have a message go along with it (announcing) that everyone should go there, to the meeting place,[301] with the *reiða* payment for the bishop.

33.2 He has those men who settle this[302] welcomed. But those who do not do this, and do not go there with the bishop's *reiða* payment, he shall summon to the meeting in the next *herað*.

33.3 He may welcome all of those who settle this. But those who do not fulfil this obligation, he may summon[303] to the meeting in the third settlement.

33.4 And if they do not fulfil their obligations there, then (the collector) shall travel to the *hǫfuðkirkja* and make it known that he has undertaken the collection of the bishop's *reiða* payment. 'And all those men who fulfilled their obligations to me, I received. But those who did not fulfil their obligations, I summoned to meet me here, to fulfil their obligations. Now if they will still fulfil their obligations here, then I will welcome them. If they will not now fulfil their obligations, then they owe three marks to the bishop.'

Chapter thirty-four

34.1 And if a church falls to the ground, or burns down, then the farmers shall take timber to the plot within a half-year,[304] and build it within twelve months.

34.2 And if it is not built by then, fifteen marks lie at stake for all the men of the third.[305]

34.3 For the consecration of the church, the bishop shall have three nights of hospitality (procuration)[306] with thirty men and thirty horses in summertime, at the expense of the farmers, but fifteen horses in wintertime, and the farmers shall get him food and ale, for him and his men, and also for those men who serve and wait upon him. He shall have that for the consecration, unless the farmers and the bishop settle on something else.

300 *stæfnu boð.*
301 *stæfnu byar.*
302 *gera skil.*
303 NB 317 4o stops suddenly here, in the middle of a word: *stæmfna þeim æpti.* The manuscripts containing the shorter version of this law includes further paragraphs shared with AM 68 4°.
304 *a missare.*
305 *þriðiungs mannum.*
306 *ueizslu.*

Chapter thirty-five

35.1 The priest at the *hǫfuðkirkja*[307] shall take care of the fire which he has for his duties, when he sings services for men. He owes three marks in nine-ell ounces (if he does not take proper care of the fire).

35.2 And if he carries fire in the church for any other reason, and it burns down due to this, then he shall have a church built, and have it consecrated, and have it finished as it was before.

35.3 And if he does not have the means to do this, or he is neglectful,[308] then the farmers shall have all his property, for the building of the church.

35.4 And if the resources of the priest are not enough for this, then the farmers shall add their own resources, so that the church may be finished. Then the priest shall leave the church, and (only) come back when he can repay each (farmer) for the harm (to his resources).

Chapter thirty-six

36.1 And if the church burns down due to another man's fire, then he (the one responsible) shall have it built up and finished at his expense.

36.2 And if he does not have the means to do this, or if he neglects this, then he should become an outlaw and unholy, and the farmers should have all his property, for the building of the church.

36.3 And if he does not have enough resources for this, then the farmers should draw on their resources for this, so that it may be finished. But he should leave, and (only) come back to the land when he can repay the farmers for the cost of this.

36.4 Now it is the responsibility of any farmer who has a servant if that servant burns down a church.[309]

Chapter thirty-seven

37.1 If a man inflicts bleeding or a wound on (another) man in enmity,[310] and (blood) touches a church,[311] he shall have the church (re)consecrated, and use his resources to pay the bishop.

37.2 And if he does not care, or does not have enough resources to do this, then he should leave the land, outlaw and unholy, and the farmers shall have their church (re)consecrated. And he should (only) come back to the land when he can compensate the farmers for the damage.

307 Short version in AM 58 4°: 'Every priest at a church . . .'

308 *uill æi røgt hafa.*

309 *Nu ef* maðr *maɴnz bræɴnir up* kirkiu. *þa* er *þat j abyrgð allra boɴnda. er maɴn æigu.*

310 *af hæftugri hænde.*

311 AM 58 4°: 'a church or churchyard'.

37.3 And if (a man) should draw blood in malice[312] in a churchyard, then the one who drew blood shall have the churchyard (re)consecrated, using his own resources, or become an outlaw, as was mentioned before (of the one) who drew blood in malice.

37.4 And if a man inflicts bleeding or a wound on (another) man by accident,[313] and not intentionally, and this (blood) remains on the church floor (as a stain),[314] then the (affected) bit of wood should be cut off and cast out of the churchyard. Then (re)consecration is not necessary (but) holy water shall be sprinkled (on the church).

37.5 And if blood falls on the churchyard, holy water shall be sprinkled in that place, once (the earth) has been dug up, if this happened as the result of an accident.[315]

37.6 It is the responsibility of any man who has a servant[316] if that servant draws blood in enmity in the churchyard.[317]

Chapter thirty-eight

38.1 Now, an enclosure shall be (made) around a church. The bishop's *ármaðr* shall hold a thing assembly on a spring day, when the frost has gone from the ground. Then each (man) should go to his section (of the fence) and repair it, such that neither rain nor rot[318] may destroy it.

38.2 And if a section is lying (on the ground), then the bishop's *ármaðr* shall set a five-day time limit,[319] before which each (man) should repair his fence. If that is not done, then six ounces shall lie at stake.

38.3 And if no-one takes responsibility[320] for that section, then those who own the sections on both sides of the section which has fallen shall obtain men (to remedy this), or maintain it themselves.

38.4 And if the bishop's *ármaðr* sets five-day time limits one after another, then there is (only) one fine, if he does not pursue the case between these. But if he pursues the case between the five-day time limits, then he should have six ounces for each five-day time limit (which passes), until a third (of the fence) has fallen down.

312 *mæð ofund.*

313 *af uaða.*

314 *oc stænðr a kirkiu golfe.* Contrast the translation by Halvorsen & Rindal 2008: 'og han står på gulvet' ('and he stands on the church floor').

315 *af uaða uærki.*

316 *maðr manna.*

317 *En ef maðr manna uæckir bloð i kirkiu garðe af hæftugri hennde. þa er þat i abyrgð allra þæira manna er æigu.* This rule has a similar structure to 36.4.

318 *ræg eða rott.*

319 *gera til fimt.*

320 *gengr uið.*

38.5 And if half (of the fence) has fallen down, then seven ounces lie at stake. And if two parts have fallen down, then there are three marks (due) in fine,[321] and all men of the third[322] are responsible for (paying) this fine.

Chapter thirty-nine

39.1 And as for churches which are proprietary churches,[323] if they fall or burn down, then timber shall be taken to (each) plot within twelve months, and (each new church shall be) built within the second (twelve months), and consecrated within the third.

39.2 And (even) if timber is not taken to the plot within twelve months, then it shall be within the second (twelve months), and the church shall be built.

39.3 And if there is no timber at the plot within two twelve-month periods, and (the church has not been) made, then timber shall be taken to the plot, and the church built and consecrated, within the third twelve months.

39.4 And if that is not done, then it shall be built and consecrated within a five-day time limit. And if it is not built and consecrated within the five-day time limit, then the estate on which the church should have stood is confiscated, and the relatives and heirs (of the owner) shall redeem the ground with gold and burnt silver, and spotless resources.[324] The farmers shall go there, and evaluate the ground, in such a way that they afterwards dare to swear that it is worth (the stated amount).

39.5 And that amount shall be divided in three. The bishop takes a third; the king another; the farmers a third.

39.6 And if the man who owns the church is poor, then the ground shall provide resources for the church (building). Next, it shall provide for the fence. And once that is done, then the ground shall provide for consecration. And then he (the owner) shall take the ground himself.

39.7 And if a man sells his church ground (for whatever it is worth), but keeps the church himself, and it falls down, then his (remaining) ground shall bear exactly as much responsibility[325] (for providing resources for the church), as that he sold.[326]

39.8 And if the man who should maintain the church is poor, then the church falls to the one who lives there, (on the ground) where the church stands.

321 *at sækt.*
322 *þriðiungs menn.*
323 *høgendes kirkiur.*
324 *fe allu lasta lausu.*
325 *abyrgð.*
326 The equivalent rule in the short version of this law in AM 58 4° reads 'And if a man sells his church ground (for whatever it is worth), but keeps the church himself, to rebuild if it falls down, then he shall pledge as much land as he sold (for this)'.

Chapter forty

40.1 For the consecration of a *hǫfuðkirkja*, the bishop shall have fifteen men and fifteen horses with him in summer, and hospitality (procuration)[327] for two days. And in winter, eight horses.

40.2 And for a proprietary church,[328] the bishop should have three marks – one ounce equalling nine ells – if he consecrates both church and churchyard.

Chapter forty-one

41.1 The bishop's *ármaðr*: he may not accuse a person of witchcraft[329] – neither man nor woman – unless this is rumoured throughout the *herað*.[330] Three farmers – or more than three – shall declare this, bearing witness that it is rumoured throughout the district.[331]

42. And if he makes this accusation, but it has not been rumoured throughout the *herað*, then he shall pay three marks for that.

42.1 This accusation may be made (by the bishop's *ármaðr*) even if it has not been rumoured throughout the *herað*, if he (the accused) confesses (to witchcraft) by himself or by his wife, or if he confesses (to witchcraft) by his children or his animals, whether he accuses a man or a woman.

Chapter forty-two

42.1 Any legal case he (the bishop's *ármaðr*) wishes to raise shall be raised at home, in the house (of the accused).

42.2 Then he (the accused) shall say what he wants: whether he wishes to undergo judgement by God (ordeal) or by men.[332] He shall not have recourse to judgement by men if he first asks for judgement by God (ordeal). (If he asks for judgement by men)[333] then he shall not have recourse to judgement by God (ordeal). He shall have whichever he asks for first.

42.3 And, whether man or woman, then (the accused) shall have the witness of twelve people from the three *heruð* in which (the accused) has lived longest, to refute the accusation.[334] (The accused) shall have whichever he can get more of (for this): men or women. But if the oaths fail, then he shall have judgement by God (ordeal). And if he fails at both (sorts of trial), then he is an outlaw and unholy, along with all his property.

327 *uæizslu.*
328 *høgendes kirkiu.*
329 *fordæðo skap.*
330 *heraz fløyt.*
331 *bygð fløyt.*
332 *Guðs skirslir eða manna.*
333 The first part of this sentence has been added later.
334 *førazst undan þui male.*

42.4 A man shall go to (trial by) hearth-iron,[335] and a woman to (trial by) cauldron-taking.[336]

Chapter forty-three

43.1 (As for) a priest who delivers the blessing for a judgement by God (ordeal):[337] he shall have six marks in ounces – one ounce equalling six ells. Both shall lay down pledges:[338] the one who goes to oath, and the one who raises the case.

43.2 If (the accused) is cleared, then the one who has raised the case[339] shall pay.

43.3 If (the accused) is found guilty,[340] then the one who held the iron (the accused) shall pay.

43.4 (A man) shall have a fifteen-day period of grace[341] following judgement by God (ordeal) and following oaths.

Chapter forty-four

And when it comes to outlawed property, then the one who has raised the case[342] takes a third of that which has been outlawed. But the two parts which remain shall be divided in three. The king takes a third, the bishop another, and the lawmen[343] the third (third).

Chapter forty-five

45.1 No man should believe in Sámi (magicians) or sorcerers,[344] or in magical figures, or offerings, or roots,[345] or anything which has to do with heathen practices,[346] or seek help from these.

45.2 And if a man goes to seek Sámi (magicians), and he is found guilty of that, then he is an outlaw, and an *úbótamaðr*, and he has forfeited all his property, and it shall be divided into three parts. The king shall take a third, the bishop another, the farmers, the third (third).

335 *arens iarns.*
336 *ketills taks.*
337 *vigir Guðs skirslir.*
338 *uæl læggia.*
339 *þa* [. . .] er *til før er.*
340 *full.*
341 *.xv. natta grið.*
342 *sakar abere.*
343 *logmenn.*
344 *finna. eða fordæðor.*
345 *vit. eða blot. eða rot.*
346 *hæiðins siðar.*

45.3 And if a case is raised against such a one, and he denies (the charge), then he should clear himself with an oath sworn by six men who were born in the *herað* in which he is located. And if he does not bring forward any witnesses, then he shall be given the right to trial by hot iron. And if he fails in the trial by hot iron, then he is an outlaw and an *úbótamaðr*, as was explained before.

45.4 (As for) any woman who has magical remedies[347] and claims she can heal men: if she is found guilty of this, then she owes three marks, if she has that much.

45.5 And if she does not have enough for that, then anyone who wishes should make use of (what she does have). And if no one wishes to make use of it, then she should go into outlawry.

45.6 If she denies (the accusation), she should take a *lýrittr*-oath.[348] And if the oath fails for her, then she must pay three marks in six ounces – one ounce equalling six ells.

Chapter forty-six

46.1 If a woman is accused of witch-riding a man, or his servants:[349] if she is found guilty of that, then she owes three marks.

46.2 If she denies it, then she shall take a six-man oath.[350] But if the oath fails her, then she must pay three marks in six-ell ounces. And if she does not have enough for that, then she should go into outlawry.

Chapter forty-seven

47.1 And if a man is on his sickbed in the *herað*, and he wants a priest to deliver readings over him, he should send a horse for him, or a ship, if necessary.

47.2 Then the priest is obliged to go to him, and deliver three readings[351] over him, without payment.[352]

47.3 If he wants more readings, then a penny worth one thirtieth of an ounce shall (be paid) for each, until nine have been read. If he wants more to be read, then that shall be negotiated with the priest.

47.4 Now, if he wishes to have the Eucharist or confession administered,[353] then he should have a horse sent to the priest. Then he (the priest) should go (to him), whether it is day or night.

347 *Kona huær er fœr mæð lif.*

348 *lyrittar æið.*

349 *(E)f þat er kænnt kono. at hon riði manne. eða þionom hans.* The initial E- is not present in AM 68 4°. AM 58 4°: 'If a woman is accused of witch-riding a man or his wife, or his servants (*hionom*) . . . '.

350 *setar æið.*

351 *lester.*

352 *kaupa laust.*

353 *lata husla sik. eða scrifta.*

47.5 And if he wants to receive the Sacrament of the Anointing of the Sick (extreme unction),[354] then he (the priest) shall administer it. He should have with him a priest or deacon.[355] For that, he shall have two ounces – one ounce equalling twelve ells.

47.6 Now, if he dies of this (illness), then a message shall be sent to the main priest,[356] and a horse shall be sent for him, if he does not own one. If he does own one, he shall use that, and tie it up in the stall where the farmer's horse stood, and give it hay – the best on the farm. (It shall be) tethered (outside), if this happens in summer.

47.7 And if there is need (for a priest) in several places (at once), then he should go to three (of these), and in the last place to which he comes, he should remain for the night watch, and perform post-mortem rites over the body,[357] and go with it to the burial place. In the morning, (he shall) receive all the corpses there, and then perform Soul Mass[358] for all their souls, and bless the graves, and perform post-mortem rites[359] over their bodies. Then he has a right to[360] *legkaup* for all (of them).

Chapter forty-eight

48.1 Twelve ells are the *legkaup* for a *lendr maðr* or his wife, nine ells for his son or daughter up to the age of forty. After that, twelve[361] ells is the *legkaup*.

48.2 So too for the *hǫldr*.[362]

48.3 If he is the son of a fully freed slave,[363] then four ells is the *legkaup*.

48.4 And three ells for freed slaves.

48.5 An unfree man:[364] one weighed penny.

48.6 For a bondsman,[365] another (weighed penny).

48.7 For every person who is three winters (years) old, or is older than three winters, there is a full *legkaup*. But for anyone who is younger, it is one weighed penny.

354 *lata olia sik.*

355 *diakn.*

356 *houuð preste.*

357 *siti þar at natsetre* [. . .] *syngia þar iuir liki.*

358 *syngia* [. . .] *salo messo.*

359 *uigi grof oc syngi iuir liki þæira.*

360 *oðlaz.*

361 Short version in AM 58 4°: seven ells.

362 *haullz manne*. Short version in AM 58 4°: 'from a *hǫldr* (*hauldbornom manne*) and his wife and children'.

363 *løysingia.*

364 *Ufrialsan.*

365 *anauðgan*. On this term, see S. Brink, *Vikingarnas slavar: Den nordiska träldomen under yngre järnålder och äldsta medeltid* Stockholm: Atlantis, 2012), p. 125.

48.8 A pledge[366] of double the value of the *legkaup* shall be given to the priest, and the full amount shall have been paid by the seventh (day), or the pledge is forfeit.[367] The priest shall collect what is due to him nevertheless.

48.9 But any man who has paid his field tithe, and his main tithe,[368] need not[369] pay the *legkaup*.

48.10 And if a message comes to a priest, summoning him to go to a place where a body is lying inside, and he will not go to it, and there are no adverse circumstances preventing him from going, then he is no longer entitled to the *legkaup* which he should have had there. The priest who undertakes that work should take it (the *legkaup*).

48.11 These are adverse circumstances: if he (the priest who should attend) lies sick, or wounded. Then he shall have half (the *legkaup*), and half (shall go to the priest) who does the work.

48.12 And if a man leaves the district, or his third, and dies in another third, then the one who performs funeral rites over his body and blesses the grave shall have (half) the *legkaup*, and the other one, who blesses his food and ale in his place of origin, shall have half.[370]

Chapter forty-nine

49.1 Now a priest shall be invited to the inheritance feast[371] with his wife, along with a man. He shall sit at the high seat, with his wife beside him.

49.2 And if there are three inheritance feasts (happening) at the same time in his parish,[372] then he shall go to all three places, and bless the food and ale,[373] and remain with the ale which he prefers, unless there is a great distance between them, or adverse circumstances prevent him from going to all those places.

Chapter fifty

50.1 A *lendr maðr* shall be buried next to the church, along with the children of *lendir menn*, and the wife of a *lendr maðr*.[374]

50.2 Next (in proximity to the church), *hǫldar*[375] and their wives and children.

366 *Væð*.

367 *foruæðia*.

368 *akr tiunnd sina. oc houuð tiunnd*.

369 In common with the scribe of AM 58 4°, we have added 'not' to make sense of this rule.

370 Short version in AM 58 4°: 'and his parish priest shall have half, and he shall bless the food and ale at his inheritance feast'.

371 *ærfis*.

372 *sokn*.

373 *vigi mat oc mungat*.

374 *lænnz mannz kono*.

375 *hauldamenn*.

50.3 Then fully freed slaves[376] shall be buried (next in proximity to the church).

50.4 Then freed slaves[377] and their children shall be buried next (in proximity to the church).

50.5 And nearest to the church fence, slaves and slave-women shall be buried.[378]

50.6 Men shall lie to the south of the church, and women to the north.

50.7 Men shall dig graves in such a way that they do not dig any other (bodies) up, whilst the limbs cleave together, and the flesh and hair remain in place.[379] And if (such a body) is dug up, then six ounces lie at stake.

50.8 And (a man) shall dig in such a way that there is a whole ell of earth above the coffin (after the burial). And if anyone digs a shorter distance down, then six ounces lie at stake.

50.9 And no one should dig in anyone else's burial-place, unless he wants to be liable to pay a legal fine[380] to the heirs of the deceased.

50.10 And if a man takes another man's bone and throws it out of the churchyard, then he owes six ounces to the bishop.

50.11 Then all those who are entitled to this shall be buried in the churchyard, and all those who are not *úbótamenn*.

50.12 (As to) a man who harms[381] himself and repents of his deed, and this is witnessed,[382] and he goes to confession: then he is buried in the churchyard, if he dies of this wound.

50.13 But if he wounds himself wittingly and does not repent, then he is not buried in the churchyard. And not peace-breakers, robbers, lord-cheaters, murder-wolves, arson-wolves, a convicted thief, assassins, men who plunder openly, and banned men,[383] and those who die whilst under ban[384] by the Holy Church, and those who kill themselves. Also those who speak and promote wrongful beliefs to men. Also open usurers,[385] and those men (adults) or children who are not baptized before death.

50.14 And these men shall be buried at the high tide mark,[386] for they are all *úbótamenn*, and they should not be buried in the churchyard.

50.15 And if he (such a one) is buried (in the churchyard), then he has been wrongfully buried, and he shall be dug up, and taken from the churchyard, and three marks shall lie at stake. That belongs to the bishop.

376 *løysingia.*

377 *frialsgiafa.*

378 *manna mann. oc ambottor.*

379 *Meðan liðum loðer saman. oc fylgir holld eða har.*

380 *sæckiaz at laga rette.*

381 Editorial emendation by Halvorsen & Rindal 2008: *sæter* < *særer.*

382 *uitnis sat.*

383 *griðniðingar trygrofar. Drottens suikarar. morð uargar. Brænno uargar. Þioft dømdr. flugu menn. Openberer rans menn. oc bandsættir menn.*

384 *i forboðom.*

385 *okr karlar.*

386 *i flodar male.*

Chapter fifty-one

51.1 No one shall keep a dead man inside beyond the fifth day (after the death), except in the event of adverse circumstances: impassable ice or heavy snow.

51.2 Then (in either of these circumstances), the body shall be taken into an outhouse, and covered with sedge or straw,[387] or hung up in the outhouse, up in the rafters. And it should be taken away as soon as this is possible.

51.3 And if anyone should keep it inside beyond the fifth day, despite an absence of any adverse circumstances, then three marks for the bishop lie at stake.

Chapter fifty-two: on incest[388]

52.1 There are seventeen women due to whom a man becomes an *úbótamaðr*, if he lies with any of them, or takes her as his wife.[389] One is his mother, another is his daughter, third is his sister, fourth is his son's daughter, fifth is his daughter's daughter, sixth is his brother's daughter, seventh is his sister's daughter, eighth is his stepmother, nine is his son's wife, ten is his brother's wife, eleven is his stepdaughter, twelve is his wife's mother, thirteen is his wife's sister, fourteen is his father's mother,[390] fifteen is his mother's sister, sixteen is his father's mother, seventeen is his mother's mother.

52.2 Any man who lies with any one of these has forfeited property and peace, land and chattels.[391] He should travel to heathen land,[392] and should never enter the presence of Christian men.

Chapter fifty-three: on spiritual kin[393]

53.1 Now this is the next matter: that no man may have sexual intercourse[394] with his spiritual kin.

53.2 And there are three kinds of spiritual kinship. The first is between a child who is baptized, and the one who baptizes it, or holds it for baptism.

53.3 There is a second kind of spiritual kinship between the one who baptized a child, and those who held the child (for baptism), and the parents[395] of the child.

387 *starru. eða stræ.*
388 *frenzæmis spiall.*
389 *fær fange.*
390 Later correction: *systir.*
391 *firigort fe oc friði lannde oc lausum øyri.*
392 *lannd hæiðit.*
393 *guðciuia.*
394 *hafa at likams losta.*
395 *fæðgina.*

53.4 The third is between a child who is baptized and the natural child[396] of the one who baptized it or held it in baptism. And so priests have spiritual kinship with the parents of all of them (the children they have baptized), and the child of a priest may not have sexual intercourse with any of those whom the priest has baptized.

53.5 If a man holds someone else's child for baptism, then the father and mother of the child, and also the child, have spiritual kinship with the wife of the man who held the child during baptism, even if she (herself) did not hold the child when it was baptized.

53.6 If a man has sexual intercourse with any of his spiritual kin, then they shall separate, and go to confession, and each of them shall pay three marks to the bishop.

396 *kiotlegs barns.*

Part VI Notes on the text

Chapter one: here it is said that every child shall be baptized

1.1–1.3

'Now, this is next' indicates that another section has preceded the Christian Law, unlike in the *Borgarthing Law*, where the initial statement ('This is first in our law') makes clear that the Christian Law was placed first. The *Eidsivathing Law* nevertheless contains some kind of preface in line with the other Scandinavian provincial laws. According to Pernler, the prefaces of the provincial laws usually comprise of liturgical or theological elements, and should not be regarded as integral parts of the legal texts themselves (Pernler 1984: 81). The preface of the *Eidsivathing Law* consists of a short statement, with a profession of Christianity and a rejection of heathendom, reminiscent of the introduction found in the Swedish *Guta Law* (Pernler 1984: 68). The initial statement is followed by two paragraphs (1.2–1.3) which sum up the content of the first eight chapters of the *Eidsivathing Law* in a few sentences. The two paragraphs mention topics like birth, deformity, baptism, and spiritual kinship, which are outlined in more detail in chapters two to eight. The structure and content thus correspond to the first four paragraphs in the *Borgarthing Law*, and indicate a common core.

Chapter two: on lay baptism

2.1–2.2

Chapter two deals with emergency baptism performed by lay people, and the ritual differs from the one prescribed in the *Borgarthing Law* in several respects (Landro 2010: 32–33). While the rite in the *Eidsivathing Law* prescribes that the sign of cross should be made 'in every place where chrism should be put', the *Borgarthing Law* prescribes use of spittle. The consecration ceremony of the water is also absent in the *Borgarthing Law*. The two emergency rites thus seem to originate in two different redactions. (See the commentary on Borg. 2.2–2.4.)

Chapter three: on a woman's labour

3.1–3.3

The chapter deals with the circumstances around birth and of stillbirth and reveals the contrast between the new and the old procedural approaches. (See the commentary on Borg. 3.2–3.3). While the equivalent paragraph in the *Borgarthing Law* focuses on the evidence and the woman's motive and state of mind, the case in the *Eidsivathing Law* should be solved with oath-taking or trial by hot iron, in accordance with the traditional procedural system (Landro 2010: 169–170; Pennington 1993: 135).

Chapter four: on baptism by a couple

Participation in a baptismal ritual created a spiritual kinship, which forced the couple to abstain from sexual relations. (See the commentary on Borg. 2.1.)

Chapter five: on deformity

Chapter six: on monstrous form

Chapters five and six are obviously related to the equivalent ones in the *Borgarthing Law* (Borg. 1) and the *Gulathing Law* (Gul. 21), and indicate either a common core of original paragraphs or a later exchange of regulations. But while the backwards descriptions in the *Borgarthing Law* are linked directly to the Evil One, this perspective is not directly articulated in the chapter in the *Eidsivathing Law*, which only mentions the children's ungodly shapes. The conclusion is also different and more lenient. The children in the *Eidsivathing Law* and the *Gulathing Law* are allowed to be baptized as long as they have human heads and voices, despite their ungodly shapes. Helle takes this as a step towards total prohibition of child exposure (Helle 2001: 190). (See the commentary on Borg. 1.2–1.3 for a different interpretation.)

Chapter seven: on the labour of a bondwoman

This chapter presents no translation problems and needs no commentary.

Chapter eight: on baptism of children

While the baptismal terms in the *Borgarthing Law* seem to follow the four *gagnfǫstur* (see the commentary on Borg. 4.1–4.2), the *Eidsivathing Law* prescribes an arrangement where the year is split up into more than four termini. The *Eidsivathing Law* is also the only one of the Norwegian Christian laws which has introduced Pentecost among the baptismal termini, which together with Easter, was the preferred baptismal terminus in the medieval Church (Fisher 1965: 3;

Nilsson, Bertil 2012: 138–141). Another characteristic trait is the five eves when baptism should take place, which were probably fasting eves. According to *Grágás*, Bishop Magnús Gissurson (1216–1236) introduced eight additional fasting eves: among others, Christmas Eve, Easter Eve, and the eve before Pentecost (*Grágás* (Finsen), 1870: 35, § 18; Landro 2010: 78). The arrangement in the *Eidsivathing Law* thus confirms the assumption that the Norwegian baptismal termini are linked to the fasting periods, and that a child born before or during a fast should be baptized before the expiration of that particular fasting period. (See the commentary on Borg. 4.1–4.2.)

Chapter nine: on holy days

9.1

The list of holy days in the *Eidsivathing Law* contains the traditional holy days established before the Carolingian period plus three more. (See the commentary on Borg. 14.) In Norway, one of these is only found in this law and in the *Gulathing Law* (Gul. 17), and honoured St Thomas Becket, archbishop of Canterbury (1162–1170). His cult had spread rapidly over northern Europe after he was murdered in his own cathedral on the 29th December 1170 (Duggan 1982: 21–44).

9.2

Magnus messo um uaret ('The Feast of St Magnús in the spring'): this refers to the patron saint of Orkney. His cousin, Híkon, had had Magnús killed on the 16th April 1115, during conflict over the earldom. Magnús was canonized in 1135, and his relics were eventually taken to the cathedral in Kirkwall, which was dedicated to him. The description 'in the spring' was probably included because the translation day of Magnús (13th December), when his earthly remains were removed from his grave and placed in a shrine, was also celebrated as a holy day. However, this was not explicitly mentioned in the *Eidsivathing Law* or any of the other Norwegian laws (Lárusson 1966; Antonsson 2007: 69–79).

Chapter ten: on cross carving

10.1

The term *hǫfuðkirkja* in the *Eidsivathing Law* refers to the main church in a third (*þriðjungr*) of a *fylki*. This division of the fylke into thirds is a peculiarity of the Eidsivathing legal district. It is thought that, originally, the legal district had three *fylki*, so the total number of *hǫfuðkirkjur* there was nine. It has not been possible to pinpoint where the *hǫfuðkirkjur* were located. In several places in the law, it is clear that the priest of a *hǫfuðkirkja* had some kind of superior status, which meant that he would announce the arrival of the king, for example (Smedberg 1973: 37–40). Similarly, the priest of a *hǫfuðkirkja* also had responsibility for ensuring that mass days (days other than Sundays on which High Mass was performed) were correctly proclaimed; he was to be punished if they were not. Proclamation of such days involved the carving of crosses carrying the relevant information. The custom of using such cross-shaped tokens is thought to have been borrowed from areas in which Celtic languages were spoken, and was common in Orkney, Shetland, and the Faroe Islands (Grieg 1957: 340). (On ember days, see the commentary on Borg. 13.1.)

10.2–10.6

Given that one of the bishop's responsibilities was to attend the provincial assembly (the Eidsivathing assembly), and that he had certain duties to perform there, it is reasonable to assume that the relevant bishop was present at each of the other provincial assemblies. At these, too, clerics came to 'meet the bishop' (*mote biscupi*). It is known that in Sweden, a 'meeting of priests' or 'diocese synod' or 'bishop's synod' took place in summer, at the close of the provincial assembly (Kroon 1948: 81–94). Such a meeting with priests was a chance for a bishop to ensure that priests both could and did perform their official duties concerning church services, provision of information, and education for their parishioners. (See also the commentary on Borg. 12.20–12.21.)

Chapter eleven: on failure in the passing of a (summons baton) cross

11.1–11.6

This whole chapter shows the great significance which was attached to respecting the sanctity of various types of holy day in addition to Sundays. Parishioners should not run the risk of eating the wrong food on a particular day, nor allow themselves to be involved in work on a day when this was forbidden. This type of rule was not new by the time of the creation of the *Eidsivathing Law*, but rather had a history stretching back to the very origins of the Church (Hall & Crehan 1983: 48–55).

11.1

lyrittar œið (from *lýrittareiðr* 'lýrittr-oath'): An oath of denial which was made with two compurgators and was thus a three-man oath (von See 1964: 57–63).

Chapter twelve: on the holy period of Sunday

12.1

none (from *nón* 'nones') (*hora nona*): the ninth hour, which began at 3pm, so that the Sunday holy period thus lasted for more than thirty-six hours, until daylight on

Monday. The duration of the holy period therefore varied significantly, depending on the time of year. *dagr er af himni* ('daylight is in the sky'): this expression is not thought to have been especially common in legal language, and otherwise appears only in the *Younger Borgarthing Law* (NBorg. 9). It adds an almost poetic dimension to the legal language here.

12.2–12.7

See the commentary on Borg. 14.6–14.16.

12.3

biscups armanne (from *biskups ármaðr*): see the commentary on Borg. 11.2.

Chapter thirteen: on men's traps

13.1–13.3

The regulations on what was permitted (or not permitted) during the Sunday holy period continue, here with respect to matters other than work in the fields or woods. Some actions relating to the acquisition of food were permitted. At the same time, there were certain limitations, which meant that one could not involve oneself in such activities as on an ordinary day. This may be a case of the inclusion of artificial rules which were never meant to be put into practice (Landro 2010: 200–202).

Chapter fourteen: on guests

Here, too, the point is that certain activities were permitted when it came to receiving guests – but only with limitations. Judging by the way in which this has been formulated, such hospitality could be offered on the condition that the householder himself did not eat whatever had been baked (which was for the guests alone) or carry out the butchery in such a way that the meat was preserved for future use.

Chapter fifteen: on isolated land

15.1–15.2

stoklond (*stokkland* 'isolated land'): a cleared plot in common woodland. The word appears only in the *Eidsivathing Law*, and nowhere else in either the oldest Norwegian laws or legislation more generally. It has been assumed that such an area was so named because it still contained large stumps from previously chopped trees (NgL V: 610 s.v. *stokkland*). No messenger therefore had any responsibility to go to such a place.

Chapter sixteen: on holy periods

16.1–16.6

The rules on travel in relation to Sundays and holy days contain no difficulties of interpretation.

Chapter seventeen: work which may be done during a holy period

17.1–17.3

The structure of this chapter appears peculiar, since 17.2–17.3 bear no relation whatsoever to the rubric. This shows that content relating to two very different topics has been blended into this single paragraph, making this a good example of the unsystematic nature of the *Eidsivathing Law*, compared to the *Borgarthing Law*. The content in 17.1, 19, and 26 is certainly related, but has been spread throughout various paragraphs, and bears witness to the same lack of systematization.

17.2

af lannde þui. er lit er kristit ('a little-converted area'): Precisely what was meant by this expression at the time of writing of this law is impossible to determine. It is certainly not impossible to imagine that particular areas in Norway were still perceived as having been less fully Christianized than others. In addition, there is a narrative in *Sverris saga* (from the very beginning of the thirteenth century) in which his travels of 1177 are described. According to this, he travelled through an area in the western and innermost parts of Dalarna in Sweden, which was then still regarded as heathen (see Lönnroth 1996: 155–156).

The demand that a person should know the name of the priest who christened him might appear unreasonably harsh. Certainly, someone who had been christened might conceivably remember this after adult baptism in a 'little-converted area' but, on the other hand, a godmother and godfather (godparents) are mentioned, and this applied when the person being christened was in infancy. We do not know how the name of the priest or the godparents would have been conveyed to the person who had been christened in the case of an infant who grew up. This must have varied according to circumstances. In a small community with low mobility this can hardly have been much of a problem. We lack adequate source material to determine how and when the practice of child baptism was introduced in connection with the Christianization process. It is possible that there was some variation in the number of godparents, and whether they were men or women. For example, a boy could (or should) have two men and one woman as godparents. It seems that the most usual number of godparents in Scandinavian areas was two (a man and a woman), as described here in the *Eidsivathing Law* (see Kilström 1958: 55–78).

17.3

fimt ('a five-day time limit'): the time limit found most commonly in the laws. This term appears in several of the oldest Norwegian laws, and could also be used to denote the meeting which would happen on the fifth day, when the five-day time limit would conclude with some form of gathering, called a *fimtarstefna*, (NgL V: 188–189).

Chapter eighteen: on holy days

18.1

From the regulations in the Norwegian laws, it appears that a burial usually took place the day after the death. This would apparently have varied somewhat, however, depending upon the time of day when the death happened. (See Nilsson, Bertil 1987: 136–137; see what follows, the commentary on 51.1–15.3.) Apart from Christmas Day, which was a feast day of the highest possible rank in the Church calendar, there were three further days when the ban on burial applied, due to the so-called *triduum sacrum*. This period, which was dedicated to the memory of the time during which Christ lay in the tomb, was characterized by deep seriousness and was viewed as a period of mourning, lasting from nones on the afternoon of the day before Easter Sunday (Björkman 1957: 198–332). Similarly, the celebratory theme of Easter Sunday could prevent burial from being carried out. However, there appears to be some variation within the oldest Norwegian laws (as there is within the younger laws and regulations in younger ecclesiastical statutes) which cannot be fully explained (Nilsson, Bertil 1989: 294–296).

Chapter nineteen

Clearly, people knew that deaths amongst livestock required immediate action; therefore, Sabbath regulations did not apply under such circumstances. Since the animal described here was butchered and used for food, this regulation cannot have been about animals which had died of illness. (See the commentary on Borg. 5.) Perhaps it applied to animals which had died after accidents or attacks by wild beasts.

Chapter twenty

20.1–20.6

The structure of this chapter is somewhat unnatural. While 20.1–20.5 concerns laundry and cloth, 20.6 belongs with the regulations in chapter twenty-one on sexual intercourse.

20.6

This rule is clear as regards the nights during which intercourse was forbidden. By contrast, it is unclear as to who should pay any fine. While the woman was given the responsibility in AM 68 4to, the man is fined in NB 317 4o. The paragraph should probably be read in light of paragraphs 21.3 and 21.5, which deal with similar cases. In these cases, which also concern intercourse at certain forbidden times, the man was fined. The Norwegian provincial laws reveal some gender differences when it comes to penalties for the same offence, but the *Gulathing Law* places responsibility with the man in cases of offences such as incest and bigamy (Helle 2001: 144).

The legislator has here proceeded on the assumption that intercourse took place during the night. This must be understood in the context of canon law, which made intercourse during daylight a sin (see figure 4.1 in Brundage 1987: 162), following regulations in the Pentateuch (the first five Books of the Old Testament).

Chapter twenty-one

21.1–21.5

Further periods during which intercourse was forbidden are specified here, in addition to the nights and times mentioned in 20.6. A comparison of the periods and particular times with intercourse bans indicates that the number of such twenty-four-hour periods must have been close to three hundred. The most important penitentials (penance handbooks which priests used to determine the nature of particular sins and which forms of penance penitents were to be allotted) only permitted married couples to have intercourse a few times a year, if they wished to avoid sinning (Brundage 1987: 154–164 with figure 4.1, p. 162). In this chapter, there is nothing to suggest that it was the woman in a sinning couple who had to pay a fine (as in 20.6); who was meant is specified in 21.4 and 21.5.

Chapter twenty-two

The question of what was necessary to make entry into and exit from a marriage legitimate took up significant space in medieval Church legislation and theology, with clear points of conflict between various Church authorities (see Christensen-Nugues 2003: 158–194; Korpiola 2004: 56–98). During the eleventh and twelfth centuries, especially, different opinions clashed. In certain respects, this is reflected in the rules found in this chapter of the *Eidsivathing Law*.

22.1

at Guðs lagum rettom ('according to God's rightful law'): this expression refers to canon law. One of the manuscripts of the *Eidsivathing Law* (NB 317 4o) points instead towards the provincial law: *at rettom landzlagum*. This difference probably reflects the tension which existed between the desire of the Church to subsume marriage law under its own jurisdiction and an alternative view of marriage law as a wholly civil matter.

Whether the consent (*consensus*) of both parties was enough to make a marriage valid was a question discussed energetically by theologians and canon lawyers during the twelfth century. Some maintained that, in addition to giving consent, the couple had to enter into union through sexual intercourse, in accordance with a view of marriage as a sacrament. During the latter half of the twelfth century, the consent theory was firmly established by Pope Alexander III (1159–1181), and was further strengthened by later popes (Plöchl 1962: 331; Christensen-Nugues 2003: 135–139, 158–165; Korpiola 2004: 88–96).

The fact that the wishes of relatives could also be involved reflected older conceptions of marriage which remained in place in canonical doctrine until the second half of the twelfth century. After that point, the demand for consent came to apply to the couple alone. According to this thinking, family members and other relatives would no longer play any part when it came to the legitimacy of a marriage (Christensen-Nugues 2003: 177–182; Korpiola 2004: 70–77). Here, the *Eidsivathing Law* is still based on an older view of marriage law.

In principle, separation was not permitted by canon law. By contrast, it is thought that, in pre-Christian times, separation had been legally possible in Scandinavian areas (although no relevant contemporary legal sources have survived to prove this). It seems that, in pre-Christian society, people were not forced to give grounds for separation (Skånland 1970: 505–506). This is probably what lies behind the formulation 'even if they change their minds'. In other words, at some earlier point, a change of mind when it came to living together as a married couple had previously probably been enough to end a marriage. More indirectly, one might also draw the conclusion that either a man or a woman, acting alone, could ask to end a marriage, since the law says, 'neither man nor woman shall separate them'. Once the Church was fully established, this possibility no longer existed. (On divorce, see Brundage 1987: 199–203, 370–376.)

22.2

The statement that the male partner (or both, according to a younger addition) could announce a separation is no more in line with canon law than other material here. Canon law stated that 'separation' was only permitted if it could be confirmed that the marriage had been entered into in an uncanonical fashion in the first place: in other words, that it had never been a true marriage in the eyes of the Church. The legal terminology relevant to the determination of invalid marriage had not been clarified by canon lawyers by the time of writing of the *Eidsivathing Law*. (See Plöchl 1962: 330–336; Christensen-Nugues 2003: 165–177.)

Neither partner had the right to marry again, which was a consequence of the fact that marriage was seen as indissoluble. What was meant by 'the law of man' in this case is not clear, and probably cannot be established more precisely.

22.3

This paragraph likewise reflects a situation in which the ideals of canon law had not entirely been translated into practice. Here, the law was based on an assumption that a person might remarry – despite the fact that this was forbidden by the

Church – while the partner from the previous marriage (which would not have been considered dissolved by the Church) was still alive.

22.4

Exactly what was meant by the suggestion that one of the partners 'caused' the separation is difficult to say. No clues are to be found in any of the older Norwegian laws. However, according to certain canon lawyers writing around this time, separation was permitted in a case of unconsummated marriage: for example, if one of the partners had made an oath of chastity, or entered a cloister, or could not consummate the marriage sexually due to physical difficulties. In fact, twelfth-century canon lawyers suggested several additional reasons why separation might be permissible, but no consensus had been reached by this point (see Plöchl 1962: 331–332; Christensen-Nugues 2003: 165–177).

The stipulation that a fine should be paid, and that the money should go to the bishop reflects a process which continued throughout the whole of the Middle Ages, as the Church sought to subsume marriage under its own jurisdiction entirely, so that all matters relating to marriage should be viewed as Church affairs.

22.5

On hindrances to marriage, see the commentary on Borg. 15.

22.6

Corresponding rules stating that a suitor should approach the relatives of the woman he wished to marry are found in various West Swedish laws: namely, the *Older* and *Younger Law of Västergötland* (Gb 2) and the *Dala Law* (Gb 1). The basis for this legislation was the principle that the so-called 'marriage man' was the woman's guardian, since she did not have full legal authority of her own. Usually, the 'marriage man' was her father. According to some Swedish laws, even women could be 'marriage men' despite the fact that they did not have full legal authority. This was the case if the father of the bride-to-be had died. Then, it was the mother – or possibly one of her brothers – who acted in his place (Carlsson 1965: 51–59; Frimannslund 1959: 233–236; Korpiola 2004: 9–17). The bride-to-be herself came in second place when it came to choosing her partner, despite the fact that she had to be asked and could say no – as can be seen here and in 22.7–8. In some places, the wording in this paragraph corresponds with the legislation of Classical Roman law (see the quotation by Christensen-Nugues 2003: 140–141), but canonists worked against this to promote an understanding that it was the consent of the couple-to-be which was the sole true foundation for marriage (Christensen-Nugues 2003: 177–182).

22.7

No more detailed rules concerning the so-called 'betrothal meeting' are found anywhere in the oldest Norwegian laws. Detailed regulations appear first in younger legislation (Carlsson 1965: 59–63; Frimannslund 1959: 233–236; Korpiola 2004: 17–24). Here in the *Eidsivathing Law* 22.7 (in contrast to 22.2), it is explicitly stated that a married couple can only be separated by death. The Church view that marriage was lifelong was based on the writings of the evangelists and the teachings of Jesus (Matt. 19:6; Mark. 10:6–12). However, there is a passage which came to be known as the 'Matthew exception' (Matt.19:9), which became the origin of various interpretations that survived into the Middle Ages. This exception meant that a man had the right to separate from his wife if she had committed adultery. This exception was removed from canon law in the middle of the twelfth century. This ended the only type of gender-differentiated marriage legislation in canon law. (See Christensen-Nugues 2003: 173–177; Brundage 1987: 58, 199–203, 294–295.)

22.8

Even though a woman did not have full legal authority, her status was not reduced to nothing. She had a legal right to refuse to enter into a marriage. By contrast to older law in northern Europe, canon law underlined the absolute freedom of the spouse-to-be to enter into (or refuse) a marriage (Christensen-Nugues 2003: 139–145).

Chapter twenty-three

23.1–23.2

In canon law, rules had been developed to prevent force from causing people to enter into marriage. This was closely related to the demand for consent to marriage, and regulation of the ways in which such consent was uttered or announced. Pope Alexander III established a rule which meant that consent could be declared invalid if it had been uttered in fear, or under threat, or by compulsion. In practice, however, it must have been difficult to determine whether or not this had been the case (see Christensen-Nugues 2003: 182–186).

Chapter twenty-four

Prohibitions against heathen practice were high priorities for the Church (Helle 2001: 183). The term *blót* could refer both to the ritual of sacrificing to heathen gods and to the sacrificed object itself (NgL V: 104 s.v. *blót*).

Chapter twenty-five

The general practice was that the bishop received fines of up to three marks for violations of the Christian regulations. Heavier fines had to be split. The *Eidsivathing Law* perhaps reveals the oldest arrangement, in which the property of a person who had been outlawed was to be split equally between the bishop, the king, and the farmers involved in the judgement. (See also 8.3.) In the *Borgarthing Law* the bishop received only three marks, and the king the remaining part of the property (see Borg. 11.2). In the *Gulathing Law* the property was split equally between the bishop and the king – an arrangement which prevailed in the later Christian laws from the thirteenth century (Helle 2001: 197).

Chapter twenty-six

Chapter twenty-six contains the same two canon law traditions as Borg. 5, and likewise consists of two different strata. Paragraph 26.1 introduces the tradition originating in East-Francia. (See the commentary on Borg. 5.1–5–12.)

suida (*svidda*): The Old Norse term *svidda* has caused much confusion for historians and philologists. In dictionaries and translations of the laws, *svidda* is translated as 'self-dead' (Landro 2010: 95). This translation is quite logical and probably in line with the etymological meaning of the word. As de Vries explains, the prefix *svi-* means 'by oneself': that is, 'dead due to oneself'. In addition, the different manuscripts of the laws switch between *suida, suiddauð*, and *sialf daudar* (NKS 1642 4to, § 5.9, Halvorsen & Rindal 2008: 164), which makes 'self-dead' a reasonable translation. Taranger also claimed that the term *svidda* corresponded to the Latin term *morticinus*, which is normally translated as 'self-dead' (Johanssen et al. 2002: 412 s.v. *morticinus*). What has eluded philologists and legal historians, though, is the fact that the term *svidda* has taken on various connotations, and illustrates one of the challenges in translation of laws. As Rodolfo Sacco indicates: 'The real difficulties of translation arise when the relationship between word and concept is not identical in different languages. Word and concept may be related in different ways and any theory of legal translation must consider them' (Sacco 1991: 14). An important phenomenon according to Sacco is the 'synecdoche, a linguistic form in which the speaker refers to a part to indicate the whole' (Sacco 1991: 14). This linguistic trope is prevalent in medieval dietary regulations, in both Old Norse and Latin sources, and a paragraph from *Paenitentiale Pseudo-Gregorii* illustrates the phenomenon: '*Suffocatum* we call that which dies without blood being shed outwards, or which is killed by a slope. If anything is found *suffocatum* by wolf or dog, or in a rope, it should under no circumstances be eaten'. (*Suffocatum dicimus, quod sine sanguinis effusione perimitur, vel quod in laqueo necatur. Si quis a lupo vel a cane, aut in laqueo suffocatum invenerit, nullatenus manducetur* (*Paenitentiale Pseudo-Gregorii III 29.* Wasserschleben 1958: 545).)

Although the etymological meaning of *suffocatum* is 'strangled', the previous paragraph reveals that the concept of *suffocatum* had taken on a wider meaning and included animals that had died without emission of blood, or animals killed by a wolf or a dog. There are also examples that illustrate that *suffocatum* and *morticina* are used as synonyms: '*Suffocatum* we call an animal which is torn apart or strangled by wolf, bear, or other animals' (*Suffocatum vocamus animal, quod a lupo seu urso et aliqua bestia strangulatum vel laceratum est* (MGH Epistolae (in Quart) 5: Epistolae Karolini aevi (III): 633). This is how the anonymous cleric from East-Francia defined *suffocatum*. A paragraph in Burchard of Worms'

Decretum, however, renders the very same content, but in this context *suffocatum* is replaced by *morticina*: 'Have you eaten *morticina*, that is animals which are torn apart by wolves or dogs, and found dead in such a way?' (*Comedisti morticina, id est animalia quae a lupis seu a canibus dilacerabantur, et sic mortua inventa sunt?* (Burchard of Worms, *Decretum*, lib. XIX, Cap. 5: De ilicitis cibis. PL 141: 968D.)).

The two previous paragraphs have the very same content, but apply two different concepts (*suffocatum* and *morticina*) to describe what is forbidden to eat. What has happened, both in the Old Norse and the Latin sources, is that the key concepts (*svidda, morticina, suffocatum*) have gone through a metonymic process. Metonymy occurs 'when an expression that normally designates one entity is used to designate another, associated entity' (Langacker 1993: 29). In other words, one entity is designated by pointing to the most prominent feature of the phenomenon. The synecdoche, to which Sacco referred, is usually treated as a subcategory of metonymy, and makes use of a part to indicate a whole. *Paenitentiale Pseudo-Gregorii* thus uses *suffocatum* ('strangled') to indicate a greater whole, which in addition to strangled animals also involves animals that have died without visible blood, or animals killed by a wolf or a dog. The Old Norse term *svidda* has gone through the same process, which becomes apparent if the three different definitions are listed consecutively: Borg. 5.5: Everything which has died without intervention by human hand is called *svidda*. Eid. 26.2: But (as for) anything which is killed by 'frenzy sickness' or which is struck by lightning or by falling sickness, that is *svidda*. Gul. 31: That we call *svidda* whose death is not known to man (partly based on Larson's translation; see Larson 2008: 58, § 31).

Taranger was wrong when he claimed that *svidda* is defined in the same way in all the Norwegian Christian Laws (Taranger 1890: 393). While the only guiding line in the *Gulathing Law*, inspired by an Augustinian notion (see the commentary on Borg. 5), is to *know the cause* of the animals' death, the *Borgarthing Law* is not that liberal. Here the criterion is that *human hands* have caused the death. As explained in the commentary to Borg. 5.1–12, two different canonical interpretations come to the fore in the different definitions of the term *svidda*. Therefore, if the interpretation of *svidda* is confined to the etymological meaning alone, parts of the content will be lost. To use the language of logic: *svidda* should not be interpreted as *defininens*, but as *definiendum*.

26.2

In this translation, we have chosen to follow the division of the chapters into smaller paragraphs made by Halvorsen & Rindal – a division that is not original. In this particular chapter, however, the division makes no sense. The final sentence in 26.1 ('It is permitted to eat anything which has a clear cause of death') conveys the Augustinian notion described earlier, and is intended to introduce the content in paragraph 26.2. The dietary chapter in the *Eidsivathing Law* thus contains the same two strata as the *Borgarthing Law*.

Chapter twenty-seven

27.1

On the ember days, see the commentary on Borg. 6.3. In most cases, the provincial laws set fifteen years (*15 vetra gamall*) as the age of majority. (See for instance the *Frostathing Law* IV 34, or NgL V: 708 s.v. *vetr* for references to other paragraphs in the Norwegian provincial laws.) The lower age limit for taking part in Church rituals was, however, younger in most cases. The rite of confirmation was usually received between the ages of seven and twelve (Helle 2001: 191), and the later *Borgarthing Law* requires that every twelve-year-old boy or girl go to confession during Lent and receive communion on Easter Day (N Borg. 14) according to the decrees of the Fourth Lateran Council in 1215.

27.2

During the ember days, there was a ban not only on meat, but also on *huit*, which corresponds to the Latin *lacticinia*: milk, egg, and food made thereof (NgL V: 308 s.v. *hvítt*; Spørck 2009: 192).

27.3

See the commentary on Borg. 6.5.

Chapter twenty-eight

See the commentary on Borg. 6.

Chapter twenty-nine

The same phrase 'then he shall eat the dog, rather than the dog eat him' is found both in the *Borgarthing Law* and the *Gulathing Law*, and suggests a common core. See the commentary on Borg. 5.14–5.15.

Chapter thirty

30.1

On marriage and 'incest prohibition', see the commentary on Borg. 15.

30.2–30.3

The manuscripts differ when it comes to the counting of the knees in these two paragraphs. While Paragraph 30.2 in AM 68 4o states that their kinship shall be counted to 'the fifth knee, and he may marry at the seventh', AM 58 4o prescribes a counting to 'the sixth knee, and marry at the seventh', which makes more sense. Likewise, while paragraph 30.3 states that the 'kinship shall be counted to the third knee, and he may marry at the fifth', regarding a widow of a relative, manuscripts AM 58 4o and NB 317 4o prescribe a counting to 'the fourth knee, and marry at the fifth'.

The limitation to the seventh degree shows that the *Eidsivathing Law*, unlike the *Borgarthing Law*, has not been brought up to date with the provisions from the Fourth Lateran Council in 1215 on this particular point.

30.11

See the commentary on chapter twenty-five.

Chapter thirty-one: on the bishop's seat

31.1

As far back as the earliest years of the Church (before the fourth century) the bishop's place in a church space had been on a special seat, or throne. Later, the term 'seat' began to be transferred to the bishop's seat in his diocese (Hellström 1971: 176–177). The idea that a king would have the final say on a bishop's appointment conflicted with the demands of the Church for 'freedom' as this was formulated by the so-called 'Gregorian Reform' movement of the latter half of the eleventh century, using the expression *libertas ecclesiae*. Collaboration between bishops and kings had a long tradition behind it, stretching back on the continent to the Early Middle Ages. In Scandinavia, there is evidence (especially from Denmark and Norway) that kings had great influence over the appointment of bishops in the Early Middle Ages (Hellström 1971: 161–174, 213–214. On the appointment of bishops in international canon law before 1215, see Ciardi 2016: 150–159, 167).

A bishop had to be *retkosen* ('correctly chosen'). What was meant in this case was that he had to be chosen by the clergy and the people, *per clerum et populum* (Ciardi 2016: 149–176). It was considered obvious that he should be consecrated using the liturgy, which was developed during the Early Middle Ages and was most often called *consecratio episcopi*. Without this consecration, he could not undertake his duties properly – especially those which related to his *potestas ordinis*: for example, performing ordinations of priests. (On a bishop's status in Church law, and on his *potestates*, see Hellström 1971: 256–259. See also the commentary on 31.2.)

til starfs oc stols ('for this work and this seat'): This expression, which only appears here in the *Eidsivathing Law* and in Swedish law texts, concerns the bishop's office and estate which were symbolically transferred to him through an act known as 'enthronement'. During this, he received his crosier (crook-shaped staff) and was seated in the bishop's throne (Hellström 1971: 176–186).

31.2

Amongst the bishop's official duties (for which he was paid, for example when householders ('we') transferred resources (*fé*) to the 'bishop's table' (*mensa episcopalis*) were ordinations of people to various levels in the ecclesiastical hierarchy, along with consecrations of church buildings and churchyards (*potestas ordinis*). In accordance with his powers of jurisdiction (*potestas iurisdictionis*), the bishop had to carry out visitations to the parishioners in his diocese very regularly, and make judicial decisions concerning clerics as well as, to a certain degree, lay people. Finally, his *potestas magisterii* concerned the education he provided both for clerics and for lay people, for instance through preaching during the services he conducted (*hann skal oss tiðir uæita*). (On the meaning of the word *tíðir* see NgL V: 640 s.v. *tíð*; Smedberg 1973: 195–199.)

31.3–31.5

The bishop's tithe could be controversial; householders did not always wish to pay this at all, and sometimes only up to a point. As a result, there is variation as to agreement with bishops over this within different Scandinavian areas. A bishop's tithe is also mentioned in the other older Norwegian laws (Gul. 8, 9; Borg. 11; Frost. II:18). (See also the commentary on Borg. 11.1; Hellström 1971: 291–296.)

31.4

Judging by the wording here, the bishop was to appoint the parish priests. In several Scandinavian areas, this matter was the subject of conflicts and compromises regarding the sorts of influence the bishop and parishioners demanded, relative to each other. This question is also related to ownership of private churches in the Early Middle Ages, in Scandinavia, and, later, to the rights of patrons, as they were formulated in international canon law around 1200 (Landau 1975: 3–15). There is no uniformity amongst the laws when it comes to appointment of priests (Hellström 1971: 376–378; Nilsson, Bertil 2014: 177–181).

That priests had to have sufficient knowledge to carry out their duties was obvious in theory, so it might appear odd that this had to be pointed out in law. This knowledge was tested by the bishop before the ordination of each priest, and also at each 'meeting of priests' (synod). (See 10.2–10–5.) However, this does not rule out the possibility that parishioners might have complained about the abilities of priests to fulfil their duties, in certain cases.

Here, the law rests on an assumption that a child was being baptized. This means that adult baptism (baptism of converts) no longer took place within the Eidsivathing legal province.

31.5

On this type of tithe, see the commentary on Borg. 11.1.

Chapter thirty-two

32.1

On the division of the tithe, see the commentary on Borg. 11.1.

32.6

biscups armaðr (*biskups ármaðr*): see the commentary on Borg. 11.2.
fimt: see 17.3.

32.7

According to canon law, a bishop's duties included performing an annual visitation to his parishioners. This was established by the *Decretum Gratiani* in the middle of the twelfth century, but can be traced back to decisions made in the fourth century (C.10 q.1 c.11; see Friedberg 1879; Inger 1961: 122). Given the geographical and climatic conditions in Norway and Sweden, such frequency of visitations could not be maintained. It was therefore considered enough if a bishop came to the main church in each third of a district once per year: in other words, to nine churches in total (see 10.1). We might imagine that priests and parishioners from the remaining parishes would have assembled at the main churches on such occasions.

Canon law also determined what should happen during a visitation. Here, all that is mentioned is what was necessary for the bishop to retain his *fé*: namely, the performance of a service and confirmations (See Hellström 1971: 297–300). The latter type of activity played a special role, since the sacrament of confirmation could only be carried out by a bishop. (See the commentary on Borg. 10.5.) In addition, there was usually a series of checks relating to the priests, church buildings, and economic matters (see Inger 1961: 122–128).

32.8–32.9

ræiðu (from *reiða*): this word had several meanings in legal language (see Brendalsmo & Riisøy 2014: 22–29). Here, it concerns the oblation which was received by the bishop from the householders. This can be viewed as a sort of contract between the relevant parties. Such contracts with bishops are also represented in the *Gulathing Law* (Gul. 9, 22) and are thought to reflect a stage in the development of the legal relationship between congregation and Church, before the introduction of tithes. However, according to the rules in this chapter of the *Eidsivathing Law*, these were parallel sources of income for the bishop. (See also 32.1.) There are several examples of oblation for bishops linked to their liturgical functions (for example church consecration) – despite the fact that tithes had already been introduced – in both the oldest Norwegian laws and the Swedish provincial laws (See Hellström 1971: 287–291).

32.10

On summons batons, see 10.1.

32.11

In international Church law, there were regulations on the size of retinue a bishop could take with him on official visits to his diocese, how long he was allowed to stay in one place, and how many necessities the parish priest and parishioners should provide for him and his followers ('procuration'). (See Inger 1961: 128–131.) These rules were the subject of various local controversies throughout the Middle Ages – not least due to episcopal misuse of such rights. The variations between laws from Scandinavian areas provide a clear picture of both controversy and compromise. (See Inger 1961: 415–443; Nilsson, Bertil 2014: 169–174.) During the recurrent annual visitation by the bishop to each third, it was the priest at the main church who had to pay the costs.

Chapter thirty-three

33.1–33.4

This chapter contains rules on the procedure followed by the man responsible for ensuring that the oblation for the bishop was collected. These provisions contain no complexities of interpretation, and clearly show how a scheme involving a whole district could be designed in such a way that no one could avoid making the payment he was obliged to make.

Chapter thirty-four

34.1–34–2

See the commentary on Borg. 8.2.

34.3

Here we have another example of what was involved in procuration for a bishop. (See 32.11.) In this case, the occasion is a church consecration. For such an event, the bishop was permitted to ride out with a significantly larger following than during his annual visitations to the main churches. Church consecration was an activity reserved for bishops and cannot have happened especially often – even if we remember that churches could fall into ruin or burn down, as in 34.1. Further, a church could be desecrated in such a way that the effect of the consecration was lost, so that reconsecration (*reconsecratio*) was necessary. Despite all this, there must have been long gaps between episcopal visits to a parish for church consecration. It was therefore all the men of the parish – not the priest alone – who had to provide the considerably more substantial procuration necessary on such an occasion. The wording at the end ('unless the farmers and the bishop settle on something else') strengthens an impression suggested by other laws and by the practicalities of the situation: it was far from always clear what would actually happen in any particular case when it came to the question of what the bishop would receive. Sometimes (perhaps often) negotiations must have taken place between the bishop and men of the parish. (See Nilsson, Bertil 2014: 169–174.)

Chapter thirty-five

35.1

In the shorter version of the *Eidsivathing Law* in the manuscript AM 58 4o, 'every priest with a church' is mentioned, which makes more sense than if the rule had only been meant to apply to priests of main churches.

syngr mannum tiðir ('when he sings services for men'): this expression has been translated slightly differently by Halvorsen & Rindal ('når han synger tidebønner for folk') and differently again by Meißner ('wenn er den Leuten Messe singt'). Considering the wide semantic range of the word *tíðir* (see 31.2) 'services' is the least precise and most inclusive translation. It probably also fits best with the purpose of the law, as shown by the wording in 35.2 'for any other reason', indicating something over and above 'services' in general.

35.2–35.4

The basic punishment for a priest who had been careless with fire, causing a church to burn down, was equivalent to the damage he had thereby caused. It must have been extremely challenging economically for an individual to bear, and must have meant, in the worst-case scenario, that the priest had to leave his office after having been made utterly destitute.

Chapter thirty-six

36.1–36.3

The punishment for a lay person who had caused a church to burn down was the same as that for a priest, in principle, but with the addition of exile from the land. This may be seen as equivalent to loss of office by a priest. In a similar way, a lay person lost his entire income when he was exiled.

fare . . . utlægr (from *fara útlagr* 'become an outlaw'): see the commentary on Borg. 8.13.

uhæilagr ('unholy'): this word is used in several places in this law, in the phrase *utlægr oc uhæilagr* (Eid. 24, 27, 36, 37, 42), in the *Frostathing Law* (Frost. IV:41), and in the *Gulathing Law* (Gul. 28, 30, 35, 98, 178, 189). The person in question had a duty to leave 'land' and had also lost the protection of the law. (Regarding the 'land', see the commentary on Eid. 17.2 and Borg. 11.2.)

36.4

The householders' collective responsibility for 'offences' by thralls in this case seems to have been the consequence of the great cost involved in rebuilding a church, which the wording of the paragraph appears to imply should happen, without stating this outright. (On the relative degrees to which thralls and their owners were held responsible for crimes for the purposes of punishment, according to the Norwegian laws, see Iversen 1994: 90–95.)

Chapter thirty-seven

37.1–37.3

af hæftugri hænde (*af heiptugri hendi*, 'in enmity'): this expression was common in legal language, and also appears in the *Gulathing Law* (Gul. 98, 99, 195) and the *Frostathing Law* (Frost. II:10, IV:16–19, 21, 22). In addition, it is found in *King Sverrir's Christian Law* (Sv. 18) and in *Archbishop Jón's Christian Law* (J 11–13) as well as in the *National Law*. The basic meaning is 'with hostile hands, in hostility'. Blood which was splashed on a church due to criminal activity caused the church and churchyard to be seen as having lost their consecrated status, which meant that they could no longer be used. This principle was expressed in canon law, and although it is impossible to establish how far back it went, it was held to be self-evident by the time of writing of the Norwegian laws. The consequence of such loss of consecrated status was that the previous condition of the church and churchyard had to be restored. According to the law, this required a new consecration (*reconsecratio*), which could only be carried out by a bishop (not a parish priest), and therefore entailed significant costs for the guilty party. (See Nilsson, Bertil 1989: 85–106, 107–121 and the commentary on Borg. 18.1–2.) The reason that responsibility for this was transferred to the parishioners collectively if the guilty party could not (or would not) arrange for a new consecration – and had therefore been exiled – was that they needed a functioning church and churchyard.

37.4–37.5

Blood itself could cause harm to the part of the consecrated church or churchyard where it fell. It therefore had to be removed, along with the affected piece of wood on the floor or patch of ground. It is impossible to know for certain what lay behind these ideas. It is possible that folk and perhaps also pre-Christian beliefs could have contributed to such thinking (Nilsson, Bertil 1989: 96–97). It would have seemed natural to use holy water in such a situation. This was used in the most diverse contexts, and with various purposes, and here it seems likely that it would have had a protective function. (On holy water, see Piltz 2016: 50–54.)

37.6

See 36.4.

Chapter thirty-eight

38.1–38.5

See the commentary on Borg. 9.1.

Chapter thirty-nine

39.1–39.4

høgendes kirkiur ('proprietary churches'): see the commentary on Borg. 8.11.

This paragraph shows the stages in the building of a small, private wooden church, during the three-year period this would have taken to complete. Consecration was a necessity, as a matter of principle, in order for the church to be used for its intended purpose, so a rule on the time limit for carrying this out is included here. The paragraphs which follow make it even clearer how urgent it was for a church to be restored, even if (as here) it had been built by an individual on his private property.

39.7–39.8

These paragraphs show partly that there was not only a plot immediately around a church but also other land which belonged to it, and partly that a church owner had the legal right to dispose of that land and could do so. At the same time, he sometimes – although evidently not always – had his own land in addition to the church land, which he had to use to keep the church in good condition even after he had sold his church land. (For more on this, see Smedberg 1973: 130–131.)

Chapter forty

40.1–40.2

On the bishop's right to compensation, see 34.3.

ef hann uigir bæðe kirkiu oc kirkiu garð ('if he consecrates both church and churchyard'): this reference to consecration of *both* church and churchyard should be understood in the context of the complexity of the question of churchyard consecration, around the time of writing of the *Eidsivathing Law*. A churchyard could, in principle, be the subject of three different consecrations or benedictions (see Nilsson, Bertil 2007), depending to a certain extent on exactly when during the Middle Ages this happened. As soon as it had been decided that a church would be built and where, the bishop was supposed to perform a liturgical act marking the site of the coming church, sprinkling it with holy water. This also applied to a limited area around the place where the church would stand: the so-called 'church plot'. Following this, the consecrated church plot could be used for burials, even before the church building had been completed. The next stage was that the church was consecrated, at which point the bishop could also consecrate the churchyard through a more formal liturgical act than the one he had performed during the blessing of the church plot. Alternatively, he could consecrate the church building alone, if the churchyard had been perceived as having been consecrated during the foundational liturgical act and used for burials after that point. It was also possible for the bishop to consecrate a churchyard separately, on an occasion other than the consecration of the church itself. Not all private chapels had burial rights (*ius funerandi*), and those without lacked true graveyards in the sense of legitimate burial places. (See Nilsson, Bertil 1989: 49–55, 70–84.)

Chapter forty-one

41.1

heraz fløyt ('rumoured throughout the *herað*'): a procedural principle that required a rumour to be publicly known, or notorious, to initiate a legal process. The *Eidsivathing Law* states that three or more farmers had to know about the offence to define it as *heraz fløyt* (Hertzberg 1874: 212; Evans 1997).

41.2

The *lex talionis* was an integral part of the accusatorial process, and implied that an 'accuser might be condemned to the same punishment that the defendant would have received if he were convicted' (Brundage 1996: 331). The *lex talionis* followed a principle of equilibrium, and its purpose was to avoid allegations made due to malice (*malitia*). In this particular case, the bishop's *ármaðr* had to pay three marks if he had made an accusation without the rumour being *heraz fløyt*. There is, however, an imbalance regarding consequence, since the accused, if convicted, was outlawed (Landro 2010: 174; Fraher 1984: 582).

Chapter forty-two

42.2

The accused could decide whether he wanted to be tried by God (ordeal) or by man. The *Eidsivathing Law* reveals no systematic approach to the use of ordeal, unlike the *Borgarthing Law* (see Introduction).

42.3

Although the first paragraph (42.1), by using the phrase 'any legal case', leaves the impression that chapter forty-two describes the general legal procedure of the

Eidsivathing Law, the particular procedure rendered in this chapter is probably attached to the preceding chapter (chapter forty-one), dealing with witchcraft. The *tylftareiðr*, which required eleven compurgators, was usually reserved for the severest crimes, like murder or treason (Helle 2001: 104). The severe consequences if the accused failed (outlawry and loss of property) point in the same direction.

42.4

The *Guðs skirslir* referred to in 42, called 'the great witness' in the *Gulathing Law* (Gul. 156; Helle 2001: 104), was a trial in which 'God condemned the guilty and exonerated the innocent through clergy-conducted physical tests' (Leeson 2012: 692). *Arinsjárn* ('hearth-iron'), which the *Eidsivathing Law* reserved for men, meant walking on or carrying hot iron a certain distance. *Ketiltak* ('cauldron-taking'), reserved for women, implied picking up an object from a cauldron with boiling water. The skin was examined by a priest after a certain amount of days, and if the skin was unharmed, the proband was proven innocent (Leeson 2012: 694; Helle 2001: 104).

Chapter forty-three

43.4

grið ('grace'): a temporary personal safety granted to individuals, valid in certain time periods or places, such as mass days (Frost. II 10) or thing assemblies, or to convicted offenders, either to renegotiate punishment or (for outlaws) to leave the country (NgL V: 248 s.v. *grið*; Helle 2001: 74, 95, 96, 101, 144).

Chapter forty-four

See the commentary on chapter twenty-five.

Chapter forty-five

45.1–45.2.

On *finna* ('Sámi') and the description of magic, superstition, and sorcery in ecclesiastical sources, see the commentary on Borg. 16.

45.3

This paragraph shows the inconsistencies in procedural matters. While paragraph 42.3 requires the witness of 12 people for a similar offence (*fordæðoskap*, 'witchcraft' mentioned in 41.1), paragraph 45.3 prescribes an oath sworn by six men for a group of offenders (named in 45.1) that includes *fordæðor* ('witches').

Chapter forty-six

Although both men and women could be accused of witchcraft, sorcery, and magic, the Norwegian provincial laws reveal the assumption that women were more often involved in these kinds of activities than men (Helle 2001: 144). Both the *Eidsivathing Law* and the *Borgarthing Law* (chapter sixteen) contain chapters dealing with witchcraft specifically linked to women, and the *Gulathing Law* prescribes that a woman who has been convicted of being a *troll oc manneta* must be taken to the sea and stabbed in the back (Gul. 28; Helle 2001: 144).

Chapter forty-seven

47.1–47.3

See the commentary on Borg. 12.14.

47.4–47.5

It is assumed here that the sick person was so ill that death might come as a result of the sickness, and he must prepare himself for this. Such preparation took place with the participation of the Church and was important for a person's last moments on earth. It was therefore essential that the correct rites were performed. Preparation included confession and receiving the sacrament of Holy Communion (Sundmark 2008: 153–164). It is for this reason that it is stated that a horse must be given to the priest, and that he had a duty to come at any time of the day or night. The preparations for death also included the so-called 'extreme unction', and unusually, it is assumed here that another priest or deacon is present. This is different from the rules preserved in the Swedish laws, in which a single priest is assumed to attend to all of this by himself. (On the priest's assistants, see Sundmark 2008: 45–48.) Another difference is that the delivery of the sacrament of unction costs money. The law thus reflects the practice of a period during which tithes had not yet fully replaced contracts between priests and parishioners, regarding priestly duties. (On payment, see Sundmark 2008: 66; see also the commentary on Borg. 12.10–12.12.)

47.6

The reason that the priest of the main church had to be summoned if the ill person died was that the main church originally had special status as the only church in the district with burial rights (*ius funerandi*) (Nilsson, Bertil 1989: 49–52).

47.7

On the 'post-mortem rites', see the commentary on Borg. 12.13.
On the 'night watch', see the commentary on Borg. 12.18.
On the *legkaup*, see the commentary on Borg. 12.3–12.8.

Chapter forty-nine

49.1

It might be noted that this law rests on the assumption that the priest was married, which suggests that, at the time of writing, Church demands for clerical celibacy had not yet had much impact on Norway. By contrast, canon law had included relevant clarifications during the twelfth century, particularly in connection with the three Lateran Councils of 1123, 1139, and 1179. These laid the foundations for intensified efforts by the Church to put celibacy demands into practice – although this was never fully implemented during the Middle Ages (Nilsson, Bertil 2008: 43–46; regarding Norway, see Gunnes 1982).

ærfis, erfi, erfiǫl, erfðarǫl ('funeral ale', 'inheritance feast'): the term for the gathering held either on the occasion of the burial or when the inheritance was passed on. In the *Gulathing Law*, it is called *saloǫl* ('soul ale') (Gul. 23): that is, something which benefited the soul of the person who had died. It could also be called *sjaund* (Gul. 23), since it was held on the seventh day after a death. The Church tried to prevent such gatherings from turning into drinking bouts, as in the case of wakes (Bø 1960: 450–452; Nilsson, Bertil 1987: 136).

annduege (*andvegi, ǫndvegi*, 'high seat'): this was the foremost place in the house, and was normally occupied by the householder and his wife. The high seat also played a legal role in the transfer of inheritance in that, when an heir took his place in the high seat after a death, he technically took over the inheritance. (See the *Gulathing Law* (Gul. 115) and the *Frostathing Law* (Frost. VIII: 17, and Birekli 1932: 42–46.) Why the priest and his wife should sit in the high seat on such an occasion, according to the *Eidsivathing Law*, remains unclear, and there are no other sources for this.

49.2

If he did not have a legally valid excuse for absence, the priest had a duty to be present at the inheritance feast, even if he could not remain there for its whole duration. This should be understood in the light of his duty to 'consecrate' the food and drink: in other words, to call down God's blessing on them. This was essential for the inheritance feast. Without the priest's blessing, it was not an inheritance feast, but simply an ordinary meal.

Chapter fifty

50.1–50.5

On the division of the churchyard for various categories of people in the social hierarchy, see the commentary on Borg. 9.2–9.10.

50.6

When it comes to the Norwegian laws, division of the churchyard by gender appears only here; there is nothing similar in the Danish or Swedish laws or in canon law. However, archaeological excavations have shown that division by gender was employed not only in the Eidsivathing area but throughout continental Scandinavia as well as Iceland and Greenland – albeit with some inconsistency and changes over time. This phenomenon has been carefully noted in recent research. (See Nilsson, Bertil 1989: 138–143; Nilsson, Bertil 1994; Jonsson 2009: 77–93; Mejsholm 2017.)

50.7–50.10

See the commentary on Borg. 9.11–9.12.

50.11–50.13

The question of who should be denied churchyard burial was thoroughly dealt with in canon law, both in normative texts and in discussions of doctrine (Nilsson, Bertil 1989: 255–269). Similar rules are also found in the other older Norwegian laws, except the *Borgarthing Law*. Seen from this perspective, the list in the *Eidsivathing Law* is very careful and thorough (Nilsson, Bertil 1989: 269–275).

50.14

flodar male (*flœðarmál* 'the high tide mark'). Amongst the oldest Norwegian laws, this term is also used in connection with burial in the *Gulathing Law* (Gul. 23). It remains unclear why this place was stipulated for the burial of *úbotamenn* (Nilsson, Bertil 1989: 276).

50.15

misgrafen (from *misgrafa* 'wrongfully bury'). This term occurs only in the *Eidsivathing Law*, amongst the oldest Norwegian laws. The procedure itself is absolutely in line with the Church's view of the churchyard as a holy place which must be kept 'pure' and which could suffer pollution (*pollutio*) (Nilsson, Bertil 1989: 276–278).

Chapter fifty-one

51.1–51.3

Judging by rules in both the Norwegian and the Swedish provincial laws, it seems that it was normal for a burial to take place the day after a death. However, this was obviously dependent on a variety of circumstances, such as when the death had taken place and (as here in the *Eidsivathing Law*) the weather: when weather prevented the deceased from being taken to the church and churchyard, the time before the burial could be extended as necessary (Nilsson, Bertil 1987: 136–137; see also the commentary on 18.1). The normal five-day time limit should be understood in the context of the role which a five-day period (*fimt*) played in several other contexts in the oldest Norwegian laws. (See 17.3.)

Chapter fifty-two: on incest

52.2

a lannd hœiðit ('to heathen land'): see the commentary on Borg. 11.4 and 17.2.

Chapter fifty-three: on spiritual kin

53.1–53.6

On spiritual kinship (*cognatio spiritualis/guðsifjar*), see also the commentary on Borg. 15; 15.9–15.13. By contrast with the *Borgarthing Law* and the *Gulathing Law*, the *Eidsivathing Law* specifies only the sacrament of baptism as a cause of spiritual kinship. The comparatively full wording in the *Eidsivathing Law* makes it especially clear how spiritual kinship could create complications in small communities and parishes with low levels of mobility.

Part VII Sources, literature, and abbreviations

A = Biskop Arnes kristenret for Island [Bishop Árni's Church Law for Iceland]. In Gustav Storm & Ebbe Hertzberg (eds.), *Norges gamle love indtil 1387*. Vol. 5. 16–56. Christiania 1895.

Adam, Adolf. 1979. *The Liturgical Year*. New York: Pueblo Publishing Company.

AM = Arnamagnæan Manuscript Collection. University of Copenhagen.

Andrén, Carl Gustaf. 1957. *Konfirmationen i Sverige under medeltid och reformationstid*. Lund: Gleerups Förlag (Bibliotheca Theologiae Practicae 1).

Andrén, Carl Gustaf. 1963. *De septem sacramentis. En sakramentsutläggning från Vadstena kloster c:a 1400*. Lund: Gleerups förlag (Bibliotheca Theologiae Practicae 15).

Antonsson, Haki. 2007. *St. Magnús of Orkney: A Scandinavian Martyr-Cult in Context*. Leiden-Boston: Brill (Northern World. North Europe and the Baltic c. 400–1700 AD. Peoples, Economies and Cultures 29).

Archbishop Árni's Statute. In R. Keyser & P.A. Munch (eds.), *Norges gamle love indtil 1387*. Vol. 3. 295–301. Christiania 1849.

Archbishop Eilífr's Third Statute. In R. Keyser & P.A. Munch (eds.), *Norges gamle love indtil 1387*. Vol. 3. 249–270. Christiania 1849.

Archbishop Eilífr's Fifth Statute. In R. Keyser & P.A. Munch (eds.), *Norges gamle love indtil 1387*. Vol. 3. 275–277. Christiania 1849.

Archbishop Eiríkr's Statute. In Gustav Storm (ed.), *Norges gamle love indtil 1387*. Vol. 4. 98–100. Christiania 1885.

Archbishop Jón's Statute. In R. Keyser & P.A. Munch (eds.), *Norges gamle love indtil 1387*. Vol. 3. 229–241. Christiania 1849.

Archbishop Jǫrundr's First Statute. In R. Keyser & P.A. Munch (eds.), *Norges gamle love indtil 1387*. Vol. 3. 241–243. Christiania 1849.

Archbishop Páll's First Statute. In R. Keyser & P.A. Munch (eds.), *Norges gamle love indtil 1387*. Vol. 3. 277–281. Christiania 1849.

Archbishop Páll's Third Statute. In R. Keyser & P.A. Munch (eds), *Norges gamle love indtil 1387*. Vol. 3. 284–294. Christiania 1849.

Auf der Mauer, Hansjörg. 1983. *Feiern im Rhythmus der Zeit 1: Herrenfeste in Woche und Jahr*. Regensburg: Friedrich Pustet Verlag (Gottesdienst der Kirche. Handbuch der Liturgiewissenschaft 5).

BÆK = *Borgarthings ældre kristenret i fotolithografisk gjengivelse efter Tönsbergs Lovbog fra c. 1320* (Det Norske Historiske Kildeskriftfonds skrifter 19). Oslo 1886.

Bagge, Sverre. 1998. *Mennesket i middelalderens Norge. Tanker, tro og holdninger 1000–1300*. Oslo: Aschehoug.

Bagge, Sverre. 2001. *Da boken kom til Norge*. Oslo: Aschehoug (Norsk Idéhistorie 1).
Bagge, Sverre. 2010. *From Viking Stronghold to Christian Kingdom: State Formation in Norway, c. 900–1350*. Copenhagen: Museum Tusculanum Press.
Birekli, Emil. 1932. *Høgsætet: Det gamle ondvege i religionshistorisk belysning*. Stavanger: Dreyers grafiska anstalt.
Bj. = The Older Town Law. In R. Keyser & P.A. Munch (eds.), *Norges gamle love indtil 1387*. Vol. 1. 301–336. Christiania 1846.
Björkman, Ulf. 1957. *Stilla veckan i gudstjänst och fromhetsliv: Med särskild hänsyn till svenska medeltida tradition*. Lund: Gleerups Förlag (Bibliotheca Theologiae Practicae 2).
Bjørkvik, Halvard. 1970. Settung. In *Kulturhistoriskt lexikon för nordisk medeltid* 15: 164–165.
Bø, Olav. 1960. Gravøl, Norge. In *Kulturhistoriskt lexikon för nordisk medeltid* 5: 450–452.
Bøe, Arne. 1959. Fasta, Norge. In *Kulturhistoriskt lexikon för nordisk medeltid* 4: 189–190.
Bøe, Arne. 1961. Helligbrøde, Noreg. In *Kulturhistoriskt lexikon för nordisk medeltid* 6: 385–388.
Borg. = The Borgarthing Law. In R. Keyser & P.A. Munch (eds.), *Norges gamle love indtil 1387*. Vol. 1. 337–372. Christiania 1846.
Braga, Corin. 2008. Psychoanalytical Geography. In *Journal for the Study of Religions and Ideologies* 7 (20): 134–149.
Brandt, F. 1880. *Forelæsninger over den norske retshistorie*. Bind 1. Kristiania: N. W. Damm & Søn.
Breisch, Agneta. 1994. *Frid och fredlöshet. Sociala band och utanförskap på Island under äldre medeltid*. Stockholm: Almqvist & Wiksell International (Acta Universitatis Upsaliensis. Studia Historica Upsaliensia 174).
Brendalsmo, A. Jan. 2001. *Kirkebygg og kirkebyggere. Byggherrer i Trøndelag ca. 1000–1600*. [Unpublished PhD-thesis. University of Tromsø].
Brendalsmo, A. Jan & Riisøy, Anne-Irene. 2014. Reida: En diskusjon av dens karakter og upphav. In Å. Ommundesen et al. (red.), *En prisverdig historiker: Festskrift til Gunnar I. Pettersen*. Oslo: Riksarkivet, 1–39 (Riksarkivaren. Skriftserie 41).
Brendalsmo, A. Jan & Stylegar, Frans-Arne. 2003. Runde kirkegårder. In *Fortidsminnesforeningen. Årbok* 157: 164–176.
Brink, Stefan. 2012. *Vikingarnas slavar. Den nordiska träldomen under yngre järnålder och äldsta medeltid*. n.p: Bokförlaget Atlantis.
Brommer, Peter (ed.). 1984. *MGH Leges, Capitula Episcoporum, Teil 1*. Hannover: Hahn.
Brundage, James A. 1987. *Law, Sex, and Christian Society in Medieval Europe*. Chicago: The University of Chicago Press.
Brundage, James A. 1996. Proof in Canonical Criminal Law. In *Continuity and Change* 11 (3): 329–339.
Carlsson, Lizzie. 1965. *"Jag giver dig min dotter". Trolovning och äktenskap i den svenska kvinnans äldre historia* I. Stockholm: A.-B. Nordiska bokhandeln (Rättshistoriskt Bibliotek. Serie 1 Nr. 8).
Christensen-Nugues, Charlotte. 2003. *Och de skall vara ett hjärta. Konsensusdoktrinen i medeltida kanonisk rätt*. Lund: Lunds universitet (Ugglan, Minervaserien 7).
Ciardi, Anna Minara. 2016. *On the Formation of Cathedral Chapters and Cathedral Culture: Lund, Denmark, and Scandinavia, c. 1060–1225*. Lund: Lund University (Bibliotheca Historico-Ecclesiastica Lundensis 60).
Cleasby, Richard. 1957. *An Icelandic-English Dictionary*. 2nd ed. Oxford: Clarendon Press.

Crawford Cree, A. T. 1906. Back-footed Beings. In *Folklore* 17 (2): 131–140.

Degnbol, Helle et al. (eds.). 1995. *Ordbog over det norrøne prosasprog*. Vol. 1. København: Den arnamagnæanske kommission.

DL = The Dala Law. In C.J. Schlyter (ed.), *Samling af Sweriges gamla lagar*. Vol. 5. 1–66. Lund 1844.

Douglas, Mary. 1996 (2005). *Purity and Danger: An Analysis of the Concepts of Pollution and Taboo*. London: Routledge.

Duggan, Anne. 1982. The Cult of St Thomas Becket in the Thirteenth Century. In M. Jancey (ed.), *St Thomas Cantilupe Bishop of Hereford: Essays in His Honour*. 21–44. Hereford: Friends of Hereford Cathedral.

Duggan, Anne. 2011. Eystein and the World of the Learned Law. In Tore Iversen (ed.), *Archbishop Eystein as Legislator – The European Connection*. 23–56. Trondheim: Tapir Academic Press.

Eid. = The Eidsivathing Law. In R. Keyser & P.A. Munch (eds.), *Norges gamle love indtil 1387*. Vol. 1. 373–406. Christiania 1846.

Eisenhofer, Ludwig. 1932–1933. *Handbuch der katholischen Liturgik*. Vol. 1–2. Freiburg im Breisgau: Herder & CO G.M.B.H. Verlagsbuchhandlung.

Eliassen, Sven G. & Norseng, Per G. 2005. *I Borgarsysle*. Østfolds historie. Bind 2. Sarpsborg: Østfold fylkekommune.

Ericsson, Georg J. V. 1967. *Den kanoniska rätten och äldre Västgötalagens kyrkobalk. En jämförande studie*. Stockholm: A-B Nordiska Bokhandeln (Rättshistoriskt Bibliotek. Serie 1 Nr. 12).

Evans, G.R. 1997. Notoriety: A Mediaeval Change of Attitude. In *Ecclesiastical Law Journal* 20 (4): 629–638.

Fehr, Bernhard (ed.). 1966 (1914). *Die Hirtenbriefe Ælfrics in altenglischer und lateinischer Fassung*. Darmstadt: Wissenschaftliche Buchgesellschaft.

Fisher, J.D.C. 1965. *Christian Initiation: Baptism in the Medieval West: A Study in the Disintegration of the Primitive Rite of Initiation*. Alcuin Club Collections No. XLVII. London: S.P.C.K.

Friedberg, Æmilius. 1879. Decretum Gratiani. In *Corpus Iuris Canonici*. Vol. 1. Lipsiae.

Frost. = The Frostathing Law. In R. Keyser & P.A. Munch (eds.), *Norges gamle love indtil 1387*. Vol. 1. 119–258. Christiania 1846.

Flom, George Tobias. 1911. Tunsberg Bylog from the Codex Tunsbergensis (Cod. Reg. n. s. 1642, 4to.). In *Journal of English and Germanic Philology* X: 214–235, 415–428.

Flom, George Tobias (ed.). 1925. *The Borgarthing Law of the Codex Tunsbergensis C. R. 1642 4to. An Old Norwegian Manuscript of 1320–1330*. Urbana: University of Illinois Press.

Foote, Peter. 1975. Træl, alment, Norge og Island. In *Kulturhistoriskt lexikon för nordisk medeltid* 19: 13–19.

Foote, Peter. 2003. *1117 in Iceland and England*. London: Viking Society for Northern Research.

Fraher, Richard M. 1984. The Theoretical Justification for the New Criminal Law of the High Middle Ages. *University of Illinois Law Review*: 577–597.

Franz, Adolph. 1909. *Die kirchlichen Benediktionen im Mittelalter*. Vol. 1–2. Freiburg im Breisgau: Herdersche Verlagshandlung.

Frimannslund, Rigmor. 1959. Festemål, Norge. In *Kulturhistoriskt lexikon för nordisk medeltid* 4: 233–236.

Gallén, Jarl. 1963. Kanonisk ålder. In *Kulturhistoriskt lexikon för nordisk medeltid* 8: 226–229.

Gb = Giftermålsbalken [the Section on Marriages].

Gjerløw, Lilli. 1962. Imbredagene. In *Kulturhistoriskt lexikon för nordisk medeltid* 7: 361–363.

Gjerløw, Lilli. 1963. Kalendarium II, Norge. In *Kulturhistoriskt lexikon för nordisk medeltid* 8: 98–106.

GL = The Guta Law. In C.J. Schlyter (ed.), *Samling af Sweriges gamla lagar*. Vol. 7. 1–112. Lund 1852.

Gr. = *Grágás, Islædernes Lovbog i Fristatens Tid, udgivet efter det Kongelige Biblioteks Haandskrift*. Vilhjálmur Finsen (ed.). Bind 1–2. København: Det nordiske Literatur-Samfund 1852.

Grágás, Islædernes Lovbog i Fristatens Tid, udgivet efter det Kongelige Biblioteks Haandskrift. Omsetjing 1. Omsett av Vilhjálmur Finsen. København 1870.

Gräslund, Anne-Sofie. 2004. Dogs in Graves – a Question of Symbolism? In Barbro S. Frizell (ed.), *Pecus: Man and Animal in Antiquity. Proceedings of the Conference at the Swedish Institute in Rome, September 9–12, 2002*. 171–180. Rome: The Swedish Institute (The Swedish Institute in Rome. Projects and Seminars 1).

Grieg, Sigurd. 1957. Budstikke (eller budkavl). In *Kulturhistoriskt lexikon för nordisk medeltid* 2: 338–340.

Grøtvedt, Per Nyquist. 1939. *Lydverket i lovhåndskrifter fra Borgertingslag 1300–1350 med ett tillegg om sørøstnorske diplomer*. Oslo: Jacob Dybwad (Skrifter utgitt av Det Norske Videnskaps-Akademi i Oslo 2 Hist.-Filos. klasse 1938: 7).

Gul. = The Gulathing Law. In R. Keyser & P.A. Munch (eds.), *Norges gamle love indtil 1387*. Vol. 1. 1–118. Christiania 1846.

Gummerus, Jaakko (ed.). 1902. *Synodalstatuter och andra kyrkorättsliga aktstycken från den svenska kyrkoprovinsen*. Uppsala: Norstedt. (Skrifter utgifna af kyrkohistoriska föreningen II: 2).

Gunnes, Erik. 1982. Prester og deier – sølibat i norsk middelalder. In Steinar Imsen & Gudmund Sandvik (eds.), *Hamarspor. Eit festskrift til Lars Hamre 1912–23 januar – 1982*. 20–44. Oslo, Bergen und Tromsø: Universitetsforlaget.

H = Hirðskrá. In R. Keyser & P.A. Munch (eds.), *Norges gamle love indtil 1387*. Vol. 2. 387–450. Christiania 1848.

Hagland, Jan Ragnar. 1984. *Riksstyring og språknorm: Spørsmålet om kongens kanselli i Norsk språkhistorie på 1200- og første halvdel av 1300-tallet* (Unpublished PhD-thesis. University of Trondheim).

Hagland, Jan Ragnar. 1998. Innskrifta på Kulisteinen: Ei nylesing ved hjelp av Jan O. H. Swantessons mikrokarteringsteknologi. In Audun Dybdahl & Jan Ragnar Hagland (eds.), *Innskrifter og datering*. 129–139. Trondheim: Tapir forlag.

Hagland, Jan Ragnar. 2002. Dialects and Written Language in Old Nordic 1: Old Norwegian and Old Icelandic. In *IHHNGL* 1: 1015–1018.

Hagland, Jan Ragnar. 2004. Norwegians and Europe: The Theme of Marriage and Consanguinity in Early Norwegian Law. In Jonathan Adams & Katherine Holman (eds.), *Scandinavia and Europe 800–1350: Contact, Conflict, and Coexistence*. 209–218. Turnhout: Brepols.

Hagland, Jan Ragnar & Sandnes, Jørn (eds.). 1994. *Frostatingslova*. Oslo: Det Norske Samlaget.

Hall, Stuart George & Crehan, Joseph H. 1983. Fasten/fasttage III. Biblisch und kirchenhistorisch. In *Theologische Realenzyklopädie* 11: 48–59.

Halvorsen, Eyvind Fjeld. 1989. Litt om endelsesvokalene i Eidsivatings kristenrett i OUB 317 4o. In *Festskrift til Finn Hødnebø 29. desember 1989*. 102–118. Oslo: Novus.

Halvorsen, Eyvind Fjeld & Rindal, Magnus (eds.). 2008. *De eldste østlandske kristenrettene. Tekst etter håndskriftene, med oversettelser*. Oslo: Riksarkivet (Norrøne Tekster 7).

Hamre, Lars. 1958. Edgärdsman, Norge. In *Kulturhistoriskt lexikon för nordisk medeltid* 3: 492–499.

Hamre, Lars. 1974. Tiend, Noreg. In *Kulturhistoriskt lexikon för nordisk medeltid* 18: 280–287.

Hamilton, Sarah. 2001. The Unique Favour of Penance: The Church and the People c. 800-c. 1100. In Peter Linehan & Janet L. Nelson (eds.), *The Medieval World*. 230–245. London: Routledge.

Haugen, Odd Einar. 2002. The Development of Latin Script 1: In Norway. In *IHHNGL* 1: 824–832.

Helle, Knut. 1995. Down to 1536. In Rolf Danielsen et al. (eds.) & Michael Drake (transl.), *Norway: A History from the Vikings to Our Own Times*. 3–119. Oslo: Scandinavian University Press.

Helle, Knut. 1999. Lov og rett i middelalderen. In Else Mundal & Ingvild Øye (eds.), *Norm og praksis i middelaldersamfunnet*. 7–22. Bergen: Senter for europeiske kulturstudier.

Helle, Knut. 2001. *Gulatinget og Gulatingslova*. Leikanger: Skald.

Hellquist, Elof. 1980. *Svensk etymologisk ordbok*. Vol. 1–2. 3rd ed. Lund: LiberLäromedel.

Hellström, Jan Arvid. 1971. *Biskop och landskapssamhälle i tidig svensk medeltid*. Stockholm: A-B Nordiska Bokhandeln (Rättshistoriskt Bibliotek. Serie 1 Nr. 16).

Helmholz, R. H. 1996. *The Spirit of Classical Canon Law*. Athens and London: The University of Georgia Press.

Hertzberg, Ebbe. 1874. *Grundtrækkene i den ældste norske proces*. Kristiania: Brøgger.

[Hirdskrá] = *Hirdskråen. Hirdloven til Norges konge og hans håndgangne menn. Etter AM 322 fol.* Steinar Imsen (ed.). Oslo: Riksarkivet 2000.

HL = The Hälsinge Law. In C.J. Schlyter (ed.), *Samling af Sweriges gamla lagar*. Vol. 5. 1–93. Lund 1844.

Holm = Kungliga Biblioteket. Stockholm.

Holmsen, Andreas. 1961 (1939). *Norges historie fra eldeste tider til 1600*. Oslo: Universitetsforlaget.

Holtsmark, Anne (transl.). 1961. *Sverres saga — En tale mot biskopene*. Oslo: H. Aschehoug & Co.

Holzmann, Robert (ed.).1935. *MHG Scriptores: Scriptores rerum Germanicarum. Nova series 9: Die Chronik des Bischofs Thietmar von Merseburg und ihre Korveier Überarbeitung*. Berlin: Weidmann.

IHHNGL = *An International Handbook of the History of the North Germanic Languages*. Oskar Bandle, Kurt Braunmuller and Ernst Hakon Jahr (eds.). (The Nordic Languages 22). Vols 1–2. Berlin: De Gruyter Mouton 2002–2005.

Inger, Göran. 1961. *Das kirchliche Visitationsinstitut im mittelalterlichen Schweden*. Lund: Gleerup (Bibliotheca Theologiae Practicae 11).

Iversen, Tore. 1994. *Trelldommen. Norsk slaveri i middelalderen*. Bergen: Historisk institutt. Universitetet i Bergen.

Iversen, Tore. 2003. Fra trell til leilending — frigivning, bosetning og herredømme i Norge, Norden og Vest-Europa i tidlig middelalder. In *Trälar. Ofria i agrarsamhället från vikingatid till medeltid*. 22–49. Stockholm: Nordiska museets förlag.

J = Archbishop Jón's Church Law. In R. Keyser & P.A. Munch (eds.), *Norges gamle love indtil 1387*. Vol. 2. 339–386. Christiania 1848.

J = Jordabalken [Land Section in the Västgöta Laws].

Janson, Henrik. 2010. What Made the Pagans Pagan? In Stepanov Tsvetelin & Georgi Kazakov (eds.), *Medieval Christianitas: Different Regions, 'Faces', Approaches*. 13–30. Sofia: Voenno izdatelstvo Publishing House.

Jochens, Jenny. 1998. *Women in Old Norse Society*. Ithaca: Cornell University Press.

Johanssen, Jan, Nygaard, Marius & Schreiner, Emil. 2002 (1998). *Latinsk-norsk ordbok*. Oslo: Cappelens Forlag.

Johnson, Maxwell E. 1999. *The Rites of Christian Initiation: Their Evolution and Interpretation*. Collegeville, MN: The Liturgical Press.

Jonsson, Kristina. 2009. *Practices for the Living and the Dead: Medieval and Post-Reformation Burials in Scandinavia*. Stockholm: Stockholm University (Stockholm Studies in Archaeology 50).

Kålund, Kristian. 1889–1894. *Katalog over den Arnamagnæanske Håndskriftsamling*. Vol. 1–2. Copenhagen: Gyldendal.

Kålund, Kristian. 1897–1900. *Katalog over de Oldnorsk-Islandske Håndskrifter i Københavns offentlige biblioteker udenfor den Arnamagnæanske Samling*. Copenhagen: Gyldendal.

Kilström, Bengt Ingmar. 1958. *Den kateketiska undervisningen i Sverige under medeltiden*. Uppsala: Almqvists & Wiksells Boktryckeri AB (Bibliotheca Theologiae Practicae 8).

Kk = Kyrkobalken [the Church Law Section].

Knudsen, Trygve. 1967. Om det eldste bevarte sørøstnorske skriftspråk. In *Skrifttradisjon og litteraturmål: Artikler og avhandlinger i utvalg. Festskrift i anledning av professor dr. Trygve Knudsens 70 års dag 23. juni 1967*. 9–52. Oslo: Universitetsforlaget.

Korpiola, Mia. 2004. *Between Betrothal and Bedding: The Making of Marriage in Sweden, ca. 1200–1610*. Saarijärvi: Gummerus Kirjapaino Oy.

Kroon, Sigurd. 1948. *Det svenska prästmötet under medeltiden. Dess uppkomst och ställning i samhälle och kyrka*. Stockholm: Svenska kyrkans diakonistyrelses bokförlag (Acta Historico-Ecclesiastica Suecana 18).

L = King Magnús Lawmender Hákonarson's National Law. In R. Keyser & P.A. Munch (eds.), *Norges gamle love indtil 1387*. Vol. 2. 1–178. Christiania 1848.

Landau, Peter. 1975. *Jus Patronatus. Studien zur Entwicklung des Patronats im Dekretalenrecht und der Kanonistik des 12. und 13. Jahrhunderts*. Köln Wien: Böhlau Verlag.

Landro, Torgeir. 2005. *De eldste norske kristenrettene. Innhald og opphav* [Unpublished master-thesis. University of Bergen].

Landro, Torgeir. 2010. *Kristenrett og kyrkjerett. Borgartingskristenretten i eit komparativt perspektiv*. [Unpublished PhD-thesis. University of Bergen].

Landro, Torgeir. 2011. Dietary Regulations in Norwegian Christian Law – a Case Study. In Tore Iversen (ed.), *Archbishop Eystein as Legislator: The European Connection*. 123–132. Trondheim: Tapir Academic Press.

Landro, Torgeir. 2013. Kristendomen i lovs form. In Geir Atle Ersland & Øystein Hellesøe Brekke (eds.), *Fragment frå fortida*. 124–148. Oslo: Dreyers Forlag.

Landro, Torgeir. 2019. The Use of Alliteration in a Norwegian Medieval Law – Just for Fun?, *European Journal of Scandinavian Studies* 49: 232–251.

Lang, Uwe Michael. 2009. *Turning Towards the Lord: Orientation in Liturgical Prayer*. San Francisco: Ignatius Press.

Langacker, Ronald W. 1993. Reference-Point Constructions. *Cognitive Linguistics* 4 (1): 1–38.

Langseth, Sissel Rydman. 1974. Termin, Norge. In *Kulturhistoriskt lexikon för nordisk medeltid* 18: 210–213.

Larrington, Carolyne. 1996. *The Poetic Edda*. Oxford: Oxford University Press.

Larson, Laurence M. 2008 (1935). *The Earliest Norwegian Laws: Being the Gulathing Law and the Frostathing Law*. Clark, NJ: The Lawbook Exchange.

Lárusson, Magnús Már. 1966. Magnús. In *Kulturhistoriskt lexikon för nordisk medeltid* 11: 221–222.

Leeson, Peter T. 2012. Ordeals. In *Journal of Law and Economics* 55: 691–714.

Levesque, Joseph L. 1995. The Theology of the Postbaptismal Rites in the Seventh and Eighth Century Gallican Church. In Maxwell E. Johnson (ed.), *Living Water, Sealing Spirit: Readings on Christian Initiation*. 159–201. Collegeville, MN: The Liturgical Press,

Liber Extra. In Æmilius Friedberg (ed.), *Corpus Iuris Canonici*. Vol. 2. Lipsiae 1881.

Lindberg, Gustaf. 1937. *Kyrkans heliga år. En historisk-principiell undersökning med särskild hänsyn till det svenska kyrkoåret*. Stockholm: Svenska diakonistyrelsen bokförlag.

Lindkvist, Thomas. 1979. *Landborna i Norden under äldre medeltid*. Stockholm: Almqvist & Wiksell International (Acta Universitatis Upsaliensis. Studia Historica Upsaliensia 110).

Lönnroth Lars. 1996. En fjärran spegel. Västnordiska berättande källor om svensk hedendom och om kristningsprocessen på svenskt område. In Bertil Nilsson (ed.), *Kristnandet i Sverige. Gamla källor och nya perspektiv*. 141–158. Uppsala: Lunne Böcker (Projektet Sveriges kristnande. Publikationer 5).

Lönnroth, Lars, Ólason, Vésteinn & Piltz, Anders. 2003. Literature. In Knut Helle (ed.), *The Cambridge History of Scandinavia 1: Prehistory to 1520*. 487–520. Cambridge: Cambridge University Press.

Lutterbach, Hubertus. 1998. Die Speisegesetzgebung in den mittelalterlichen Bußbüchern. In *Archiv für Kulturgeschichte* 80: 1–37.

Lynch, Joseph H. 1998. *Christianizing Kinship – Ritual Sponsorship in Anglo-Saxon England*. Ithaca: Cornell University Press.

Maurer, Konrad. 1881. *Über die norwegisch-isländischen Gagnföstur*. München.

Meens, Rob. 1995. Pollution in the Early Middle Ages: The Case of the Food Regulations in the Penitentials. In *Early Medieval Europe* 4 (1): 3–19.

Meens, Rob. 1998. Magic and the Early Medieval World View. In Joyce Hill & Mary Swan (eds.), *The Community, the Family and the Saint: Patterns of Power in Early Medieval Europe*. 285–295. Turnhout: Brepols.

Meens, Rob. 2002. Eating Animals in the Early Middle Ages: Classifying the Animal World and Building Group Identities. In Angela N. H. Creager & William Chester Jordan (eds.), *The Animal-Human Boundary: Historical Perspectives*. 3–28. New York: University of Rochester Press.

Meißner, Rudolf. 1941. *Die norwegische Volkskirche nach den vier alten Christenrechten*. Weimar: Verlag Hermann Böhlaus (Deutschrechtlisches Archiv, Zweites Heft).

Meißner, Rudolf. 1942. *Bruchstücke der Rechtsbücher des Borgarthings und des Eidsivathings*. Bearbeitet von Rudolf Meißner. Weimar: H. Böhlau (Germanenrechte. Neue Folge).

Mejsholm, Lotta. 2017. Kvinnor och män mellan himmel och jord. Segregering av de döda som kyrkopolitisk strategi. In Sten Tesch (red.), *Skiftet. Vikingatida sed och kristen tro. Ett mångvetenskapligt perspektiv på kristnandeprocessen i Mälarområdet*. 157–184. Skellefteå: Artos & Norma Bokförlag.

Metz, René 1976. L'enfant dans le droit canonique Medieval: Orientations de recherche. In *L'enfant 2: Europe médiévale et modern*. 9–96. Bruxelles: Société Jean Bodin (Recueils de la societé Jean Bodin pour l'histoire comparative des institutions 36).

Metzler, Irina. 2006. *Disability in Medieval Europe: Thinking About Physical Impairment During the High Middle Ages, c. 1100–1400*. London: Routledge.

MGH = Monumenta Germaniae Historica.

Mikkelsen, Egil. 2019. *Looting or Missioning: Insular and Continental Sacred Objects in Viking Age Contexts in Norway*. Oxford and Philadelphia: Oxbow Books.

Morgenroth, Matthias. Woche/Wochentage. In *Theologische Realenzyklopädie* 36: 264–267.

Murphy, James Brnhard. 2006. The Lawyer and the Layman: Two Perspectives on the Rule of Law. In *The Review of Politics* 68: 101–131.
NB = Nasjonalbiblioteket. Oslo.
Nedkvitne, Arnved & Norseng, Per G. 1991. *Oslo bys historie 1: Byen under Eikaberg fra byens oppkomst til 1536*. Oslo: J. W. Cappelen.
Nevéus, Clara. 1974: *Trälarna i landskapslagarnas samhälle. Danmark och Sverige*. Uppsala: Acta Universitatis Upsaliensis. Studia Historica Upsaliensia 58.
NgL = *Norges gamle love indtil 1387*. Vols. 1–5. Christiania 1846–1895.
Nilsson, Bertil. 1987. Död och begravning. Begravningsskicket i Norden. In Olle Ferm & Göran Tegnér (red.), *Tanke och tro. Aspekter på medeltidens tankevärld och fromhetsliv*. 133–150. Stockholm: Riksantikvarieämbetet (Studier till det medeltida Sverige 3).
Nilsson, Bertil. 1989. *De sepulturis. Gravrätten i Corpus Iuris Canonici och medeltida nordisk lagstiftning*. Stockholm: Almqvist & Wiksell International (Bibliotheca Theologiae Practicae 44).
Nilsson, Bertil. 1994. *Kvinnor, män och barn på medeltida begravningsplatser*. Uppsala: Lunne Böcker (Projektet Sveriges kristnande. Publikationer 3).
Nilsson, Bertil. 2001. Gudsdomar i Skandinavien under vikingatid och medeltid. In Michael Stausberg (ed.), *Kontinuitäten und Brüche in der Religionsgeschichte. Festschrift für Anders Hultgård zu seinem 65. Geburtstag am 23.12.2001*. 503–535. Berlin and New York: Walter de Gruyter (Ergänzungsbände zum Reallexikon der germanischen Altertumskunde 31).
Nilsson, Bertil. 2007. Guds åker beredd till skörd. Något om det medeltida ritualet för invigning av kyrkogård. In Johnny Hagberg (ed.), *Ett fönster mot den himmelska kyrkan. En vänskrift till Alf Härdelin*. 63–69. Skara: Skara stiftshistoriska sällskap (Skara stiftshistoriska sällskaps skriftserie 34).
Nilsson, Bertil. 2008. Förbjudna kvinnor och barn i medeltida prästgårdar. Celibatskrav och motstånd i Sverige. In *Saga och sed. Kungl. Gustav Adolfs Akademiens Årsbok*. 41–70. Uppsala: Kungl. Gustav Adolfs Akademien för svensk folkkultur.
Nilsson, Bertil. 2010. Den tidiga medeltidens likbegängelse och begravningsbruk i Västkyrkan. Liturgi och kyrkorätt. In Bertil Nilsson (ed.), *Från hedniskt till kristet. Förändringar i begravningsbruk och gravskick i Skandinavien c:a 800–1200*. 9–56. Stockholm: Sällskapet Runica et Mediævalia (Opuscula 14).
Nilsson, Bertil. 2012. Vem döpte, när och var? Doprättigheter under tidig medeltid i västkyrkan. In Stephan Borgehammar & Jes Wienberg (eds.), *Locus Celebris. Dalby kyrka, kloster och gård*. 129–150. Göteborg and Stockholm: Makadam Förlag, Centrum för Danmarksstudier, Lunds universitet.
Nilsson, Bertil. 2014. The Church Law of Scania on the Consecration of Churches and the Appointment of Parish Priests: International Canon Law and That of Scania. In Kerstin Hundahl, Lars Kjær & Niels Lund (eds.), *Denmark and Europe in the Middle Ages, c. 1000–1525: Essays in Honour of Professor Michael H. Gelting*. 157–182. Farnham, Surrey: Ashgate.
Nilsson, Göran B. 2011. Handskriften B 59 och Yngre Västgötalagen. In Per-Axel Wiktorsson (ed.), *Äldre Västgötalagen och dess bilagor i Cod. Holm. B 59*. Vol. 1. 45–59. Skara: Föreningen för Västgötalitteratur.
Nilsson, Göran B. 2012. *Nytt ljus över Yngre Västgötalagen. Den bestickande teorin om en medeltida lagstiftningsprocess*. Stockholm: Rönnells Antikvariat (Rättshistoriskt bibliotek 69).
NKS = Den nye kongelige samling, Det Kongelige Bibliotek. Copenhagen.

Nordeide, Sæbjørg Walaker & Steinar Gulliksen. 2007. First Generation Christians, Second Generation Radiocarbon Dates: The Cemetery at St. Clement's in Oslo. In *Norwegian Archaeological Review* 40 (1): 1–25.

Norseng, Per G., Pedersen, Ellen Anne & Stylegar, Frans-Arne. 2003. *Øst for Folden.* Østfolds historie. Bind 1. Sarpsborg: Østfold fylkeskommune.

Ødegaard, Marie. 2013. State Formation, Administrative Areas, and *Thing* Sites in the Borgarthing Law Province, Southeast Norway. In *Journal of the North Atlantic* 5: 42–63.

ÖgL = The Östgöta Law. In H.S. Collin & C.J. Schlyter (eds.), *Samling af Sweriges gamla lagar*. Vol. 2. 1–232. Stockholm 1830.

Olavsson, Torleiv. (transl.). 1914a. *Ældre Eidsivatingslov: Kristenretten tillikemed et opbevaret brudstykke av den verdslige lov*. Oslo: Soelberg.

Olavsson, Torleiv. 1914b. *Ældre Borgartingslov: Vikens kristenret, tillikemed endel ældre lovregler om ekteskapsstiftelse og trolovelse m.m., som er indført deri fra Eidsivalovens eller Borgartingslovens verdslige del.* Oslo: Soelberg.

Olsson, Alfa. 1960. Gröt. In *Kulturhistoriskt lexikon för nordisk medeltid* 5: 524.

Orning, Hans Jacob & Bjørn Poulsen. 2019. Holding Royal Office and the Creation and Consolidation of the Elites in Scandinavia c. 1050–1250. In B. Poulsen, H. Vogt & J. Sigurðsson (eds.), *Nordic Elites in Transformation, c. 1050–1250*. Vol. 1. 212–247. New York: Routledge.

Ottosson, Kjartan. 2002. Old Nordic: A Definition and Delimitation of the Period. In *IHHNGL* 1: 787–793.

Pálsson, Hermann. 1999. The Sami People in Old Norse Literature. In *Nordlit. Arbeidstidsskrift i litteratur* 5: 29–53.

Payer, Pierre J. 1984. *Sex and the Penitentials: The Development of a Sexual Code 550–1150.* Toronto, Buffalo and London: University of Toronto Press.

Peel, Christine 2009. *Guta Lag: The Law of the Gotlanders*. Christine Peel (ed. and transl.). London: Viking Society for Northern Research University College.

Peel, Christine 2015. Guta Lag and Guta Saga. In Christine Peel (ed.), *The Law and History of the Gotlanders*. London and New York: Routledge (Medieval Nordic Laws).

Pellijeff, Gunnar. 1967. *Lag om gård i västgötalagarna*. Stockholm: Almqvist & Wiksell (Nordiska texter och undersökningar 22).

Pennington, Kenneth. 1993. *The Prince and the Law 1200–1600: Sovereignity and Rights in the Western Legal Tradition*. Berkeley: University of California Press.

Pennington, Kenneth. 1997. The Spirit of Legal History. In *The University of Chicago Law Review* 64 (3): 1097–1116.

Pernler, Sven-Erik. 1984. De svenska kyrkobalkarnas inledningsord. In *Kyrkohistorisk årsskrift*: 61–99.

Piltz, Anders O.P. 2016. Örat tar över. Trons avmaterialisering på 1500-talet. In Fredrik Heiding & Magnus Nyman (eds.), *Doften av rykande vekar: Reformationen ur folkets perspektiv*. 45–92. Skellefteå: Artos & Norma.

PL = *Patrologia Latina*. J.-P. Migne (ed.). Vol. 221. Paris 1844–1864.

Plöchl, Willibald M. 1962. *Geschichte des Kirchenrechts 2: Das Kirchenrecht der abendländischen Christenheit 1055 bis 1517*. Wien and München: Verlag Herold.

Pryce, Huw. 2000. Lawbooks and Literacy in Medieval Wales. In *Speculum* 75 (1): 29–67.

R = Rättslösabalken [The Book About Lawlessness in the Västgöta Laws].

Rafnsson, Sveinbjörn. 1985. The Penitential of St Þorlákur in its Icelandic Context. In *Bulletin of Medieval Canon Law* 15: 19–30.

Riisøy, Anne Irene. 2005. Kristenrettene og sosialhistorien. In Steinar Imsen (ed.), *Den kirkehistoriske utfordring*. 59–74. Trondheim: Tapir. Akademisk forlag.

Riisøy, Anne Irene. 2014. Outlawry: From Western Norway to England. In Stefan Brink & Lisa Collinson (eds.), *New Approaches to Early Law in Scandinavia*. 101–129. Turnhout: Brepols.

Riisøy, Anne Irene & Bjørg Dale Spørck. 1999. Dateringen av nyere Borgartings kristenretter. In *Collegium Medievale* 12: 57–74.

Rindal, Magnus (ed.). 1981. *Barlaams og Josaphats saga*. Oslo: Kjeldeskriftfondet (Norrøne Tekster 4).

Rindal, Magnus. 1987. Dei eldste fragmenta av dei norske landskapslovene. In Jan Ragnar Hagland, Jan Terje Faarlund & Jarle Rønhovd (eds.), *Festskrift til Alfred Jakobsen*. 130–136. Trondheim: Tapir.

Rindal, Magnus (ed.). 1997. *Selja – heilag stad i 1000 år*. Oslo: Universitetsforlaget.

Rindal, Magnus. 2002. The History of Old Nordic Manuscripts 2: Norwegian (incl. Faroese). In *IHHNGL* 1: 801–808.

Rindal, Magnus. 2004. Dei eldste norske kristenrettane. In Jón Viðar Sigurðsson, Marit Myking & Magnus Rindal (eds.), *Religionsskiftet i Norden. Brytingar mellom nordisk og europeisk kultur 800–1200 e.Kr.* 103–137. Oslo: Senter for studier i vikingtid og nordisk middelalder (Skriftserie 6).

Rodríguez, Jesús Fernando Guerrero. 2007. *Old Norse Drinking Culture* [Unpublished PhD-thesis. University of York].

Runer, Johan. 2012. Huvudtionde, odal och prästgårdar. In *Historisk tidskrift* 132(4): 595–623.

Sacco, Rodolfo. 1991. Legal Formants: A Dynamic Approach to Comparative Law. In *The American Journal of Comparative Law* 39 (1): 1–34.

Sanmark, Alexandra. 2004. *Power and Conversion – A Comparative Study of Christianization in Scandinavia*. Uppsala: University of Uppsala (Occasional Papers in Archaeology 34).

Sanmark, Alexandra. 2005. Dietary Regulations in Early Medieval Norway. In *Viking and Medieval Scandinavia* 1: 203–224.

SAOB = *Ordbok öfver svenska språket*. Vol. 1. Stockholm 1898.

Schulte, Michael. 2002. The Phonological Systems of Old Nordic I: Old Icelandic and Old Norwegian. In *IHHNGL* I: 882–895.

SdmL = The Södermanna Law. In C.J. Schlyter (ed.), *Samling af Sweriges gamla lagar*. Vol. 4: 1–183. Lund 1838.

See, Klaus von. 1964. *Altnordische Rechtswörter: Philologische Studien zur Rechtsauffassung und Rechtsgesinnung der Germanen*. Tübingen: Max Niemeyer Verlag.

Seip, Jens Arup. 1942. *Sættargjerden i Tunsberg og kirkens jurisdiksjon*. Oslo: Jacob Dybwad.

Seip, Didrik Arup. 1954. *Palæografi B: Norge og Island*. Brøndum-Nielsen Johs (ed.). Stockholm, Oslo and Copenhagen: Bonnier, Aschehoug, Schultz (Nordisk Kultur 28:B).

SjKk = Church Law of Zeeland. In *Danmarks gamle landskapslove med kirkelovene*. Erik Kroman (ed.). Vol. 8: 443–504. København: Gyldendalske Boghandel, Nordisk forlag 1941.

Skånland, Vegard. 1970. Skilsmisse, Alm. o. Norge. In *Kulturhistoriskt lexikon för nordisk medeltid* 15: 505–508.

SkKk = Church Law of Scania. In *Danmarks gamle landskapslove med kirkelovene*. Svend Aakjær & Erik Kroman (eds.), Vol. 1. 819–954. København: Gyldendalske Boghandel—Nordisk forlag 1933.

Skre, Dagfinn. 1995. Kirken før sognet. Den tidligste kirkeordningen i Norge. In Hans-Emil Lidén (ed.), *Møtet mellom hedendom og kristendom i Norge*. 170–233. Oslo: Universitetsforlaget.

Skre, Dagfinn. 1996. *Herredømmet. Bosetning og besittelse på Romerike 200–1350 e. Kr.* [Unpublished Dr Phil-thesis. University of Oslo].

Skyum-Nielsen, Niels. 1975. Træl, Danmark. In *Kulturhistoriskt lexikon för nordisk medeltid* 19: 19–21.

Smedberg, Gunnar. 1973. *Nordens första kyrkor. En kyrkorättslig studie*. Lund: Gleerups Förlag (Bibliotheca Theologiae Practicae 32).

Spørck, Bjørg Dale. 2009. *Nyere norske kristenretter (ca. 1260–1273)*. Oversatt med noter og etterord av Bjørg Dale Spørck. Thorleif Dahls kulturbibliotek. Oslo: Aschehoug.

Spurkland, Terje. 2005. *Norwegian Runes and Runic Inscriptions*. Woodbridge: The Boydell Press.

Söderwall, K.F. 1884–1918, 1925–1973. *Ordbok öfver svenska medeltidsspråket* (Supplement 1–2). Lund: Berlingska boktryckeri- och stilgjuteri-aktiebolaget.

Storm, Gustav (ed.). 1895. *Hirdskraa i fotolithografisk gjengivelse efter Tønsbergs lovbog fra c. 1320*. Oslo: Grøndahl (Norske historiske kildeskriftfonds skrifter 29).

Sunde, Jørn Øyrehagen. 2010 (2005). *Speculum legale — rettsspegelen. Ein introduktion til den norske rettskulturen si historie i eit europeisk perspektiv*. Bergen: Fagbokforlaget.

Sundmark, Stina Fallberg. 2008. *Sjukbesök och dödsberedelse. Sockenbudet i svensk medeltida och reformatorisk tradition*. Skellefteå: Artos & Norma bokförlag (Bibliotheca Theologiae Practicae 84).

Sv. = King Sverrir's Church Law. In R. Keyser & P.A. Munch (eds.), *Norges gamle love indtil 1387*. Vol. 1: 407–434. Christiania 1846.

Svensson, Lars. 1974. *Nordisk paleografi: Handbok med transkriberade och kommenterade skriftprov*. Lund: Studentlitteratur.

Ström, Per. 1997. *Paradisi recuperatio. Den romersk-germanska kyrkoinvigningens form och innebörd, med en textutgåva till PRG XL baserad på nya handskriftsstudier*. [Unpublished ThD-thesis. University of Uppsala].

Tangl, Michael. (ed.). 1916. *MGH Epistolae: Epistolae selectae 1: Die Briefe des heiligen Bonifatius und Lullus*. Berlin: Weidmannsche Verlag.

Taranger, Absalon. 1890. *Den angelsaksiske kirkes indflydelse paa den norske*. Kristiania: Den norske historiske forening.

Thietmar of Merseburg see in Holtzmann, Robert.1953. *MHG Scriptores: Scriptores rerum Germanicarum. Nova series 9: Die Chronik des Bischofs Thietmar von Merseburg und ihre Korveier Überarbeitung*. Berlin: Weidmann.

Thijssen, J. M. M. H. 1996. Master Amalric and the Amalricians: Inquisitorial Procedure and the Suppression of Heresy at the University of Paris. In *Speculum* 71: 43–65.

Thors, Carl-Eric. 1957. *Den kristna terminologin i fornsvenskan* (Studier i nordisk filologi 45). Helsingfors und København: Svenska Litteratursallskapet i Finland.

TiL = Church Law Section of Tiohärad. In C.J. Schlyter (ed.), *Samling af Sweriges gamla lagar*. Vol. 5: 95–110. Lund 1844.

Trusen, Winfried. 1988. Der Inquisitionsprozeß. Seine historischen Grundlagen und frühen Formen. In *Zeitschrift der Savigny-Stiftung für Rechtsgeschichte. Kanonistische Abteilung* 74: 168–230.

Tveito, Olav. 2007. Erkebiskop Wulfstan av York og de eldste norske kristenrettene. In *Norsk Teologisk Tidsskrift* 108: 170–186.

Ugulen, Jo Rune. 2006. Haulden: Bonde eller aristokrat. In Jørn Øyrehagen Sunde (ed.), *Rettstekstar i mellomalderen – Idé og praksis*. 55–79. Oslo: Unipub (Rettshistoriske studier 17).

UL = The Uppland Law. In C.J. Schlyter (ed.), *Samling af Sweriges gamla lagar*. Vol. 3. 1–275. Stockholm 1834.

VgL I = Older Västgöta Law. In H.S. Collin & C.J. Schlyter (eds.), *Samling af Sweriges gamla lagar*. Vol. 1. 1–14. Stockholm 1827.

VgL I = Older Västgöta Law. In Per-Axel Wiktorsson (ed. and transl.), *Äldre Västgötalagen och dess bilagor i Cod. Holm. B 59*. Vol. 1–2. Skara: Föreningen för Västgötalitteratur. 2011.

VgL II = Younger Västgöta Law. In H.S. Collin & C.J. Schlyter (eds.), *Samling af Sweriges gamla lagar*. Vol. 1. 75–222. Stockholm 1827.

Viðar Sigurðsson, Jón. 2009. *Norsk historie 800–1300*. 3rd ed. Oslo: Det Norske Samlaget.

Vogt, Helle. 2005. *Slægtens funktion i nordisk højmiddelalderret: kanonisk retsideologi og fredsskabende lovgivning*. København: Jurist- og Økonomforbundets forlag.

Vogt, Helle. 2009. 'Secundum consuetudinem et leges patri': The Concept of Law and Custom in Thirteenth Century Denmark. In Per Andersen & Mia Münster-Swendsen (eds.), *Custom: The Development and Use of a Legal Concept in the Middle Ages*. 67–80. København: DJØF Publishing.

Vries, Jan de. 2000. *Altnordisches etymologisches Wörterbuch*. Leiden: Brill.

Wasserschleben, F.W H. (ed.). 1958 (1851). *Die Bußordnungen der abendländischen Kirche*. Graz: Akademische Druck- u. Verlagsanstalt.

Winkler, Gaabriele. 1995. The Original Meaning of the Prebaptismal Anointing and Its Implications. In Maxwell E. Johnson (ed.), *Living Water, Sealing Spirit: Readings on Christian Initiation*. 58–81. Collegeville, MN: The Liturgical Press.

Wisløff, Carl Fredrik 1966. *Norsk kirkehistorie*. Vol. 1. Oslo: Lutherstiftelsen.

Wood, Susan. 2006. *The Proprietary Church in the Medieval West*. Oxford: Oxford University Press.

Glossary

ármaðr person working on behalf of a king or bishop
belgborinn adjective describing a child with a specific disability
forvé unholy place
fylki administrative area, larger than a *herað*
fylkiskirkja *fylki* church
gerð a type of public duty
graptarkirkja burial church
***halfrétti* oath** a type of oath
***halfrétti* payment** a type of penalty payment
herað administrative area, smaller than a *fylki*
heraðskirkja *herað* church
heraðsþing *herað* thing assembly
heraðsmenn men of the *herað*
hauldr, hǫldr person of specific, fairly high status
hǫfuðkirkja a church with special status
hǫfuðprestr priest at a *hǫfuðkirkja*
hǫfuðtíund a type of oblation to the Church
kvennaleiðir someone who accompanies a woman
legkaup a type of payment made to a priest
lendr maðr person of specific, fairly high status
***lýrittr* oath** a type of oath
lǫg, lag legal province (area larger than a *fylki*), related to *lǫg* (law)
lǫgfé a type of legal payment
mannsgildi, mannsgjǫld a type of penalty payment
Ólafssáð a type of oblation to the Church
reiða a type of payment made to a bishop
sáld unit of measurement for agricultural produce
séttungr unit of measurement for agricultural produce
sveiti, svidda, svídauðr forbidden food
trygðakaup a type of penalty payment
þegngildi a type of penalty payment
þræll person of extremely low status, thrall, slave
úbótamaðr person who has committed an unatonable offence
úbotaverk unatonable offence

Index

For Product Safety Concerns and Information please contact our EU representative GPSR@taylorandfrancis.com
Taylor & Francis Verlag GmbH, Kaufingerstraße 24, 80331 München, Germany

www.ingramcontent.com/pod-product-compliance
Ingram Content Group UK Ltd.
Pitfield, Milton Keynes, MK11 3LW, UK
UKHW022019180926
475701UK00005B/923

* 9 7 8 0 3 6 7 6 4 6 4 4 8 *